JBoss 3.2 Deployment and Administration

Meeraj Kunnumpurath

JBoss 3.2 Deployment and Administration

ISBN (pbk): 1-59059-281-6

Printed and bound in the United States of America 12345678910

Trademarked names may appear in this book. Rather than use a trademark symbol with every occurrence of a trademarked name, we use the names only in an editorial fashion and to the benefit of the trademark owner, with no intention of infringement of the trademark.

Technical Reviewer: Craig Berry

Editorial Board: Dan Appleman, Craig Berry, Gary Cornell, Tony Davis, Steven Rycroft, Julian Skinner, Martin Streicher, Jim Sumser, Karen Watterson, Gavin Wray, John Zukowski

Assistant Publisher: Grace Wong

Project Manager: Tracy Brown Collins

Copy Editor: Kim Wimpsett

Production Manager: Kari Brooks

Production Editor: Kelly Winquist

Proofreader: Lori Bring

Compositor: Molly Sharp

Indexer: Bill Johncocks

Cover Designer: Kurt Krames

Manufacturing Manager: Tom Debolski

Distributed to the book trade in the United States by Springer-Verlag New York, Inc., 175 Fifth Avenue, New York, NY, 10010 and outside the United States by Springer-Verlag GmbH & Co. KG, Tiergartenstr. 17, 69112 Heidelberg, Germany.

In the United States: phone 1-800-SPRINGER, email orders@springer-ny.com, or visit http://www.springer-ny.com. Outside the United States: fax +49 6221 345229, email orders@springer.de, or visit http://www.springer.de.

For information on translations, please contact Apress directly at 2560 Ninth Street, Suite 219, Berkeley, CA 94710. Phone 510-549-5930, fax 510-549-5939, email info@apress.com, or visit http://www.apress.com.

The information in this book is distributed on an "as is" basis, without warranty. Although every precaution has been taken in the preparation of this work, neither the author(s) nor Apress shall have any liability to any person or entity with respect to any loss or damage caused or alleged to be caused directly or indirectly by the information contained in this work.

The source code for this book is available to readers at http://www.apress.com in the Downloads section. You will need to answer questions pertaining to this book in order to successfully download the code.

Contents at a Glance

Contents

About the Author

Meeraj Kunnumpurath
Meeraj works as a senior information specialist with Electronic Data Systems. He has been using enterprise Java for more than four years. He's a Sun Certified Java Programmer and Web Component Developer. He also writes for popular web sites and journals.

He loves football (as it's called outside the United States). He's a big fan of Chelsea Football Club and hopes they win the premiership this season.

You can reach Meeraj at meeraj@lycos.com

I thank Allah for making this possible.

I'd like to thank the JBoss Group and all the JBoss developers for producing such a wonderful product and making the source open. Without their source, I wouldn't have been able to write this book.

I'd also like to thank Craig for helping me do this book as well as all the other projects I've been involved with at Wrox and Apress with Craig.

I also thank Abdul Rahim for the friend and brother he has been.

I'd like to dedicate the work I've done for this book to my brothers and sisters, who have been refugees in their own land, for 50 years of endless suffering and misery. Allah says, "Verily hardship follows ease."

Introduction

Over the past five years, Java 2 Enterprise Edition (J2EE) has evolved as one of the most popular technologies for building enterprise-class applications. J2EE provides a platform for building robust, high-performing, scalable, manageable, maintainable, and portable enterprise-class applications. One of the key factors that has contributed significantly to the success of J2EE as an enterprise platform is portability.

Specifically, J2EE is an open standard and isn't tied to any proprietary vendor-specific implementation. It takes the "write once, run anywhere" spirit of Java to new heights. J2EE provides portability of applications across J2EE vendors by externalizing the runtime behavior of the components such as transactions, security, persistence, lifecycle management, and so on from the compiled binaries of the components into Extensible Markup Language (XML)–based deployment descriptors.

One of the important features of J2EE is that it lets the container providers decide how to implement the aforementioned runtime services that they provide to the components. In most cases, the component developers will concentrate on the business logic behind the components; application assemblers and component deployers will take these components and configure their runtime behavior based on the target platform on which they'll be deployed. Application assemblers and deployers usually do this by amending the standard deployment descriptors that come with the components and adding container-specific deployment descriptors to the components.

Hence, to develop powerful J2EE applications that fully utilize the runtime services provided by the platforms in which they run, you should be well versed with the configuration and deployment of J2EE components on specific application servers. Also, to ensure that applications run properly once they're deployed, you should be able to monitor and manage the components within the application server environments.

This book concentrates on one of the most popular open-source application servers, JBoss, with more than 50,000 downloads a month, from the JBoss Group. The book covers JBoss 3.*x* and specifically version 3.2, which supports most of the J2EE 1.3 features. This book covers how to configure various J2EE components to fully utilize the runtime services provided by the JBoss server and shows how to configure, manage, and administrate the JBoss server itself.

Throughout this book, I'll use the petstore application version 1.3.1 from Sun Microsystems to illustrate the various deployment aspects of J2EE components on the JBoss server. The petstore application comes preconfigured with the deployment information required for the J2EE Reference Implementation (RI) from Sun Microsystems. You'll learn how to configure these components to fully utilize the runtime services provided by the JBoss server. In the process, you'll also identify the key issues involved in porting J2EE applications from one application server to another. You can download the petstore application from http://java.sun.com/j2ee/download.html.

What's Covered in This Book?

Chapter 1 covers the JBoss 3.*x* server features that you'll need to know. The rest of the chapters cover topics that can be broadly classified into the following categories:

- ❑ Running the server
- ❑ Configuring the server
- ❑ Deploying components

Running the Server

This section covers the following topics:

- ❑ Server installation in Chapter 2
- ❑ Server architecture in Chapter 2
- ❑ Operating the server in Chapter 3

Configuring the Server

This section covers the following topics:

- ❑ The JBoss Java Management Extensions (JMX) management and administration architecture in Chapter 4
- ❑ Configuring runtime properties in Chapter 5

❑ Configuring naming services in Chapter 6

❑ Configuring security in Chapter 7

❑ Configuring Java Database Connectivity (JDBC) datasources in Chapter 8

❑ Configuring Java Message Service (JMS)–administered objects in Chapter 9

❑ Configuring mail sessions in Chapter 10

❑ Configuring the Tomcat and Jetty web containers and web servers in Chapters 11 and 12

❑ Configuring cluster environments in Chapter 13

❑ Configuring logging properties in Chapter 14

Deploying Components

This section covers the following topics:

❑ The JBoss deployment architecture in Chapter 15

❑ Deploying web components and the JBoss web deployment descriptor in Chapter 16

❑ Deploying Enterprise JavaBean (EJB) components and the JBoss EJB deployment descriptors in Chapters 17 and 18

❑ Deploying Enterprise Archive (EAR) applications and the JBoss EAR deployment descriptor in Chapter 19

❑ Deploying custom JBoss components in Chapter 20

Reading XML Structures

Throughout this book, you'll see diagrams generated using XMLSpy from Altova (http://www.altova.com) that illustrate the structure of the various XML documents that are used to configure JBoss and the various components deployed within JBoss. This section provides a brief overview of the notations and icons used by XMLSpy for representing the various aspects of an XML content model. Please note that this section isn't a tutorial on XML, XML Schema, or Document Type Definitions (DTDs).

XMLSpy uses the notation highlighted in the following diagram for representing "sequence" in an XML schema:

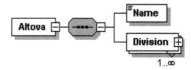

In the previous diagram, this therefore means that the Altova element will contain a Name and Division subelement as so:

```
<Altova>
  <Name/>
  <Division/>
</Altova>
```

The notation highlighted in the following diagram represents "choice" in an XML schema:

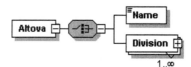

In the previous diagram, this therefore means that the Altova element will contain *either* a Name or a Division subelement.

An element that can appear exactly once in its parent's content model is represented by a solid border:

An element that can optionally appear in its parent's content model is represented by a dashed border:

The following notation represents an element that can appear from zero to many times in its parent's content model:

0..∞

The following notation represents an element that can appear from zero to a fixed number of times in its parent's content model. In the following diagram, the element may appear zero to ten times:

0..10

The following notation represents an element that can appear from one to many times in its parent's content model:

1..∞

The following notation represents an element that can appear from one to a fixed number of times in its parent's content model. In the following diagram, the element may appear one to ten times:

1..10

1

JBoss Server 3.x Features

JBoss is an open-source and free Java 2 Enterprise Edition (J2EE) application server from the JBoss Group, implemented purely in Java. The JBoss Group, headed by Marc Fleury, is composed of more than 100 developers all over the world. The current major version of JBoss, 3.2, supports most of the J2EE 1.3 features.

1.1 JBoss Components

The JBoss server uses an extremely modular architecture built around **Java Management Extensions (JMX)**. Out of the box, JBoss provides a JMX implementation, an Enterprise JavaBean (EJB) container, and the basic JBoss server. JBoss also comes with a variety of pluggable components that implement the various J2EE standards such as Java Message Service (JMS), Java Naming and Directory Interface (JNDI), Java Authentication and Authorization Service (JAAS), Java Transaction API (JTA)/Java Transaction Service (JTS), and so on.

JBoss allows you to write your own components and plug them into the core JMX implementation, as long as the components you write comply with the JMX specification. This means, for example, if you're not happy with the transaction manager that comes with JBoss, you can write your own transaction manager component and plug it into the JMX bus. You can also add compliant third-party components to JBoss. You'll look at the JBoss JMX implementation in more detail in section 4.2, "JMX in JBoss."

The core components that come with JBoss, out of the box, are depicted in this diagram:

Container Managed Persistence	J2EE Web Container Integration	JTS/JTA	JCA Connectivity
JBoss CMP	**Web Container**	**JBossTX**	**JBossCX**

JMX Implementation

JBossSX	**JBossMQ**	**EJB**	**Management**
JAAS Security	JMS Messaging	EJB Container	Remote Management

These components are as follows:

- **JMX Implementation**
  JBoss provides a JMX implementation for registering and managing components. This is the heart of the JBoss server. JBoss also provides a remote management facility for the JMX server and the components running within it.

- **EJB Container**
  This provides the container implementation for the EJB 1.1 and 2.0 specifications.

- **JBossMQ**
  This component provides the JMS implementation for messaging support.

- **JBossTX**
  This component provides transaction services using JTA and JTS.

- **JBossCMP**
  This component provides Container-Managed Persistence (CMP) for entity EJB components. JBoss supports both CMP 2.0 and CMP 1.1.

- **JBossSX**
  This is the JBoss component that provides JAAS-based security.

- **JBossCX**
  This component provides Java Connector Architecture (JCA) connectivity services.

- **Web Container**
  This component provides a pluggable level for integrating J2EE web containers. Currently two web containers that integrate with JBoss are Apache Tomcat and Jetty.

1.2 JBoss Versions

At the time of writing, the current major version of JBoss version is 3.2, and the minor version is 3.2.2. JBoss 3.2 supports most of the J2EE 1.3 features, including EJB 2.0, and comes with an integrated web container, Tomcat 4.1.*x*, which supports the Servlet 2.3 and JavaServer Pages (JSP) 1.2 specifications. JBoss 3.2 is also available with Jetty.

> **Minor versions include primarily bug fixes and the occasional minor feature addition. This book focuses on the major 3.2 release of JBoss, so the minor version you have is relatively unimportant to the material covered in this book.**

1.3 J2EE Support

The latest version of JBoss, along with bundled web container (Jetty or Tomcat), supports the following J2EE Application Programming Interfaces (APIs):

❑ **EJB 2.0**
JBoss CMP supports most of the EJB 2.0 features. It's also backward compatible and supports EJB 1.1 components. This is covered in detail in Chapters 17 and 18.

❑ **Servlet 2.3**
Both Jetty and Tomcat support the Servlet 2.3 specification. This is covered in detail in Chapters 11, 12, and 16.

❑ **JSP 1.2**
Both Jetty and Tomcat support the JSP 1.2 specification. This is covered in detail in Chapters 11, 12, and 16.

❑ **JMS 1.0.2**
JBoss comes with a JMS provider that supports both point-to-point and publish/subscribe messaging, compliant with the JMS 1.0.2 specification. This is covered in detail in Chapter 9.

❑ **JTA 1.0.1/JTS 1.0**
JBoss provides a JTA/JTS–compliant transaction manager that supports distributed transactions.

❑ **JCA**
JBossCX provides a JCA implementation and uses JCA for connecting to all external resources including databases. This is covered in detail in Chapter 8.

❑ **JAAS 1.0**
JBoss provides a highly flexible security service built on top of JAAS. This is covered in detail in Chapter 7.

❑ **JavaMail 1.2**
JBoss provides an MBean service for configuring JavaMail sessions. This is covered in detail in Chapter 10.

❑ **JNDI**
JBoss provides a highly configurable naming provider that is capable of using multiple protocols including Remote Method Invocation (RMI) and Hypertext Transfer Protocol (HTTP). This is covered in detail in Chapter 6.

❑ **RMI-IIOP**
JBoss supports RMI invocation over Internet Inter-Orb Protocol (IIOP).

JBoss isn't a J2EE 1.3–certified application server. However, the controversies related to JBoss and J2EE certification are mainly political and not technical, and they have been well documented.

1.4 Custom Features

In addition to the aforementioned J2EE specific features, JBoss supports the following features:

❑ Fault tolerance and load balancing using clusters.

❑ Web services with an integrated Axis engine.

❑ Logging configuration based on Log4J.

❑ EJB invocation over Secure Sockets Layer (SSL).

❑ The JBoss server is built around a JMX bus. JBoss uses JMX MBeans for all its configuration and supports deployment of user JMX MBeans within the JBoss environment.

❑ Java Specification Request (JSR) 77 defines a management information model for the J2EE platform. The model is designed to interoperate with many management systems and protocols.

This chapter presented a high-level overview of the various features available with JBoss. In the next chapter, you'll look into the details of installing JBoss and the JBoss directory structure.

2

Installing JBoss

This chapter covers the installation process for JBoss and explores the installed files.

2.1 Installing JBoss

You can download JBoss in both binary and source formats, either from the JBoss web site at http://www.jboss.org or from the SourceForge JBoss page at http://sourceforge.net/projects/jboss/. Version 3.*x* of JBoss comes in two flavors:

❑   With an integrated Jetty web container

❑   With an integrated Tomcat 4.*x* web container

All the files available from the download site, except the ones that are suffixed with -src, are binary archives. The latest binary archive for the JBoss/Jetty bundle will be something such as jboss-3.2.2.tgz or jboss-3.2.2.zip, and the JBoss/Jetty bundle is jboss-3.2.2_jetty-4.2.11.zip, depending on the latest release. You can explode these files using any standard unzip tool such as the Java Development Kit (JDK) jar tool, WinZip, the tar command on Unix, and so on. You can also find earlier versions along with more recent beta releases of JBoss on these web sites.

> **Before you install JBoss, make sure you have installed JDK 1.3 (or higher) on your machine. Also make sure that the** JAVA_HOME **environment variable points to the JDK installation directory. JBoss uses this for adding** tools.jar **to the classpath.**

You can extract the contents of the archive file into any directory you want. However, I recommend you install into a directory name without spaces because it may cause problems with some of the Sun Virtual Machines (VMs).

2.2 JBoss Directory Structure

Once you have extracted the contents of the binary archive, the directory structure for JBoss (for both Jetty and Tomcat bundles) will look as follows:

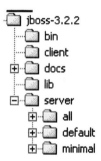

Obviously, if you have a version other than 3.2.2, your root folder will be labeled slightly differently.

The contents of the JBoss root directory are as follows:

❑ The \bin directory contains the following files required for starting and stopping JBoss:

- run.bat/run.sh
  These are the command files used for starting JBoss on Windows and *X systems respectively. This is covered in further detail in section 3.1, "Starting JBoss."

- run.jar
  This is the bootstrap Java Archive (JAR) file used for starting JBoss.

- `shutdown.sh/shutdown.bat`
  These are the command files used for shutting down JBoss on Windows and *X systems, respectively. This is covered in further detail in section 3.2, "Shutting Down JBoss."

- `shutdown.jar`
  This is the bootstrap JAR file used for shutting down JBoss.

- `deployer.jar`
  This file contains the class files required for deploying components remotely on JBoss.

- `twiddle.jar`
  This file contains the class files for a simple command-line utility for accessing the JBoss Java Management Extensions (JMX) server.

- `twiddle.bat/twiddle.sh`
  This is the batch script for running the JMX command-line utility.

- `deployer.bat/deployer.sh`
  This is the command script for running the remote deployer.

- `classpath.sh`
  This is a shell script to determine JBoss classpaths.

- `jboss_init_redhat.sh`
  This is a startup and shutdown script for Red Hat Linux.

- `run.conf`
  This script contains the bootstrap options for setting the Java Virtual Machine (JVM) options, maximum file descriptors, and so on.

❑ The \client directory contains the JAR files required by the client applications for connecting to JBoss. The files contained in this directory are as follows:

- `auth.conf`
  This is used for the Java Authentication and Authorization Service (JAAS) client-side login module.

- `cacerts`
  This is the security file with root Certificate Authority (CA) certificates.

- `concurrent.jar`
  This is a third-party library used by JBoss for collection-based classes.

- `getopt.jar`
  This is a third-party library used by JBoss for processing command-line arguments.

- `gnu-regexp.jar`
  This JAR file contains classes for evaluating regular expressions.

7

- `jacorb.jar`
  This is the one of the free Java implementations for the CORBA standard.

- `jbossall-client.jar, jboss-client.jar, jboss-common-client.jar`
  These are JBoss common client classes.

- `jbossha-client.jar`
  This contains the client classes for accessing clustered JBoss.

- `jboss-iiop-client.jar`
  This contains the client classes for using Internet Inter-Orb Protocol (IIOP).

- `jboss-j2ee.jar`
  These are Java 2 Enterprise Edition (J2EE) classes.

- `jboss-jaas.jar`
  These are JAAS classes.

- `jbossjmx-ant.jar`
  This contains the classes and interfaces for the MBean server.

- `jboss-jsr77-client.jar`
  This contains the classes for Java Specification Request (JSR) 77 for J2EE management.

- `jbossmq-client.jar`
  This contains the client classes for using the Java Message Service (JMS).

- `jbossmqha.jar`
  This contains the client classes for using a clustered JMS service—although JBossMQ currently doesn't support clustering.

- `jboss-net-client.jar`
  This contains the client classes for using JBoss .NET for web services.

- `jboss-sx-client.jar`
  This contains the client classes for using the JBoss security framework.

- `jboss-system-client.jar`
  This contains a couple of deployment exception classes.

- `jboss-transaction-client.jar`
  This contains client classes for the JBoss transaction framework.

- `jcert.jar`
  This contains classes that support public key certificates.

- `jmx-connector-client-factory.jar`
  This contains the factory classes for creating the connectors to access the JMX agent.

- `jmx-ejb-connector-client.jar`
  This contains the Enterprise JavaBean (EJB)–based connector for accessing the JMX agent.

- `jmx-invoker-adaptor-client.jar`
  This contains the client-side classes required for accessing the JMX server.

- `jmx-rmi-connector-client.jar`
  This contains the Remote Method Invocation (RMI)–based connector for accessing the JMX agent.

- `jnet.jar`
  This contains socket factories.

- `jnp-client.jar`
  This contains the Java Naming and Directory Interface (JNDI) initial context factory and related classes.

- `jsse.jar`
  This is the Java Secured Socket Extension classes.

- `log4j.jar`
  This contains the Log4J classes.

❑ The \docs directory contains the Document Type Definitions (DTDs) for the various JBoss-specific deployment descriptors, standard J2EE deployment descriptor DTDs, and examples for configuring datasources for the various Database Management System (DBMS) vendors using the JBoss Java Connector Architecture (JCA) connection factories. Please note that this directory doesn't contain any JBoss server documentation.

❑ The \lib directory contains the startup JAR files required for JBoss. You can configure the directory from which the startup classes are loaded at startup time using system properties. You'll look at this in section 3.1.2, "JBoss System Properties," when I cover the standard system properties used by JBoss. It's recommended that user JAR files *aren't* stored in this directory.

❑ The \server directory contains the various server configuration sets that can be used with JBoss. JBoss comes with three preconfigured sets: default, all, and minimal. JBoss server configuration sets are explained in detail in section 2.3, "Server Configuration Sets."

2.3 Server Configuration Sets

JBoss comes with three server configuration sets: default, all, and minimal. A **server configuration set** is used to define the services that are available for the JBoss instance that's running. You can control the configuration set that's used by a JBoss instance during startup using command-line options. Keep the following in mind:

❑   The minimal configuration set contains only the bare minimum services required to run JBoss.

❑   The default set that's used by default contains all the services except clustering, RMI-IIOP, and the Axis engine for web services.

❑   The all configuration set contains all the services.

You can also create your own configuration set by creating a new directory under the server directory and copying the contents of the default configuration set to it.

2.3.1 The Default Configuration Set

This section covers the contents of the default configuration set. The contents of the default configuration set are as follows:

A number of these directories won't appear until after you've launched this configuration set for the first time. Also, the \work directory is specific to the Tomcat variant.

The directories present in the default configuration set are as follows:

❑   \conf
    This directory contains the various configuration files. This includes the core JBoss configuration file called jboss-service.xml. However, the location of the configuration directory, and the name of the core configuration file, can be controlled during startup using command-line options. Section 3.1.1, "JBoss Startup Options," covers this in further detail.

❑   \data
This directory stores all the persistent files. This directory will be used for
storing a variety of information such as serialized EJB instances that are
passivated, the default Hypersonic database that comes with JBoss, and
persistent JMS messages that are stored to files. The location of this
directory can also be specified at runtime. Section 3.1.1, "JBoss Startup
Options," covers this in further detail.

❑   \deploy
This is the directory into which the various deployment components such
as EAR, EJB JAR, WAR, and RAR files as well as the JBoss-specific **Service
Archive (SAR)** files are copied to be deployed. Section 4.2.1.2, "JBoss SAR
Components," covers JBoss SAR files in further detail.

This directory also contains configuration files with names that follow the
pattern *-service.xml. Any of the aforementioned archives that are
copied to this directory while JBoss is running will be hot deployed to the
server. You'll have a detailed look at the contents of this and the \conf
directories of the default configuration set in section 4.2.2, "The JBoss Root
Configuration File." You can configure the hot deployment behavior by
editing some of the configuration files. Section 15.2, "Hot Deployment,"
covers this in detail.

❑   \farm
This directory contains an MBean descriptor for the clustered scheduling
service.

❑   \lib
This directory contains JAR files that are used by the server. JAR files
located in this directory are automatically added into the server's class
repository. You can use this directory for storing JAR files, such as Java
Database Connectivity (JDBC) driver classes, that are shared between
your applications. The location of the server \lib directory may also be
specified as a command-line option during server startup. This is covered
in detail in section 3.1.1, "JBoss Startup Options."

❑   \log
This directory stores the log files. The two main log files are boot log and
server log. JBoss also logs Hypertext Transfer Protocol (HTTP) access
messages. JBoss logging is based on Log4J and is on by default. Configuring
logging in JBoss is explored in section 14.3, "Configuring Logging."

❑   \tmp
This directory is used by JBoss for storing temporary files during deploying
applications. You can specify the location of this directory during server startup.

❑   \work
This directory will be present only with the Tomcat bundle. Tomcat uses
this directory to store the generated servlets for the JavaServer Pages (JSPs).

2.3.1.1 Default Configuration Set Contents

The JBoss architecture is based around the **JMX** specification. Section 4.1, "An Overview of JMX," covers the JBoss architecture and gives a brief overview of JMX. JBoss uses a variation of the standard **JMX MLet syntax** for specifying the configuration information. The next chapter provides a detailed coverage of the contents of the JBoss configuration files.

In this section, you'll look at the various configuration files that come with the default configuration set. You can find these files in the \conf and \deploy directories. You can also author and store your own configuration files in the \deploy directory following the pattern *-service.xml, which is compliant in the way JBoss configuration files are authored, and they will be deployed by the server. As mentioned earlier, files copied to the \deploy directory will be hot deployed on the server.

The contents of the \conf directory in the default configuration set are as follows:

❑ auth.conf
This file was used in the pre-3.x versions of JBoss for defining JAAS login modules. This file is now deprecated and isn't used in 3.x versions.

❑ jboss-minimal.xml
This file contains the services that are available when JBoss is started with the minimal configuration set.

❑ jbossmq-state.xml
This file is used by the JMS implementation that comes with JBoss for storing usernames, passwords, roles, information regarding durable subscription, and so on. Section 9.5, "State Manager," covers this in further detail.

❑ jboss-service.xml
This file is used for defining the core JBoss services. It contains core services such as class loading, system properties, transactions, naming, deployment, management, monitoring, administration, and so on. Section 4.2.2, "The JBoss Root Configuration File," covers this in further detail.

❑ jndi.properties
This file contains the various JNDI properties, such as initial context factory, provider Uniform Resource Locator (URL), and so on, used for connecting to the JBoss naming provider, within the JBoss server. Section 6.2.1, "Initial Context Properties," covers this in further detail.

❑ log4j.xml
This file is used for configuring Log4J for logging. By default, both file and console logging are enabled. The file logger uses a rolling log for midnight everyday. The threshold set for console messages is INFO, and this file also contains examples for logging messages to Unix Syslogs daemon, JMS destinations, e-mails, and so on. Section 14.3, "Configuring Logging," covers this in further detail.

❑ login-config.xml
This is the file used in JBoss 3.0 for storing JAAS-based security. The login modules defined in this section can be used in your web applications, EJBs, and so on for enforcing declarative security. Section 7.3.3.2, "XML Login Config MBean," covers this in further detail.

❑ server.policy
This is the Java security policy file used by JBoss.

❑ standardjaws.xml
This file contains the datasource mapping for the various DBMS vendors. The datasource mapping information is available for Interbase, DB2, Oracle, Sybase, PostgreSQL, Hypersonic SQL, PointBase, SOLID, MySQL, MS SQL Server, SAP DB, Cloudscape, and Informix. If the database you use isn't in this file, you can append the mapping information for your database to this file. JBoss Container-Managed Persistence (CMP)—EJB 1.1—uses the contents of this file.

❑ standardjboss.xml
This file contains the default configuration for all the EJBs deployed on this server. The defaults can be overridden for each EJB by using JBoss-specific deployment descriptors.

❑ standardjbosscmp-jdbc.xml
This file contains the CMP default configuration for all the CMP entity EJBs deployed on this server. The defaults can be overridden for each CMP entity EJB using JBoss-specific deployment descriptors. You'll look at this in section 18.1, "CMP Configuration Files."

❑ web.xml
This file is present only with the JBoss/Tomcat bundle and specifies the defaults for all the web applications that are deployed.

The \deploy directory contains the following files that follow the pattern *-service.xml as well as the various SAR, RAR, and JAR files. The *-service.xml files contain the JMX MBean definitions used to configure various services. It also contains some standard J2EE

JAR, WAR, and RAR components, which come with the JBoss installation. The contents of this directory are as follows:

❑ http-invoker.sar
This directory contains the MBeans that provide the service for invoking JBoss components using HTTP.

❑ jbossweb-jetty.sar or jbossweb-tomcat41.sar
These directories contain the MBeans for the embedded Jetty or Tomcat web containers, respectively.

❑ jms
This directory contains the various MBeans for the JBossMQ messaging provider.

❑ jmx-console.war
This directory contains the web application for accessing the JMX console.

❑ jmx-invoker-adaptor-server.sar
This directory contains the MBean services for the JRM-based invoker adaptor.

❑ jboss-local-jdbc.rar
This file contains the resource adaptor used for creating datasources that support local transactions.

❑ management
This directory contains the various MBeans and EJBs for enabling JSR 77–based management.

❑ jboss-xa-jdbc.rar
This file contains the resource adaptor used for creating datasources that support distributed transactions.

❑ jboss-jca.sar
This file contains the MBeans that are used for JCA resource adaptor deployment.

❑ uuid-key-generator.sar
This is an MBean service for creating unique keys.

❑ cache-invalidation-service.xml
This is an MBean used for invalidating distrib entity bean caches in a cluster.

❑ hsqldb-ds.xml
This is a datasource configuration file that provides connectivity to the local Hypersonic SQL (HSQL) database.

❑ mail-service.xml
This is an MBean for configuring JavaMail sessions.

- ❑ `properties-service.xml`
  This is an MBean for loading system properties.

- ❑ `schedule-manager-service.xml, schedule-service.xml`
  These MBeans are used for creating scheduling services.

- ❑ `sqlexception-service.xml`
  This is an MBean service for processing SQL exceptions.

- ❑ `transaction-service.xml`
  This is an MBean service that exposes the transaction manager.

- ❑ `user-service.xml`
  This is a skeleton MBean descriptor that can be used for describing user-defined MBeans

2.3.2 Creating Configuration Sets

To create your own configuration set you need to create a directory by the name you want to call the configuration set in the `\server` directory and then copy the contents of the `\default` configuration set. This will contain all the services except IIOP, clustering, and Axis-based web services.

In order for JBoss to use this configuration set, you'll need to configure its startup, as covered in section 3.1.1, "JBoss Startup Options."

In this chapter, you looked at JBoss installation and how the various directories and files are organized. In the next chapter, you'll look at JBoss operation and see how to start and stop JBoss. You'll also learn about selecting JBoss startup options, setting system properties, running JBoss as a system service, and so on.

3

Operating JBoss

Now that you have an overview of the JBoss directory structure, you'll look at how to start and stop JBoss and also the various JBoss startup options.

> By default, none of the ports used by JBoss/Jetty or JBoss/Tomcat listens on a port numbers between 0–1023. Therefore, you don't need root access to start JBoss on Unix systems.

3.1 Starting JBoss

To start JBoss, you can run the following command on Windows systems:

```
run.bat
```

On Unix systems, you need to run the following:

```
run.sh
```

Newer versions of JBoss 3.*x* also come with a specific startup file for Red Hat Linux:

```
jboss_ini_redhat.sh start
```

You can also use the bootstrap Java Archive (JAR) file as shown here:

```
java -jar run.jar
```

Make sure that you run the previous commands from the \bin directory of your JBoss installation. If you're starting JBoss with the second option, please make sure that the Java Development Kit (JDK) tools.jar file is available to the classloader. One way to do this is to copy tools.jar to the \lib directory of the configuration set you're using. The embedded web container within JBoss uses classes from this file for compiling JavaServer Pages (JSP). If everything goes fine, you won't get any stack traces in the command window running JBoss, and you'll have the output similar to the one shown here:

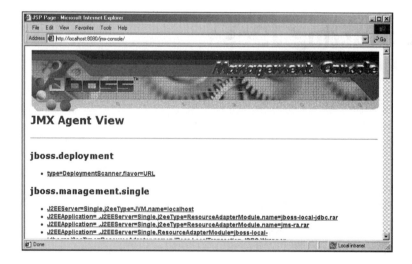

Neither JBoss/Jetty nor the JBoss/Tomcat bundle comes with a default web application. Hence, to test whether JBoss is up and running, you can access the Java Management Extensions (JMX) console web application on http://localhost:8080/jmx-console. This will list all the MBeans registered with the JBoss JMX MBean server, as shown here:

3.1.1 JBoss Startup Options

If you run JBoss without specifying any options, JBoss will use the default configuration set. However, if you run the command `run -h`, JBoss will print the various startup options. The various startup options available with JBoss are listed in the following table:

Option	Description
-V	This will print the JBoss version.
–p	You can use this option for specifying the patch directory for any server updates. If the value specified is a directory Uniform Resource Locator (URL), all the ZIP and JAR files present in the directory identified by the URL are added to the classpath. Otherwise, the URL itself is added to the classpath.
–h	This will print the various startup options.
–n	The URL specified by this option will be used as the base directory to boot remotely from the Internet.
–c	You can use this option to specify the configuration set to use. By default, JBoss uses the default configuration set. If you want to use the minimal configuration set, you can run the command `run -c minimal`. As explained in section 2.3.2, "Creating Configuration Sets," you can create your own configuration set and use that to start JBoss using the -c option. For example, if your configuration set resides in the directory `petstore`, you can issue the command `run -c petstore`.
–j	You can use this option to specify the Java API for XML Processing JAXP parser to use. The allowed values are `xerces` or `crimson`. By default, JBoss uses `crimson`.
–L	You can use this option to add extra libraries to the JBoss classpath. All the archive files present in the filename specified by this option will be added to the class repository. Section 5.1.3, "UnifiedClassLoader," covers JBoss class repositories in detail.
–C	You can use this option to add extra libraries to the JBoss classpath. The archive URL specified by this option will be added to the class repository.
–P	You can use this option to specify a URL pointing to a file containing the system properties to be loaded.
–D	You can use this option to specify system properties; see section 3.1.2, "JBoss System Properties," for more information.

19

3.1.2 JBoss System Properties

You can specify the following properties using the –D option when you start JBoss to specify the system properties that are identified by JBoss:

❑ jboss.boot.library.list
This specifies a comma-separated list of libraries required to boot the server. This defaults to all libraries specified by the jboss.lib.url property.

❑ jboss.server.type
This specifies the JBoss server implementation class. The default is org.jboss.system.server.ServerImpl.

❑ jboss.server.root.deployment.filename
This specifies the configuration file that contains the core MBean definitions. The default is the jboss-service.xml file present in the \conf directory of the configuration set that is used.

❑ jboss.home.dir
This specifies the JBoss home directory. The default value is the directory from which run.jar was loaded.

❑ jboss.home.url
This specifies the Internet URL to be used as the base directory from where to start JBoss. The default is the value of the property jboss.home.dir.

❑ jboss.lib.url
This specifies the URL that contains the libraries for the server. The default is the \lib directory under the URL specified by the property jboss.home.url.

❑ jboss.patch.url
This specifies the URL points to the location that contains the patch libraries. If the value is a file URL, all the ZIP and JAR files in the location are added to the classpath. Otherwise, the URL is added to the classpath.

❑ jboss.server.name
The value of this property will deduce the home directory for the configuration set that is used. The default value is default.

❑ jboss.server.base.dir
This property specifies the base directory for deducing the configuration sets that are available. The default value is the path created using the values for jboss.home.url and the constant server.

❑ jboss.server.home.dir
This property specifies the base directory for the configuration set that is used. The default value is the path created using the values for jboss.server.base.dir and jboss.server.name.

❑ `jboss.server.temp.dir`
    This specifies the temporary directory used in deployment. The default
    value is the path created using the values for `jboss.server.home.dir`
    and the constant `tmp`.

❑ `jboss.server.data.dir`
    This specifies the directory used for storing persistent data. The default
    value is the path created using the values for `jboss.server.home.dir`
    and the constant `db`.

❑ `jboss.server.temp.dir`
    This specifies the temporary directory used in deployment. The default
    value is the path created using the values for `jboss.server.home.dir`
    and the constant `tmp`.

❑ `jboss.server.base.url`
    This property specifies the base URL for deducing the configuration sets
    that are available. The default value is the URL created using the values for
    `jboss.home.url` and the constant `server`.

❑ `jboss.server.home.url`
    This property specifies the base directory for the configuration set that is
    used. The default value is the path created using the values for
    `jboss.server.base.url` and `jboss.server.name`.

❑ `jboss.server.config.url`
    This property specifies the URL of the configuration directory for the
    configuration set. The default value is the URL created using the values for
    `jboss.server.home.url` and the constant `conf`.

❑ `jboss.server.lib.url`
    This property specifies the URL of the `\lib` directory for the configuration
    set. The default value is the URL created using the values for
    `jboss.server.home.url` and the constant `lib`.

❑ `jboss.server.exitonshutdown`
    This property specifies whether to exit the Virtual Machine (VM) on server
    shutdown. The default value is `false`.

3.1.3 Enabling Remote Debugging

JBoss supports Java Platform Debugger Architecture (JPDA)–based remote debugging.
To enable this, you need to uncomment the following line in `run.sh/run.bat`:

```
set JAVA_OPTS=-classic -Xdebug -Xnoagent -Djava.compiler=NONE
    -Xrunjdwp:transport=dt_socket,address=8787,server=y,suspend=y
    %JAVA_OPTS%
```

You can also run the debugger in shared memory by setting the following option:

```
set JAVA_OPTS=-classic -Djava.compiler=NONE -Xnoagent -Xdebug
    -Xrunjdwp:transport=dt_shmem,server=y,address=jboss,suspend=n
    %JAVA_OPTS%
```

Now you can attach to the remote debugger through the specified port using a supported Integrated Development Environment (IDE).

3.1.4 Running JBoss As an NT Service

You can run JBoss as an NT service using any NT service wrapper for Java programs. When you choose a wrapper, you need to make sure it doesn't exit the VM on an NT logoff event. In this section, you'll look at how to use the Wrapper utility available on http://sourceforge.net/projects/wrapper/ to run JBoss as an NT service. Wrapper allows Java applications to be installed and controlled like native NT/Unix services and also provides correction software to automatically restart crashed or frozen Java Virtual Machines (JVMs).

To use the Wrapper utility to install JBoss as an NT service, perform the following steps:

1. Download the latest version of the utility from SourceForge.

2. Extract the contents of the ZIP file to a local directory.

3. Copy the file wrapper.exe from the \bin directory to the \bin directory of your JBoss home.

4. Copy wrapper.jar from the \lib directory to the JBoss \bin directory.

5. Save the following contents in a file called wrapper.conf in the JBoss \bin directory:

```
wrapper.java.command=java
wrapper.java.mainclass=com.silveregg.wrapper.WrapperSimpleApp
wrapper.app.parameter.1=org.jboss.Main
wrapper.java.classpath.1=./run.jar
wrapper.java.classpath.2=./wrapper.jar
wrapper.java.classpath.3=c:/JDK/lib/tools.jar
wrapper.java.library.path=.
wrapper.port=1777
wrapper.startup.timeout=300
wrapper.ping.timeout=300
wrapper.shutdown.timeout=300
wrapper.disable_shutdown_hook=TRUE
wrapper.request_thread_dump_on_failed_jvm_exit=TRUE
wrapper.ntservice.name=JBoss
wrapper.ntservice.displayname=JBoss Server
wrapper.ntservice.description=JBoss J2EE Server
wrapper.ntservice.starttype=AUTO_START
wrapper.ntservice.process_priority=NORMAL
```

You'll need to adjust the classpath setting to point to your Java Runtime Environment (JRE) `tools.jar` *file as appropriate.*

6. Issue the following command from the JBoss \bin directory:

```
wrapper.exe -i wrapper.conf
```

This will install JBoss as an NT service. To make sure it has been installed properly, go to the **Control Panel\Administrative Tools\Services** menu on Windows 2000 and check whether the JBoss service is displayed in the list:

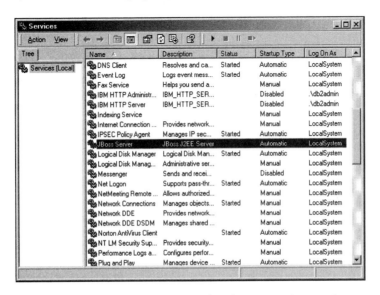

Make sure that the startup type is automatic so that the service is started on system startup. You can manually start and stop the service by right-clicking the service. You can also right-click the service to edit the properties such as startup type, the system account that will run the service, and so on. To uninstall the service, enter the following command:

```
wrapper.exe -r wrapper.conf
```

Some of the important properties supported in the `Wrapper` configuration file are as follows:

❑ `wrapper.java.command`
This is the path to the Java executable.

❑ `wrapper.java.mainclass`
This specifies the fully qualified name of the main class that should be executed if the class implements the interface. Otherwise, it should be `com.silveregg.wrapper.WrapperSimpleApp`, as in this case.

23

❑ `wrapper.java.classpath.<n>`
This is specifies an ordered list of classpath entries. You'll specify the JBoss bootstrap JAR `run.jar`, the JDK's `tools.jar`, and the `Wrapper`-specific `wrapper.jar`.

❑ `wrapper.java.library.path`
This is the path to the directory that contains `wrapper.dll`.

❑ `wrapper.java.additional.<n>`
This specifies an ordered list of arguments to the Java executable. Note that this is *not* used to pass the application parameters.

❑ `wrapper.java.initmemory`
This specifies the initial JVM heap size.

❑ `wrapper.java.maxmemory`
This specifies the maximum JVM heap size.

❑ `wrapper.app.parameter.<n>`
This specifies an ordered list of arguments to the application. In this case, the first argument denoted by `wrapper.app.parameter.1` will be the JBoss main class `org.jboss.Main`. The class `com.silveregg.wrapper.WrapperSimpleApp` will internally call the main method on the JBoss main class.

❑ `wrapper.port`
This specifies a port number used by the `Wrapper` executable to communicate with the Java application to monitor how it's running.

❑ `wrapper.startup.timeout`
This is the number of seconds to allow for the JVM to be launched and contact the wrapper before the wrapper should assume that the JVM is hung and terminate the JVM process.

❑ `wrapper.ping.timeout`
This can specify the number of seconds to allow between the wrapper pinging the JVM and the response.

❑ `wrapper.startup.timeout`
This is the amount of time the service should wait after the wrapper halts the JVM before it gives a failed status.

❑ `wrapper.disable_shutdown_hook`
This disables the JDK shutdown hook.

❑ `wrapper.request_thread_dump_on_failed_jvm_exit`
This specifies whether to dump the thread on JVM exit if the service failed.

❑ `wrapper.ntservice.name`
This specifies the NT service name.

❑ `wrapper.ntservice.displayname`
This specifies the service display name in the service window.

❑ `wrapper.ntservice.description`
This specifies the service description.

❑ `wrapper.ntservice.dependency.<n>`
This specifies the ordered list of services to be started before this service can be started. You can use this for starting data servers, mail servers, and so on before starting JBoss.

❑ `wrapper.ntservice.starttype`
This specifies the startup mode. The allowed values are `AUTO_START` and `ON_DEMAND_START` to respectively indicate whether it should be started automatically or manually.

❑ `wrapper.ntservice.process_priority`
This sets process priority. The allowed values are `NORMAL`, `LOW`, `HIGH`, and `REALTIME`.

Along with the aforementioned properties, the configuration file also supports a wide variety of properties to specify the level and locations of logging. You can use this in the initial stages to debug, if the service is not working properly, or to log the JBoss console output. However, for the day-to-day operation, it's better to disable console logging and rely on the JBoss file logging. Section 14.3, "Configuring Logging," covers JBoss logging in detail.

3.1.5 Running JBoss As an *X Daemon

In this section you'll look at how to run JBoss as Unix/Linux daemon. The example shown in this section uses SuSE Linux v8.0. Make the necessary modification for your version of Unix/Linux. To run JBoss as a daemon, you need to perform the following steps:

1. Create a script file called `jboss` that will be called during system startup and shutdown. This script is responsible for starting and shutting down JBoss. The contents of this script is as follows:

```
#!/bin/sh

. /etc/rc.status
. /etc/rc.config

export JAVA_HOME=/usr/lib/java
export JBOSS_HOME=/usr/local/jboss

export PATH=$JBOSS_HOME/bin:$JAVA_HOME/bin:/sbin:$PATH
```

```
case "$1" in
  start)
    echo "Starting JBoss"
    cd $JBOSS_HOME/bin
    startproc -l /var/log/jboss.log $JBOSS_HOME/bin/run.sh
    ;;
  stop)
    echo "Shutting down JBoss"
    cd $JBOSS_HOME/bin
    ./shutdown.sh
    rc_status -v
    ;;
  restart)
    echo "Restarting JBoss"
    cd $JBOSS_HOME/bin
    ./shutdown.sh
    sleep 10
    startproc -l /var/log/jboss.log $JBOSS_HOME/bin/run.sh
    ;;
  *)
    echo "Usage: $0 {start|stop|restart}"
    exit 1
    ;;
esac
rc_exit
```

2. Store this script in a file called `jboss` in the `/etc/int.d` directory.

3. Make the file executable by running the command `chmod 751 jboss`.

4. Create soft links in `/etc/init.d/rc3.d` and `/etc/init.d/rc5.d` for starting the script during system startup. You can do this with the commands `ln -s /etc/init.d/jboss /etc/init.d/rc3.d/S10Jboss` and `ln -s /etc/init.d/jboss /etc/init.d/rc5.d/S10Jboss`. Please note that the name of the symbolic link should start with the string SXX, where XX is a two-digit number indicating the order in which the startup script should be called during system startup.

5. Create soft links in `/etc/init.d/rc3.d` and `/etc/init.d/rc5.d` for stopping the script during system shutdown. You can do this with the commands `ln -s /etc/init.d/jboss /etc/init.d/rc3.d/K10Jboss` and `ln-s /etc/init.d/jboss /etc/init.d/rc5.d/K10Jboss`. Please note that the name of the symbolic link should start with the string KXX, where XX is a two-digit number indicating the order in which the shutdown script should be called during system shutdown.

6. Now if you restart the system, JBoss will run as a system service.

3.1.6 Startup Troubleshooting

In this section, you'll look at some of the commonly encountered problems in running
JBoss:

Problem	Solution
Exception in deploying Log4J service. Startup process throws `DeploymentException` stating no property editor found for attribute `ConfigurationURL`.	This happens only on the IBM JRE; you can solve this by upgrading to IBM JRE version 1.3.1.
Unable to access JMX console on port 8082 after starting JBoss.	From version 3.0.1 onward, the JMX console is available as a true Java 2 Enterprise Edition (J2EE) application and can be accessed on the default port 8080 by accessing the context path /jmx-console.
Startup fails with `JDom` JAR file in the `/lib` directory.	The JAR file contains an `info.xml` file in the `META-INF` directory; JBoss treats it as a deployment descriptor. Removing this JAR file will register the `JDom` JAR file in the class registry.
`ClassCircularityError` in starting JBoss.	This is because of a bug in the Sun JVM that has not been fixed even in JDK 1.4. However, a delegation-based classloading model since JBoss 3.0.1 has fixed this problem.
`FileNotFoundException` in trying to run JBoss as an NT service.	Give full access to the account used to run the service to the JBoss directories.
`BindException` when trying to start JBoss.	Make sure no other process is using ports used by JBoss.

3.2 Shutting Down JBoss

You can shut down JBoss in one of the following three ways:

❑ Press *Ctrl-C* from the command window that runs the server. JBoss will use a JDK shutdown hook to do a graceful shutdown.

❑ Use the `shutdown.sh/shutdown.bat` file to shut down the server. This will connect to the Hypertext Transfer Protocol (HTTP) adaptor of the JBoss MBean server and issue a call to call the shutdown method on the server MBean. This batch file will try to connect to the JMX HTTP adaptor listening on localhost at port 8080. You can also use this to issue a remote shutdown by specifying the host address and port number as shown here:

```
shutdown wombat.com 8000
```

❑ Use the following command to use the `shutdown.jar` file:

```
java -jar shutdown.jar
```

You can use the second and third options if the command window is not available, such as when the JBoss server is running on a remote server or as an NT service or a Unix daemon.

The JBoss Configuration Architecture

JBoss configuration is based on the **Java Management Extensions (JMX)**. To understand JBoss's configuration options well, it's important to have a good grasp of the JMX architecture. This chapter provides a brief overview of JMX and detailed coverage of the JBoss configuration architecture.

4.1 An Overview of JMX

This section provides a high-level overview of JMX. Please note that a comprehensive coverage of JMX is beyond the scope of this chapter and the book *JMX: Managing J2EE with Java Management Extensions* (Sams, 2002) may help.

JMX is a specification that has evolved through the Java Community Process (JCP) with JSR 3. JMX primarily focuses on managing and monitoring applications. You can use JMX to manage resources within your application, such as connection factories, JMS destinations, mail sessions, and so on. When you make a resource manageable, you need to provide the following pieces of information regarding the resource:

- ❑ Different ways the resource can be constructed
- ❑ Different properties the resource possesses
- ❑ Different behaviors exhibited by the resource

JMX provides a solution for this by defining a standard for representing manageable resources. It also defines:

❑ How these resources can be managed

❑ How the managed resources are made available to be managed

To address the aforementioned requirements, the JMX specification defines a management architecture that provides the following levels:

❑ An **instrumentation level** that exposes the resources managed using standard interfaces. In JMX vocabulary, the instrumentation level components are called managed beans or **MBeans**. MBeans are similar to the JavaBean component model. MBeans provide a wrapper around the application resources that are managed in order to make them manageable.

❑ An **agent level** that provides the run time in which the instrumentation-level components can run. In JMX vocabulary, the run time in which the MBean components are run is called the **MBean server**. JMX implementations are required to provide MBean server implementations that will host all the MBean components that are managed. The JMX specification mandates the agent level to provide some MBean services for monitoring, timers, dynamic loading of MBeans, and so on.

❑ A **distributed services level** that provides the communication infrastructure for management applications to connect to the agent level and view the MBean components, alter their properties, and invoke their methods. The management applications can be browser based or thick client applications.

The JMX architecture explained previously is depicted in the following diagram:

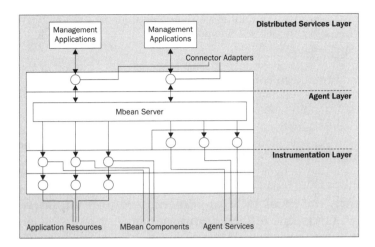

Please note that the resource that is being managed and the MBean component that exposes the resource for management do not need to be separate components; they can very well be implemented in the same component.

4.1.1 Instrumentation Level

The instrumentation level constitutes the MBean components that represent the managed resources. In the previous section, you also saw the information you need about a resource before it can be managed. From a Java perspective, this information comprises the following:

❑ The resource properties that represent the state of the resource. For example, if you were exposing a Java Database Connectivity (JDBC) connection pool as a managed resource, you would want information (such as pool size, initial capacity, increment size, shrink size, and so on) regarding the resource.

❑ The information on the constructors you can use to create the resources. In the case of the JDBC connection pool, these may include operations to get and release connections.

❑ Information regarding the various parameters that are passed to the constructors and operations of the managed resources.

❑ Notifications that are sent by MBean components through the JMX notification infrastructure. In a connection pool, the resource may need to send a notification when the data server goes down.

JMX defines a standard way of defining MBean components so that the MBean server can gather information about the MBean components. For this, JMX defines four types of MBean components:

❑ Standard MBean components

❑ Dynamic MBean components

❑ Model MBean components

❑ Open MBean components

> **Currently the JBoss JMX implementation only supports standard and dynamic MBean components.**

4.1.1.1 Standard MBeans

Standard MBeans are the most primitive form of JMX MBeans. They provide information about their attributes and operations using plain Java interfaces. The interfaces that describe the properties of the MBeans are required to have names ending with the string MBean.

4.1.1.2 Dynamic MBeans

The difference between standard and dynamic MBeans is that in standard MBeans, the JMX implementation extracts the metadata about the MBean attributes and operations from the MBean interface, whereas in dynamic MBeans, the MBean provider provides this metadata using some standard JMX classes for describing the metadata. This provides more flexibility to the MBean provider for defining the manageable behavior of the MBean.

4.1.1.3 Model MBeans

Model MBeans are similar to dynamic MBeans. Every JMX implementation is required to provide an implementation of this interface called RequiredModelMBean. The only thing the instrumentation developer needs to do for using model MBeans is to provide the required metadata classes.

4.1.1.4 Open MBeans

The dynamic and model MBeans are used when the metadata provided, as pertains to the behavior of the MBean components, can be described by primitive data types, strings, arrays of strings, or primitive types. Open MBeans are used when the metadata information is more complex. Open MBeans provide a set of generic classes to describe complex metadata so that the management applications don't need to worry about the complex data types used within the JMX system to describe the metadata for the MBeans, thus avoiding tight coupling between the management applications and the JMX system.

4.1.2 The Agent Level

The agent level provides the runtime in which the MBean components operate. At the heart of the agent level is the MBean server that acts as repository of all the MBean components running within the JMX system. This is represented by the JMX interface `MBeanServer`. The attributes and operations of every MBean registered with an MBean server are available for remote management through the distributed services layer.

Each MBean component registered with an MBean server is uniquely identified by a name represented by the JMX class `ObjectName`. Object names take the format of a domain name, separated from zero or more key-value pairs by a colon:

```
domainName:[key=value,key=value,....]
```

The key-value pairs are mainly used in querying the MBean server for MBean components. An example of an object name used in JBoss configuration for the transaction manager MBean is as follows:

```
jboss:service=TransactionManager
```

In this example, the domain is `jboss`, and it contains one key by the name `service` and value `TransactionManager`.

The MBean server interface defines a variety of methods for the following purposes:

- ❑ Creating MBean instances
- ❑ Removing MBean instances
- ❑ Registering MBean instances with the MBean server
- ❑ Querying MBean instances registered in the server
- ❑ Viewing and changing the various MBean attributes
- ❑ Invoking operations on the MBean instances

MBean server instances are created using the factory class `MBeanServerFactory`.

4.1.2.1 Agent-Level Services

The JMX specification mandates the implementations to provide the following MBean services, which are themselves MBeans, as part of the agent level:

❑ **MLet Service**
MLet is the short form of Management Applet, and this service is used to load MBean components defined in an Extensible Markup Language (XML)–like format into the MBean server. The MBean that represents the MLet service provides methods to load MBean information from remote Uniform Resource Locators (URLs). JBoss uses a variation of the MLet services to load the various configuration information and components as MBeans. You'll look at that in detail in section 4.2, "JMX in JBoss."

The following snippet shows the syntax of how an MLet service is defined:

```
<MLET
  CODE="" | OBJECT=""
  ARCHIVE=""
  [CODEBASE=""]
  [NAME=""]
  [VERSION=""]
  [ARG TYPE="" VALUE=""]
</MLET>
```

An `MLET` tag is used for each MBean that is dynamically loaded. The `CODE` attribute defines the fully qualified class of the MBean that needs to be loaded. Alternatively, you can specify a file that contains the serialized MBean object using the `OBJECT` attribute. The `ARCHIVE` attribute defines the list of Java Archive (JAR) files that will contain the definitions for the MBean class and any dependent classes.

The `CODEBASE` attribute can define the relative path to the archives. The `NAME` attribute defines the unique object name for the MBean. The `VERSION` attribute defines an optional version number. The `ARG` tag defines the arguments that are passed to the MBean constructor.

❑ **Monitoring Services**
This service monitors MBean attributes at predefined intervals. This service will send a notification to registered listeners if the attribute value changes above a predefined limit during successive observations. The services provide different types of monitors such as counter monitors for monitoring a non-negative integer, gauge monitors for monitoring arbitrarily changing integer values, string monitors for monitoring string attributes, and so on.

❑ **Timer Service**
This is for sending timer-based notifications.

❑ **Relation Service**
This is used to associate MBean instances with each other.

4.1.3 Distributed Service Level

The distributed services level enables management applications to connect to the agent level and manipulate the MBean components registered with the MBean server. Most of the distributed service layer details are standardized in a separate JSR (#160) on JMX Remoting 1.2. This provides a client-side Application Programming Interface (API) for management applications to discover both local and remote JMX agent levels and interact with them.

4.2 JMX in JBoss

The JBoss server uses a JMX-based configuration architecture. It provides an MBean server implementation that acts as a repository for all the JBoss components. All the JBoss components, including the JBoss server, are written as JMX MBean components. The JBoss server, when it starts up, creates an MBean server instance. All the JBoss components are then registered with this MBean server. The default domain name used by the JBoss MBean server instance is jboss.

It then registers both the server and the server configuration instances as MBean components with the MBean server. As you have seen in section 2.3, "Server Configuration Sets," the server configuration instance defines various properties such as the JBoss home directory, server configuration set, boot library path, root configuration file, and so on.

Then JBoss creates and registers the following MBean components:

❑   A service controller MBean that controls the lifecycle of other MBean components registered with the server.

❑   An MBean component that represents the main deployer within JBoss. This component will deploy all the MBeans specified in the root configuration file identified by the jboss.server.root.deployment.filename system property. This defaults to jboss-service.xml file found in the \conf directory of the configuration set that is used. Section 2.3, "Server Configuration Sets," covers JBoss configuration sets. The MBeans defined in this file control the behavior of the JBoss instance that is running. The contents of this file use an XML format similar to the one used by the standard JMX MLet service.

❑   MBean components capable of deploying various types of components such as Enterprise Archive (EAR), Java Archive (JAR), and SAR. **SAR** is the acronym for **service archive**, which is a component model JBoss introduces for packaging MBean components. See section 4.2.1.2, "JBoss SAR Components" for more details.

4.2.1 MBeans in JBoss

In JBoss, you can write two different types of MBeans:

❑   The first one is either one of JMX standard or dynamic MBean types. These MBeans are not dependent on any of the JBoss services. You can use these MBeans if you don't expect JBoss to manage the lifecycle for the MBean.

❑   You can also write MBeans that are dependent on the JBoss services. These MBeans are written in a format specific to JBoss MBean services. JBoss MBean services expose methods that can be used to manage the lifecycle of the MBean instances to notify the MBean when it can create, destroy, and start itself. You can use these MBeans if your MBeans depend on other MBeans and you want to define lifecycle dependencies. The service lifecycle of every JBoss service MBean is controlled by the following MBeans:

- MBean responsible for SAR deployment

- A service configurator MBean

- A service controller MBean

4.2.1.1 JBoss Service MBeans

MBean components that utilize JBoss services are required to implement the `org.jboss.system.Service` interface. The service controller MBean will call the methods defined in this interface on various MBean components at appropriate times:

❑   `create()`
The service controller MBean calls the `create()` method on MBean components on the occurrence of an event that affects the state of the MBean component. This will also trigger the invocation of the `create()` method on all other MBean components on which this MBean depends. Section 4.2.1.2, "JBoss SAR Components," covers MBean dependencies in detail.

❑   `start()`
The `start()` method is invoked on the MBean when it's ready to start its service. This will be called only after calling the `start()` method on all other MBeans on which this MBean depends.

- stop()
  The stop() method is called when the service controller requires the MBean to stop its service. You can use this method for cleaning up resources.

- destroy()
  The destroy() method is called when the service controller requires to destroy the MBean. You can use this method for cleaning up resources.

4.2.1.2 JBoss SAR Components

JBoss introduces the notion of **SAR** components for packaging and deploying MBeans. The SAR deployer MBean is responsible for the deployment of SAR components. SAR components can be deployed either in packaged or in exploded formats.

When a SAR component is deployed in the packaged format, it should be a JAR file with the extension sar. The META-INF directory of the JAR file should contain an XML file called jboss-service.xml. This file uses an XML syntax similar to the one used by the JMX MLet service for defining MBean definitions. The JAR file should also contain the MBean class as well as any other dependent classes. In the exploded format, the MBean definitions should be stored in a file with the name ending with the string -service.xml.

The structure of the SAR deployment descriptor is as follows:

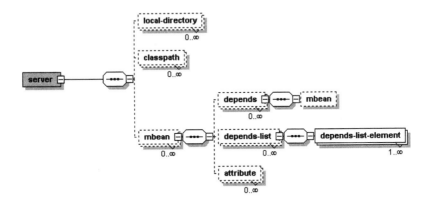

It's important that you understand the structure of the SAR deployment descriptor Document Type Definition (DTD) because you'll be using it often for configuring the various MBean services that come with JBoss as well as writing your own MBean services.

The root element of the deployment descriptor is called `server`. This element can have one or more `local-directory` and `classpath` elements. The `local-directory` element has a `path` attribute, which describes the path within the SAR file that should be copied to the directory within the server that is used for persistent storage. The `classpath` element defines external JAR files that should be deployed with the MBean components defined in the SAR. The `classpath` element has an `archives` attribute used to define a comma-separated list of JAR files and a `codebase` attribute used to define a URL that contains the JAR files.

4.2.1.2.1 Defining MBeans

You define MBeans using **mbean** elements within the `server` element. The mandatory `code` attribute defines the class that represents the MBean component. The `name` attribute defines the unique object name that is used to identify the MBean within the MBean server. The `mbean` element may contain zero or more `attribute` elements to define the MBean attributes. The `name` attribute of the `attribute` element defines the attribute name, and the text content of the element defines the attribute value. The element content may be any arbitrary XML if the type of the attribute is `org.w3c.dom.Element`.

An example of an MBean definition is as follows:

```
<mbean code="org.jboss.naming.NamingService"
       name="jboss:service=Naming">
  <attribute name="Port">1099</attribute>
</mbean>
```

This snippet defines an MBean by the name `jboss:service=Naming` and the class `org.jboss.naming.NamingService` with an attribute `Port` set to the value `1099`.

4.2.1.2.2 Defining Dependencies

When you define MBean services, the service you define may depend on other services. This means you want to make sure all those services on which your service is dependent are deployed and started before your service is started. For example, if you define an MBean service that uses JNDI lookup, you would want to make sure that the JBoss naming MBean service is started before your service is started.

Dependencies are resolved by the service configuration and service controller MBeans by using the lifecycle callbacks defined for the MBean services and the dependencies defined in the SAR deployment descriptor for the MBean. The SAR deployment descriptor defines two ways of defining dependencies:

❏ The mbean element may contain zero or more depends elements to define dependencies on other MBean services. You can use the text content of this element for defining the object name of an MBean on which this MBean ID depends. The following snippet shows how the depends element defines dependencies:

```
<mbean code="org.jboss.deployment.cache.DeploymentCache"
       name="jboss.deployment:type=DeploymentCache">
    <depends optional-attribute-name="Deployer">
    jboss.system:service=MainDeployer
    </depends>
    <depends optional-attribute-name="Store">
    jboss.deployment:type=DeploymentStore,flavor=File
    </depends>
</mbean>
```

You can use the optional-attribute-name attribute to bind the service depended upon to an attribute of the dependent service. You can also use the nested mbean element to define the MBean on which this MBean depends:

```
<mbean
  . . .
    <depends optional-attribute-name="someAttribute">
        <mbean code="someCode" name="someName">
            <attribute name="attrib">value</attribute>
            . . .
        </mbean>
    </depends>
</mbean>
```

❏ Alternatively, you can use the depends-list element to define multiple object names for the MBean service on which this MBean service depends:

```
<mbean
  . . .
    <depends-list optional-attribute-name="someName">
        <depends-list-element>
            someDomain:key1=value1
        </depends-list-element>
        <depends-list-element>
            someDomain:key2=value2
        </depends-list-element>
    </depends-list>
</mbean>
```

4.2.2 The JBoss Root Configuration File

When JBoss starts, the main deployer starts the MBean services defined in the root configuration file. By default, this file is the `jboss-service.xml` file in the `\conf` directory of the configuration set that is used. However, you can control the location of this file using the system property `jboss.server.root.deployment.filename`.

The MBean services specified in this file define the behavior of the server instance that is running. In this section, you'll look at the core services that are defined in the root configuration file for the default configuration set. The following listing shows the MBean services defined in the `jboss-service.xml` file present in the `%JBOSS_HOME%\server\default\conf` directory:

```xml
<?xml version="1.0" encoding="UTF-8"?>

<server>

  <!-- Load all jars from the JBOSS_DIST/server/<config>/ -->
  <classpath codebase="lib" archives="*"/>
```

This service provides the JSR 77 management domain for the JBoss server:

```xml
<mbean
      code="org.jboss.management.j2ee.LocalJBossServerDomain"
      name="jboss.management.local:j2eeType=J2EEDomain,name=Manager">
    <attribute name="MainDeployer">
      jboss.system:service=MainDeployer
    </attribute>
    <attribute name="SARDeployer">
      jboss.system:service=ServiceDeployer
    </attribute>
    <attribute name="EARDeployer">
      jboss.j2ee:service=EARDeployer
    </attribute>
    <attribute name="EJBDeployer">
      jboss.ejb:service=EJBDeployer
    </attribute>
    <attribute name="RARDeployer">
      jboss.jca:service=RARDeployer
    </attribute>
    <attribute name="CMDeployer">
      jboss.jca:service=ConnectionFactoryDeployer
    </attribute>
    <attribute name="WARDeployer">
      jboss.web:service=WebServer
    </attribute>
    <attribute name="MailService">
      jboss:service=Mail
    </attribute>
    <attribute name="JMSService">
```

```
      jboss.mq:service=DestinationManager
   </attribute>
   <attribute name="JNDIService">
      jboss:service=Naming
   </attribute>
   <attribute name="JTAService">
      jboss:service=TransactionManager
   </attribute>
   <attribute name="UserTransactionService">
      jboss:service=ClientUserTransaction
   </attribute>
   <attribute name="RMI_IIOPService">
      jboss:service=CorbaORB
   </attribute>
</mbean>
```

The following is a service to enable logging using Log4J. This service supports attributes for specifying the Log4J configuration file and the refresh period for reloading Log4J configuration. You'll look at this MBean more closely in section 14.1, "The Logging MBean."

```
<mbean
   code="org.jboss.logging.Log4jService"
   name="jboss.system:type=Log4jService,service=Logging">
   <attribute name="ConfigurationURL">resource:log4j.xml</attribute>
   <attribute name="Log4jQuietMode">true</attribute>
</mbean>
```

This is the service to enable dynamic class loading:

```
<!-- Class Loading -->
<mbean
   code="org.jboss.web.WebService"
   name="jboss:service=Webserver">
   <attribute name="Port">8083</attribute>
   <attribute name="DownloadServerClasses">true</attribute>
</mbean>
```

This is the Java Naming and Directory Interface (JNDI) service to enable naming and directory lookup. You'll look at these MBeans more closely in section 6.1, "The JBoss Naming Service," and section 6.3, "JNDI View:"

```
<!-- JNDI -->
<mbean
   code="org.jboss.naming.NamingService"
   name="jboss:service=Naming">
   <attribute name="Port">1099</attribute>
</mbean>

<mbean
   code="org.jboss.naming.JNDIView"
   name="jboss:service=JNDIView"/>
```

The following are services to enable Java Authentication and Authorization Service (JAAS)–based security. You'll look at this MBean more closely in section 7.3.2, "Configuring the JAAS Security Manager:"

```
<!-- Security -->
<mbean
  code="org.jboss.security.plugins.SecurityConfig"
  name="jboss.security:name=SecurityConfig">
  <attribute name="LoginConfig">
    jboss.security:service=XMLLoginConfig
  </attribute>
</mbean>
<mbean
  code="org.jboss.security.auth.login.XMLLoginConfig"
  name="jboss.security:service=XMLLoginConfig">
  <attribute name="ConfigResource">login-config.xml</attribute>
</mbean>

<!-- JAAS security manager and realm mapping -->
<mbean
  code="org.jboss.security.plugins.JaasSecurityManagerService"
  name="jboss.security:service=JaasSecurityManager">
  <attribute name="SecurityManagerClassName">
    org.jboss.security.plugins.JaasSecurityManager
  </attribute>
</mbean>
```

These are MBean services for transactions:

```
<!-- Transactions -->
<mbean
  code="org.jboss.tm.XidFactory"
  name="jboss:service=XidFactory">
</mbean>

<mbean
  code="org.jboss.tm.TransactionManagerService"
  name="jboss:service=TransactionManager">
  <attribute name="TransactionTimeout">300</attribute>
  <depends optional-attribute-name="XidFactory">
    jboss:service=XidFactory
  </depends>
</mbean>

<mbean
  code="org.jboss.tm.usertx.server.ClientUserTransactionService"
  name="jboss:service=ClientUserTransaction">
</mbean>
```

The following is an MBean service for the Enterprise JavaBean (EJB) deployer:

```
<!-- EJB deployer -->
<mbean
   code="org.jboss.ejb.EJBDeployer"
   name="jboss.ejb:service=EJBDeployer">
   <attribute name="VerifyDeployments">true</attribute>
   <attribute name="ValidateDTDs">false</attribute>
   <attribute name="MetricsEnabled">false</attribute>
   <attribute name="VerifierVerbose">true</attribute>
   <attribute name="StrictVerifier">true</attribute>
   <depends optional-attribute-name="TransactionManagerServiceName">
      jboss:service=TransactionManager
   </depends>
   <depends optional-attribute-name="WebServiceName">
      jboss:service=WebService
   </depends>
</mbean>
```

This is an MBean service for the EAR deployer. You'll look at this MBean more closely in section 19.1, "The EAR Deployer:"

```
<!-- EAR deployer -->
<mbean
   code="org.jboss.deployment.EARDeployer"
   name="jboss.j2ee:service=EARDeployer">
</mbean>
```

This is the MBean for JMX invocation. The JRMP invoker is used for remote invocation and the local invoker is used for in-VM invocation. The pooled invoker enhances performance by pooling resources.

```
<!-- Invokers to the JMX node -->

<!-- RMI/JRMP invoker -->
<mbean
   code="org.jboss.invocation.jrmp.server.JRMPInvoker"
   name="jboss:service=invoker,type=jrmp">
   <depends>jboss:service=TransactionManager</depends>
</mbean>

<mbean
   code="org.jboss.invocation.local.LocalInvoker"
   name="jboss:service=invoker,type=local">
   <depends>jboss:service=TransactionManager</depends>
</mbean>

<mbean code="org.jboss.invocation.pooled.server.PooledInvoker"
      name="jboss:service=invoker,type=pooled">
   <attribute name="NumAcceptThreads">1</attribute>
```

```
<attribute name="MaxPoolSize">300</attribute>
<attribute name="ClientMaxPoolSize">300</attribute>
<attribute name="SocketTimeout">60000</attribute>
<attribute name="ServerBindAddress"></attribute>
<attribute name="ServerBindPort">0</attribute>
<attribute name="ClientConnectAddress"></attribute>
<attribute name="ClientConnectPort">0</attribute>
<attribute name="EnableTcpNoDelay">false</attribute>

<depends optional-attribute-name="TransactionManagerService">
    jboss:service=TransactionManager
</depends>
</mbean>
```

The following are MBeans for hot deployment. You'll look at these MBeans more closely in section 15.2, "Hot Deployment:"

```
<!-- Deployment Scanning -->
<mbean
  code="org.jboss.deployment.scanner.URLDeploymentScanner"
  name="jboss.deployment:type=DeploymentScanner,flavor=URL">
  <depends optional-attribute-name="Deployer">
    jboss.system:service=MainDeployer
  </depends>
  <attribute name="URLComparator">
    org.jboss.deployment.DeploymentSorter
  </attribute>
  <attribute name="Filter">
    org.jboss.deployment.scanner.DeploymentFilter
  </attribute>
  <attribute name="ScanPeriod">5000</attribute>
  <attribute name="URLs">./deploy</attribute>
  <attribute name="RecursiveSearch">True</attribute>
</mbean>
```

4.3 Accessing the JMX Agent

In this section, you'll look at how to access the JBoss JMX agent level and manipulate the registered MBeans. You can access the JBoss JMX agent using the JMX Hypertext Markup Language (HTML) adaptor provided with JBoss. This is provided as a standard J2EE web application and can be accessed using the context path /jmx-console. The console web application is available as an exploded WAR in the \deploy directory of the default configuration set. The home page for the console displays all the MBean services registered with JBoss sorted by domain name. The following image displays the initial page of the JMX console:

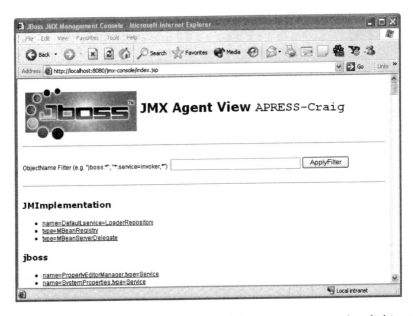

From the Agent View page, you can view any of the MBean services by clicking the link representing the service. The following image displays the MBean service for viewing the JNDI tree:

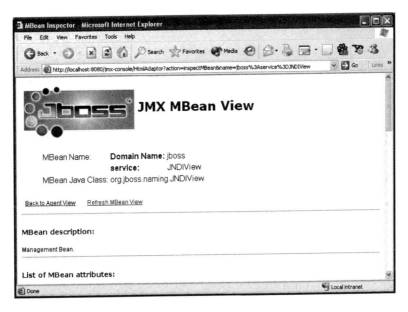

From this page, you can set the attributes on the MBean as well as invoke operations on the MBean. The following image displays the results of invoking the list() method on the JNDIView MBean:

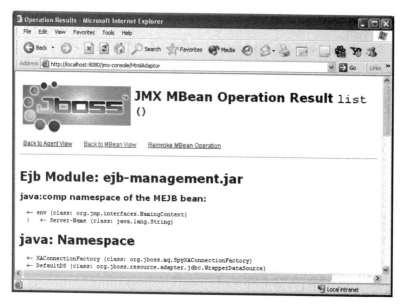

JBoss also provides an Remote Method Invocation (RMI) adaptor for connecting to the JMX agent level. This allows remote clients to connect to the JMX agent and invoke MBean operations. This can be useful if you have clients that rely on MBeans deployed within the JBoss server instances. However, for pure administration of the server, it's best to connect to the browser-based interface for invoking MBean operations.

4.3.1 Securing the JMX Console

JBoss installation provides anonymous access to the JMX console application. However, you may want to permit access to the console only to authorized users. To do this, you need to secure the console by specifying a security domain in the jboss-web.xml JBoss web deployment descriptor for the console web applications. Security domains are covered in detail in section 7.2, "The JBoss Security Layer," and the JBoss-specific web deployment descriptor is covered in section 16.1, "The JBoss Web Deployment Descriptor."

You can enable security by editing the `jboss-web.xml` file in the `\deploy\`
`jmx-console.war\WEB-INF` directory in the `\deploy` directory. Add the following
code to the XML file:

```
<jboss-web>
   <security-domain>java:/jaas/jmx-console</security-domain>
</jboss-web>
```

> *You'll probably find this line is already present but commented so all
> you'll need to do is uncomment it.*

This will use a preconfigured security domain and use basic authentication for the
console application allowing access only to the username `admin` and password `admin`.
You may have to restart the server. This domain uses the `user.properties` and
`role.properties` files available in the `\WEB-INF\classes` directory. You also
need to uncomment the `security-constraint` defined in the `web.xml` file in the
`\jmx-console.war\WEB-INF` directory in the `\deploy` directory:

```
<security-constraint>
  <web-resource-collection>
    <web-resource-name>HtmlAdaptor</web-resource-name>
    <description>
       An example security config that only allows users with the
       role JBossAdmin to access the HTML JMX console web
       application
    </description>
    <url-pattern>/*</url-pattern>
    <http-method>GET</http-method>
    <http-method>POST</http-method>
  </web-resource-collection>
  <auth-constraint>
    <role-name>JBossAdmin</role-name>
  </auth-constraint>
</security-constraint>
```

Now if you try to access the console, the browser will prompt you for a username and password:

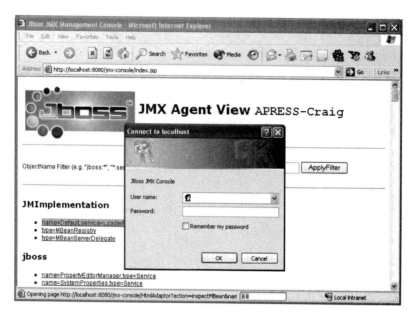

5

Runtime Properties

Application servers generally adopt different classloading strategies to resolve dependencies between various classes used in an enterprise application as well as their dependencies on external libraries. Even though Java 2 Enterprise Edition (J2EE) defines standards on classloading issues, such as using the classpath manifest attribute and Servlet 2.3 classloading model, it is extremely important that you understand the classloading model adopted by your application server because it significantly influences how you package your various components.

In this chapter you will have a detailed look at the JBoss classloading architecture. The chapter will also cover configuring various runtime properties such as the Java Virtual Machine (JVM) heap, profiling, setting the classpath, and so on.

5.1 JBoss Classloading

Before delving into the intricacies of the JBoss classloading architecture, you will look at how JBoss loads the system classes on startup. As you saw in section 3.1, "Starting JBoss," you start JBoss using the bootstrap Java Archive (JAR) file `run.jar`. This JAR file contains the bare minimum classes required to gain an entry point to the JBoss system classes.

5.1.1 Classloading During JBoss Startup

The class with the `main()` method in the `run.jar` file is `org.jboss.Main`. This `main()` method creates a thread group called `jboss`, adds a thread called `main`, and starts the thread. This thread will call the `boot()` method on the `org.jboss.Main` class by passing the command-line arguments passed to the `main()` method.

This series of steps is depicted in the following sequence diagram:

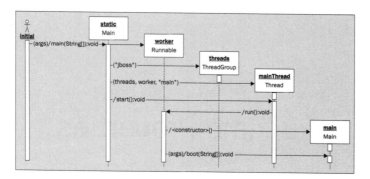

The `boot()` method will first parse the command-line arguments to identify the various pieces of information such as the library Uniform Resource Locator (URL), patch directory, and so on and add them as system properties. Section 3.1.1, "JBoss Startup Options," covers the various command-line options in detail. The `boot()` method will then create an instance of `org.jboss.system.server.ServerLoader` and add the libraries specified by the `–L` and `–C` options (as well as the Java API for XML Processing (JAXP, Java Management Extensions (JMX), and concurrent library JAR files present in the `\lib` directory at the root of the JBoss home) to the list of libraries maintained by the server loader.

> **The JAR files present in the `\lib` directory are hard-coded within JBoss; hence, copying user-defined JAR files to this directory won't make them available to the classloader.**

The server loader is a helper class to load the JBoss server instance. Then it will ask this instance to load the server by passing the thread context classloader:

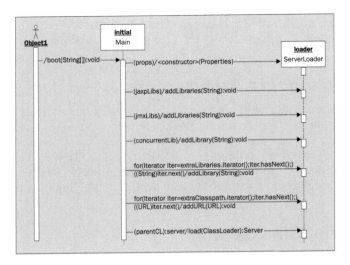

The server loader will first create an instance of the URLClassLoader with the thread context classloader as the parent, passing the following libraries:

- The URLs specified by the jboss.boot.library.list system property. The default value is the \lib directory under JBoss home.

- The JAXP JAR (crimson.jar or xerces.jar depending on the -j option). The default is crimson.jar.

- The JMX JAR jboss-jmx.jar.

- Oswego Concurrent JAR (concurrent.jar)—a third-party collections library used by JBoss.

- JARs specified as libraries via -L command-line options.

- JARs or directories specified via -C command-line options.

It then sets the newly created classloader as the thread context classloader and creates an instance of the server by creating the class org.jboss.system.server.ServerImpl. The init() method is called on the server instance by passing the list of properties created from the command-line options and system properties, and the start() method is called. Once the start() method returns, the server loader resets the thread context classloader to the old thread context classloader.

The start() method of the server first starts an MBean server and registers the server configuration and server instance itself as MBean services. It will then register the service controller MBean. After this it creates and registers the main deployer MBean. This MBean is responsible for orchestrating the deployment process. This deployer will delegate the deployment process to subdeployers responsible for deploying specific types of deployment units. JBoss provides different subdeployers for Enterprise Archive (EAR), Java

Archive (JAR), Web Archive (WAR), Enterprise JavaBean (EJB), Service Archive (SAR), and so on. Refer to section 15.1, "Deployers," for more information on deployers in JBoss.

5.1.2 Classloading Architecture

The JBoss 3.*x* classloading architecture allows the sharing of classes across multiple application components. This classloading architecture introduces the concept of an MBean service that acts as a **shared repository** of classes. The classloaders used within JBoss will first look into this repository before loading a class. To implement this strategy, JBoss introduces the UnifiedClassLoader as the primary classloader within JBoss. This class extends the Java Development Kit (JDK) URLClassLoader class.

5.1.3 UnifiedClassLoader

The UnifiedClassLoader is an MBean service that is responsible for loading classes from a single URL in conjunction with a centralized class repository. This class is initialized with the URL from which to load the classes. The classloader will look into a global shared repository whether the requested class is available before loading the class from the URL.

JBoss creates a unified classloader for each deployment unit that is deployed. The deployed units include WARs, EJBs, EARs, SARs, and Resource Archives (RARs). Each time an instance of the unified classloader is created, it is registered with the central loader repository. The loader associated with the deployed unit will be responsible for loading all the classes from that deployed unit.

The following diagram depicts the typical classloading strategy in an EAR deployment scenario:

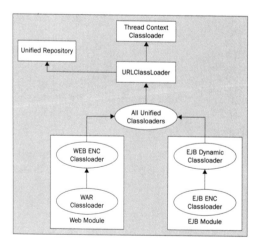

As with any other classloading scenario, the scheme depicted previously uses a hierarchical scheme. Whenever a classloader is asked to load a class, it will ask its parent classloader for the class before loading it. The diagram depicts the following classloaders:

- The thread context classloader is the system classloader.

- The URLClassLoader created by the server loader loads classes from the boot library path as explained in section 5.1.1, "Classloading During JBoss Startup."

- A pool of unified classloaders contains a classloader each for every deployed unit. The relevant deployers will create a unified classloader and register it with the loader repository when it deploys a component. These classloaders will consult with the loader repository for a class before loading the class.

- The EJB dynamic classloader, which is an instance of org.jboss.web.WebClassLoader (a simple subclass of URLClassLoader), is used in conjunction with the WebService MBean to allow dynamic loading of resources and classes from deployed EARs, EJB JARs, and WARs. A WebClassLoader is associated with a container and must have a UnifiedClassLoader as its parent.

- The EJB Environment Naming Context (ENC) classloader is a URLClassLoader, used solely for the deployed EJB's java:comp Java Naming and Directory Interface (JNDI) context.

- The WEB ENC classloader is a URLClassLoader, used solely for the deployed WAR component's java:comp JNDI context.

- The WAR classloader that loads classes from the \WEB-INF\lib and \WEB-INF\classes directories of the WAR.

Please note that if you are using Servlet 2.3 classloading, the WAR loader will try to load the classes from the \WEB-INF directories before consulting with the parent classloader. This can cause a ClassCastException if you have EJB client views in your \WEB-INF directories because the class that is looked up by the WAR loader is different from the dynamic proxy class that implements the EJB client view. This is because JBoss uses dynamic reflection proxies to implement EJBs. A possible solution to this is not to include the EJB client view in the \WEB-INF directories.

5.1.3.1 Advantages and Disadvantages

The main advantage of this classloading scheme is that the classes are shared across multiple components without the need to replicate them across the components.

> **One major disadvantage is that it is impossible to have multiple versions of the same class across different EAR files because JBoss will always use the first version that is loaded.**

This means that if you have a JAR file in the `\lib` directory of the server, JBoss will use that JAR file to load the classes even if you package a different version of the JAR file with your application. This is because the `URLClassloader` used by the server loader is the parent classloader for all the unified classloaders. Hence, whenever a unified classloader is asked to load a class, it will ask its parent classloader to load the class before trying it itself. So, if the library were present in the `\lib` directory, the URL classloader would load it before the unified classloader would get a chance to load it from the EAR file.

For example, imagine an EAR X uses version 1.0 of library A, and EAR Y uses version 1.1 of the same library. EAR X has version 1.0 bundled with it, and EAR Y has version 1.1 bundled with it. If EAR X is deployed first, even if EAR Y contains version 1.1 of the library, JBoss will use version 1.0 whenever EAR Y tries to use the library. This is because the classes from version 1.0 of the library are already available in the loader repository, and when a component in EAR Y asks the classloader to load the class, it will look in the repository first before loading it from the version 1.1 JAR file packaged with EAR Y.

However, you can circumvent this problem using scoped classloading in EAR files. You achieve using the following entry in the JBoss-specific application deployment descriptor, `jboss-app.xml`, present in the `\META-INF` directory of the EAR file:

```
<jboss-app>
  <loader-repository>MyLoaderRepository</loader-repository>
</jboss-app>
```

This EAR will use its own loader repository and looks into this repository before falling back to the default repository. See section 19.2.2, "Loader Repository," for more details on this feature.

5.2 Setting the Classpath

By default the JBoss startup script uses only the JDK `tools.jar` file and the JBoss bootstrap `run.jar` JAR file in the classpath. After that, as explained in section 5.1.1, "Classloading During JBoss Startup," JBoss will add the necessary archives and paths to the classloaders as specified by the command-line options. All the JAR files in the `\lib` directory of the configuration set you use will be available to the classloaders. Hence, rather than modifying the classpath during startup, it is recommended you copy the JAR files containing shared classes to the \lib directory of your configuration set.

> **Copying the JAR files to the \lib directory of the JBoss home won't make them available to the classloaders because these JARs are hard-coded in JBoss.**

If your class files are remote, then you can use the -L and -C options during startup to make them available to the classloaders.

5.3 Setting JVM Options

By default, the startup script doesn't use any JVM options. This means the JVM uses all the default values. You can set JVM options by editing the run.bat file. These options include the following:

- ❏ -Xmixed
  Mixed mode execution (default)

- ❏ -Xint
  Interpreted mode execution only

- ❏ -Xbootclasspath <directories and zip/JAR files separated by ;>
  Set the search path for bootstrap classes and resources

- ❏ -Xbootclasspath/a <directories and zip/JAR files separated by ;>
  Append to end of bootstrap classpath

- ❏ -Xbootclasspath/p <directories and zip/JAR files separated by ;>
  Prepend in front of bootstrap classpath

- ❏ -Xnoclassgc
  Disable class garbage collection

- ❏ -Xincgc
  Enable incremental garbage collection

- ❏ -Xbatch
  Disable background compilation

- ❏ -Xms<size>
  Set initial Java heap size

- ❏ -Xmx<size>
  Set maximum Java heap size

- ❏ -Xss<size>
  Set Java thread stack size

- ❏ -Xprof
  Output Central Processing Unit (CPU) profiling data

- ❏ -Xrunhprof
  Perform JVMPI heap, CPU, or monitor profiling

- ❏ -Xdebug
  Enable remote debugging

- ❏ -Xfuture
  Enable strictest checks, anticipating future default

- ❏ -Xrs
  Reduce use of operating system signals by Java/VM

The following snippet shows the excerpt from `run.bat` file to start JBoss by specifying an initial and maximum JVM heap size of 128 megabytes:

```
%JAVA% %JAVA_OPTS% -classpath "%JBOSS_CLASSPATH%" -Xmx128m -Xms128m
org.jboss.Main %ARGS%
```

Please refer to the JDK tools documentation for an exhaustive coverage of standard and nonstandard JVM options.

6

Configuring Naming

In this chapter, you'll look at the JBoss naming architecture and how to configure the JBoss naming service on both the server and client sides.

6.1 The JBoss Naming Service

JBoss provides a Remote Method Invocation (RMI)–based implementation for the **Java Naming and Directory Interface (JNDI)**. The clients use the Java RMI protocol for connecting to the naming service provider and performing naming and directory operations. The RMI-based implementation uses optimized invocation to use call-by-reference for in–Virtual Machine (VM) lookups. At the core of the JBoss naming implementation is the naming service MBean that is normally declared in the `jboss-service.xml` root configuration file available in the `\conf` directory of the configuration set you use. The MBean definition is as follows:

```
<mbean
  code="org.jboss.naming.NamingService"
  name="jboss:service=Naming">
```

This MBean supports the following attributes:

Attribute	Function
Port	The port on which the **JBoss Naming Provider (JNP)** server listens. The default value for this is 1099.
RmiPort	The RMI port on which the RMI naming implementation is exported. The default value of 0 means any available port is used.
BindAddress	Used on a multi–Internet Protocol (IP) host to specify the address on which the JNP server listens.
Backlog	To define the maximum number of connection requests that can be queued.
ClientSocketFactory	To specify an optional RMI client socket factory to be used. The default is java.rmi.server.RMIClientSocketFactory.
ServerSocketFactory	To specify an optional RMI server socket factory to be used. The default is java.rmi.server.RMIServerSocketFactory.
JNPServerSocketFactory	Optionally used to specify a factory for creating server sockets.

The following listing shows the definition of the naming service MBean in the root configuration file:

```
<mbean
   code="org.jboss.naming.NamingService"
   name="jboss:service=Naming">
   <attribute name="Port">1099</attribute>
</mbean>
```

6.2 JNDI Client Configuration

In this section, you'll look at the configuration required on the client side to connect to the JNP server. Two important things to keep in mind are the properties required for creating the JNDI initial context and the required client-side Java Archive (JAR) files.

6.2.1 Initial Context Properties

You don't need to specify any of the properties when you connect to the JNDI provider from within JBoss. In such scenarios, JBoss reads the properties from jndi.properties in the \conf directory. This file doesn't specify the provider Uniform Resource Locator (URL) that enables JBoss RMI-based context implementation to use an in-VM call. These are the contents of the jndi.properties file, available in the \conf directory of the default configuration set:

```
java.naming.factory.initial=org.jnp.interfaces.NamingContextFactory
java.naming.factory.url.pkgs=org.jboss.naming:org.jnp.interfaces
# Do NOT uncomment this line as it causes in VM calls to go over
# RMI!
#java.naming.provider.url=localhost
```

The properties required when a client outside the JBoss VM connects to the JNP server are as follows:

Property	Value
Context. INITIAL_CONTEXT_FACTORY	org.jnp.interfaces.NamingContextFactory.
Context.PROVIDER_URL	jnp://<your server>:port. If you don't specify the protocol, it defaults to jnp; if you don't specify the port, it defaults to 1099.
Context.URL_PKG_PREFIXES	org.jboss.naming:org.jnp.interfaces.
jnp.socketFactory	This should specify an implementation of javax.net.SocketFactory. The default value is org.jnp.interfaces.TimedSocketFactory.
jnp.timeout	This specifies the connection timeout in milliseconds. A default value of 0 means the connection will wait for the underlying transport to time out.
jnp.sotimeout	This specifies the read timeout for a connected socket. The default value of zero will perform a blocking read.

So, for example, to configure a client to call into the JBoss JNDI namespace, you would use code such as this:

Create the properties required to connect to the JBoss naming provider:

```
Properties prop = new Properties();

prop.put(Context.INITIAL_CONTEXT_FACTORY,
    "org.jnp.interfaces.NamingContextFactory");
prop.put(Context.PROVIDER_URL,
    "jnp://localhost:1099");
prop.put(Context.URL_PKG_PREFIXES,
    "org.jboss.naming:org.jnp.interfaces");
```

Create an initial context connecting to the JBoss naming provider:

```
InitialContext jbossContext = new InitialContext(prop);
```

6.2.2 Client JAR Files

To connect to the JNP server, at bare minimum, you need the following JAR files available in the client directory of your JBoss installation:

❑   jnp-client.jar

❑   log4j.jar

❑   jboss-common-client.jar

However, depending on the type of object you're looking up, you may need extra JAR files. For example, if you're looking up Java Message Service (JMS) administered objects, you'll need the jbossmq-client.jar file in the client classpath. See section 2.2, "JBoss Directory Structure," for a complete rundown of the client JAR files.

6.3 JNDI View

JBoss provides an MBean that is configured in the root configuration file to view the objects bound in its JNDI namespace. The MBean definition is as follows:

```
<mbean
  code="org.jboss.naming.JNDIView"
  name="jboss:service=JNDIView">
```

If you access the MBean from the JMX console and invoke the list() method, it will list all the contexts and objects in the JNDI namespace:

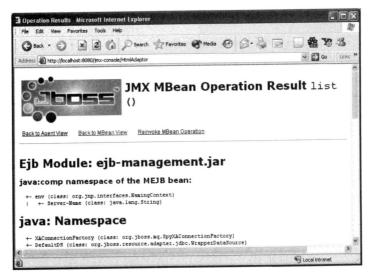

This page is useful for troubleshooting problems that occur in performing naming and lookup operations. The page lists all the contexts and subcontexts within the naming provider and all the objects that are bound within the naming provider that show the JNDI name and type of the object that is exported.

6.4 External JNDI Namespaces

JBoss provides an MBean for incorporating external namespaces into the JBoss namespace. This means that you can look up objects bound in JNDI namespaces defined outside JBoss through the JBoss naming provider. The MBean definition is as follows:

```
<mbean
    code="org.jboss.naming.ExternalContext"
    name="jboss.jndi:service=ExternalContext">
```

This MBean supports the following attributes:

Attribute	Function
JndiName	This is the JNDI name under which the external namespace is bound.
RemoteAccess	This is a flag to indicate whether the initial context of the external namespace should be bound as a serializable object. This will allow a client running outside the JBoss VM to create the external initial context. The external initial context is looked up using the standard JNDI lookup calls through the JBoss initial context.
CacheContext	This is a flag to state whether the external initial context should be created and cached when the MBean is started.
InitialContext	This is the fully qualified name of the class that implements the JNDI initial context.
Properties	This is to specify a standard properties file that contains the initial context properties required to connect to the external naming provider.

An example is as follows:

```
<mbean
  code="org.jboss.naming.ExternalContext"
  name="jboss.jndi:service=ExternalContext,jndiName=WLSContext">

  <attribute name="JndiName">WLSContext</attribute>
  <attribute name="InitialContext">
    weblogic.jndi.internal.WLInternalContext
  </attribute>
  <attribute name="RemoteAccess">true</attribute>
  <attribute name="RemoteAccess">weblogic.properties</attribute>

</mbean>
```

The previous example defines an external naming provider running within a BEA WebLogic environment. You can look up the initial context for the WebLogic JNDI namespace through the JBoss initial context. To do this, you need to first create an initial context that connects to the JBoss naming provider. Then you should use that initial context to look up the WebLogic initial context.

The code to use the external context may look as follows:

```
Properties prop = new Properties();

prop.put(Context.INITIAL_CONTEXT_FACTORY,
    "org.jnp.interfaces.NamingContextFactory");
prop.put(Context.PROVIDER_URL,
    "jnp://localhost:1099");
prop.put(Context.URL_PKG_PREFIXES,
    "org.jboss.naming:org.jnp.interfaces");

InitialContext jbossContext = new InitialContext(prop);
```

Look up the external initial context using the JBoss initial context:

```
InitialContext wlsContext =
    (InitialContext)jbossContext.lookup("WLSContext");
```

6.5 JNDI Link References

JBoss provides an MBean for creating JNDI link references. JNDI link references allow you to create symbolic links to existing JNDI names. The MBean definition is as follows:

```
<mbean
    code="org.jboss.naming.NamingAlias"
    name="myDomain:service=myService">
```

This MBean supports the following attributes:

Attribute	Function
FromName	Specifies the original JNDI name
ToName	The alias name

An example is as follows:

```
<mbean
    code="org.jboss.naming.NamingAlias"
    name="myDomain:service=myService">
    <attribute name="ToName">newName</attribute>
    <attribute name="FromName">oldName</attribute>
</mbean>
```

This MBean will link the oldName mapping to the new mapping of newName.

6.6 HTTP-Based JNDI

JBoss provides an HTTP-based implementation for using JNDI contexts. As mentioned earlier, the JNDI implementation provided by JBoss uses RMI for communication between the JNDI clients and the naming provider. However, this can pose problems if the clients that connect to the naming provider sit outside a firewall. Firewalls allow communication to a set of predefined ports. In such cases, communication based on RMI may not be possible. HTTP is one of the protocols passed through by most firewalls, and they allow remote clients to connect to port 80 of the internal servers. In such cases, rather than using RMI-based initial context factories, you can use the alternative HTTP-based JNDI implementation provided by JBoss.

This is available as a SAR component called `http-invoker.sar` in the `\deploy` directory. To use this, you need to use the following code:

```
Properties prop = new Properties();

prop.put(Context.INITIAL_CONTEXT_FACTORY,
    "org.jboss.naming.HttpNamingContextFactory");
prop.put(Context.PROVIDER_URL,
    "http://localhost:8080/invoker/JNDIFactory");
InitialContext context = new InitialContext(prop);
```

Please note that the initial context factory is different from the one mentioned earlier, and the protocol for the provider URL is HTTP rather than JNP. To use this you need to have `jboss-client.jar` file in the client classpath.

7

Configuring Security

Security is a key aspect of enterprise application development; it should be addressed with utmost importance. Java 2 Enterprise Edition (J2EE) provides a simple yet powerful means of defining role-based security in both programmatic and declarative manners. J2EE web applications are secured by defining, in the web deployment descriptor, the roles required by the subjects for accessing secured Uniform Resource Locators (URLs). As for Enterprise JavaBeans (EJBs), the security constraints are defined at method level for the home and remote interface methods in the EJB deployment descriptor.

JBoss provides a security mechanism independent of the implementation technology. JBoss security caters for standard J2EE role-based security as well as custom security requirements. In this chapter, you'll see the JBoss security architecture and look at how to configure and extend the various JBoss security features.

7.1 JBoss Security Features

This chapter will cover the security features provided by JBoss in further detail:

- **Pluggable Security Layer**
  JBoss provides a set of interfaces that define the behavior of the JBoss security layer. These interfaces define the contract between the other JBoss core modules for performing various security related tasks such as authentication, authorization, security realm mapping, and so on. These interfaces provide an implementation-independent way of integrating the security layer to the rest of the JBoss core modules. This means you can write your own security layer compliant with the JBoss security interfaces and configure JBoss to use it.

- **JBossSX Implementation**
  JBossSX is an out-of-the-box security extension that implements the JBoss security layer. JBossSX is implemented based on **Java Authentication and Authorization Service (JAAS)**. JBoss also comes with a set of built-in JAAS login modules that enable you to store security information such as principals, credentials, and roles in a variety of sources such as database servers, directory services, text files, and so on. It also allows you to write custom login modules to integrate with specialized security applications.

- **Security Proxy**
  J2EE provides a simplified form of enforcing security using users and roles mapping. However, this scheme may not solve complex security requirements where security policies are influenced by domain data. For example, in an employee information system, you may want to allow an employee to change only their address and nobody else's. Requirements such as this one are obviously difficult to implement using J2EE user role–based security. One obvious option is to implement this security requirement in your business components. However, JBoss provides a powerful scheme of externalizing security functionality from business components, using the security proxy architecture. Section 17.5.3, "Security Proxy," cover security proxies in detail.

- **Secure Remote Password (SRP) Protocol**
  SRP protocol is an Internet standards working group specification for public key exchange handshake. JBossSX provides an implementation of the SRP protocol.

- **Secure Sockets**
  JBoss supports EJB invocation using secure sockets.

7.2 The JBoss Security Layer

In this section, you look at the JBoss security layer, which is comprised mainly of the following three interfaces:

❏ org.jboss.security.AuthenticationManager
   Defines methods for validating credentials against principals

❏ org.jboss.security.RealmMapping
   Defines methods for mapping principals and roles to security information stored in a datasource such as a database or directory service

❏ org.jboss.security.SecurityProxy
   Used for implementing custom security requirements

It's important that security implementations implement the aforementioned interfaces. In addition to these interfaces, the security layer also defines the following interfaces:

❏ org.jboss.security.SubjectSecurityManager
   Extends the authentication manager interface and defines extra methods for accessing the security domain associated with the security manager and the authenticated subject associated with the current thread.

❏ org.jboss.security.SecurityDomain
   Extends the subject security manager and realm mapping interfaces and defines methods to provide support for secure invocations, keystore interactions, and so on.

> **Please note that the functionality offered by the** Security-Domain **interface is still in development and will provide comprehensive security architecture in the future versions of JBoss that support multiple domains.**

Both the web and EJB containers delegate the actual task of authentication and authorization to the security layer implementation through the interfaces defined in the security layer. At runtime, JBoss uses the security layer implementation with which it has been configured. In most cases, you'll use the default JBossSX implementation that comes with JBoss. The class following diagram depicts how the JBoss web and EJB containers interact with the security implementation through the security layer. Please note that the security layer is accessed through an interceptor-based framework that is explained in detail in section 7.3.1, "Security Interceptor Architecture:"

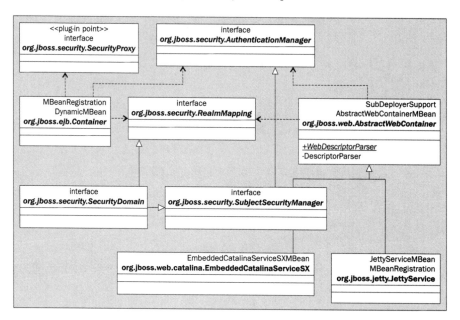

> **Enforcing declarative security constraints for web components using the JBoss security layer and JBoss-specific web deployment descriptor is covered in detail in section 16.1, "The JBoss Web Deployment Descriptor," and that for EJBs is covered in detail in section 17.5, "EJB Security."**

7.3 JBossSX Implementation

JBossSX provides an implementation to the security layer explained in the previous section using JAAS. The org.jboss.security.plugins.JaasSecurityManager class, which implements the authentication manager and realm mapping interfaces, is at the core of JBossSX. The security implementation layer that should be used within JBoss is usually defined using the security manager MBean service in the jboss-service.xml JBoss root configuration file available in the \conf directory of the configuration set you use.

In the JBoss-specific deployment descriptors for EJB and web components, `jboss.xml` and `jboss-web.xml`, respectively, you can specify the security domain to be used for authenticating and authorizing threads when they access secure methods and Uniform Resource Indentifiers (URIs). The EJB and web containers interface with the JAAS security manager to perform authentication and authorization checks. The security domain normally defines the JAAS login module to use for authentication and authorization and any information specific to the login module used. JBoss comes with a set of prebuilt login modules that can interface with security information stored in databases, Lightweight Directory Access Protocol (LDAP) directory services, and so on.

7.3.1 Security Interceptor Architecture

Both JBoss EJB and web containers use an interceptor-based architecture similar to the GoF Decorator pattern. This framework allows interceptors to be inserted between the originator of the invocation and the invocation target to add additional functionality. In JBoss, interceptors are used for a wide variety of purposes, such as imposing security, transactions, and so on. The security interceptors access the underlying security implementation through the contract exposed by the security layer to perform various security-related tasks.

The following diagram depicts how the JBoss security interceptors use the JBossSX implementation for performing security-related tasks:

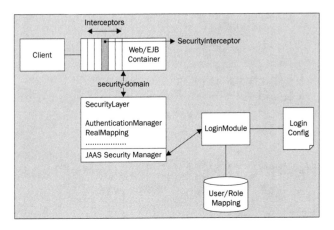

J2EE web components are secured by specifying the roles used to access URIs in the web deployment descriptor. In the same way, EJB components are secured by specifying the roles required to invoke the home and component interface methods in the EJB deployment descriptors.

However, to map these roles to the security policies in the operational environment, you need to use the JBoss-specific web and EJB deployment descriptors. These descriptors provide a `security-domain` element that's used to map the security policies defined in the JBoss environment to the declarative security specified in the standard deployment descriptors. The value of this element should be in the format `java:jaas/<domain_name>`, where domain_name is the name used to define the login configuration for the domain.

During the deployment of web and EJB components, JBoss creates an instance of the security manager for the component and sets its security domain name to the value specified by the `security-domain` element. When a client accesses a secure web resource or invokes a secure EJB method, the container delegates the process of authentication and authorization to the security manager instance.

Here, the JAAS security manager instance will use the standard JAAS Application Programming Interface (API) to use an appropriate login module to perform the necessary security tasks. The JAAS security manager creates an instance of the JAAS `LoginContext` class by passing the security domain value to the login context, and it uses the methods defined on the login context to perform authentication and authorization. Login modules are configured in external resources against the same value specified for the `security-domain` element. JBoss comes with a set of prebuilt login modules. Section 7.3.4, "Prebuilt Login Modules," explains the prebuilt login modules that come with JBoss.

> **Please note that if you're using JAAS security manager in different components, all of them will be using different instances of the `JaasSecurityManager` class. The difference is that each of them will be configured to use the security domain specified for that deployment unit in its JBoss-specific deployment descriptor.**

7.3.2 Configuring the JAAS Security Manager

In this section, you'll look at how to configure the JAAS security manager. The JAAS security manager is normally configured using the `JaasSecurityManagerService` MBean service in the JBoss root configuration file, `jboss-service.xml`, in the \conf directory of the configuration set you use. Please note that even though the name of the MBean is `JaasSecurityManagerService`, it doesn't have anything specific to do with JAAS. You can use it for defining any security manager implementation for the JBoss abstract security layer. The MBean definition is as follows:

```
<mbean
    code="org.jboss.security.plugins.JaasSecurityManagerService"
    name="jboss.security:service=JaasSecurityManager">
```

The security manager MBean provides a variety of attributes for configuring the various security related properties, such as security manager implementation, security proxy factory, caching policy, and so on.

An example of using the security manager MBean for defining the security layer implementation to be used is as follows:

```
<mbean
    code="org.jboss.security.plugins.JaasSecurityManagerService"
    name="jboss.security:service=JaasSecurityManager">
    <attribute name="SecurityManagerClassName">
        org.jboss.security.plugins.JaasSecurityManager
    </attribute>
</mbean>
```

The security manager implementation service defined previously defines the JAAS security manager as the security layer implementation to use. Please note that the class identified by the content for the `SecurityManagerClassName` attribute should implement the `AuthenticationManager` and `RealmMapping` interfaces.

> *This service also provides a JNDI Service Provider Interface (SPI) object factory implementation for creating objects in the context java:/jaas. This is to make sure that any lookup for objects in the java:/jaas context will always return instances of the JaasSecurityManager class. The EJB and web containers will look up the security manager associated with the EJB or web application to perform a security check.*

The security manager MBean service supports the following attributes:

Attribute	Function
SecurityManagerClassName	Used for defining the class that implements the org.jboss.security.AuthenticationManager and org.jboss.security.RealmMapping interfaces. If not supplied, it defaults to org.jboss.security.plugins.JaasSecurity-Manager.
SecurityProxyFactory ClassName	Used for defining the class that implements the org.jboss.security.SecurityProxyFactory class used for creating security proxies. The default value is org.jboss.security.SubjectSecurityProxyFactory. Security proxies are used for implementing custom security.

continues

71

Attribute	Function
AuthenticationCache JndiName	Used for defining the security credential caching policy. Caching policies are defined per security domain. By default, JBoss uses a timed caching policy. CachePolicy is a generic JBoss interface used for defining caching policies. Several implementations are available based on different logics such as Least Recently Used (LRU) replacement, timed caching, and so on. The value defined in this attribute is appended to the security domain name to look up the cache policy for the domain.
DefaultCacheTimeout	Used for defining the timeout value, in seconds, for the timed cache policy. The default value is 1,800 seconds. This attribute is only applicable when the AuthenticationCacheJndiName attribute isn't set. A small timeout value means that changes made to the user-role mapping information made in the underlying security store will be available to the security manager in a shorter period of time at the cost of performance.
DefaultCache Resolution	Used for defining the interval, in seconds, at which the cache is checked for resolution. The default value is 60 seconds. This attribute is only applicable when the AuthenticationCacheJndiName attribute isn't set.

The following listing shows a more exhaustive example of using the security manager service MBean to define the security layer implementation to be used:

```
<mbean
  code="org.jboss.security.plugins.JaasSecurityManagerService"
  name="jboss.security:service=JaasSecurityManager">
  <attribute name="SecurityManagerClassName">
    org.jboss.security.plugins.JaasSecurityManager
  </attribute>
  <attribute name="DefaultCacheTimeout">
    60
  </attribute>
  <attribute name="DefaultCacheResolution">
    15
  </attribute>
</mbean>
```

Shorter values defined for the timed cache policy configuration values mean that the JAAS security manager will be revalidating the cached principal, roles, and credentials information at relatively short intervals of time. This will make sure that the cached information reflects the security store information more accurately.

7.3.3 Login Configuration

In the previous section, you saw that the JAAS security manager used the login modules configured for the security domains for performing authentication and authorization. You have also seen that the information specific to the login modules are stored against the security domain names in external resources. In this section, you'll see how these external resources can be configured within JBoss.

7.3.3.1 Security Config MBean

The security config MBean defines a reference to another MBean that's used for reading login configuration information. JBoss 3.x uses an implementation of the JAAS Configuration interface, and it uses an XML file for storing the login configuration information. This information contains the mapping of security domain values to login module definitions. The following snippet shows the definition of the security config MBean in the JBoss root configuration file:

```
<mbean
  code="org.jboss.security.plugins.SecurityConfig"
  name="jboss.security:name=SecurityConfig">
  <attribute name="LoginConfig">
    jboss.security:service=XMLLoginConfig
  </attribute>
</mbean>
```

The LoginConfig attribute defines the MBean object name of the MBean that provides access to the security configuration information. If this isn't specified, JBoss will use the default implementation of the javax.security.auth.login.Configuration class. The default format used by this class is as follows:

```
1 -> identityModule {
2 ->    org.jboss.security.auth.spi.IdentityLoginModule required
3 ->    principal=Meeraj
4 ->    roles=admin,author
5 -> }
```

In this example, line 1 defines the security domain name. If this login module is used to define the security domain for your web or EJB components, the value that should be used is `java:/jaas/identityModule`. Line 2 defines the login module to be used and whether the login module is `required`, `requisite`, `sufficient`, or `optional`. Section 7.3.3, "Login Configuration," explains the significance of these attributes. The class defined on line 2 should implement the JAAS `LoginModule` interface. Lines 3 to 5 specify properties specific to the login module that's used.

7.3.3.2 XML Login Config MBean

The XML login config MBean extends the JAAS `Configuration` interface to provide the security configuration functionality based on an XML structure. The definition of this MBean in the JBoss root configuration file is as follows:

```
<mbean
   code="org.jboss.security.auth.login.XMLLoginConfig"
   name="jboss.security:service=XMLLoginConfig">
   <attribute name="ConfigResource">login-config.xml</attribute>
</mbean>
```

The `ConfigResource` attribute defines the name of the XML file containing the security configuration information. JBoss comes with a sample file called `login-config.xml` in the `\conf` directory of the default configuration set that contains some simple definitions for JAAS login modules.

The following diagram depicts the organization of the security MBeans and the login configuration file:

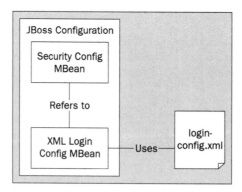

7.3.3.3 Login Configuration Data

In this section, you'll look at the structure of the XML file used for storing login configuration. The structure for the XML is shown in the following figure:

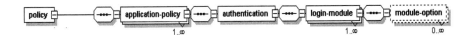

The elements are defined as follows:

Element	Function	Attributes
policy	The root element of the security policy configuration. It can contain one or more application-policy elements.	None.
application-policy	Defines the security configuration for an application domain and may contain one authentication element.	name is a mandatory attribute for the application-policy element and is used to link the login modules defined for the application policy to the security domain defined in the JBoss-specific deployment descriptors for the web and EJB components.
authentication	Used to define one or more login modules that should be used to perform authentication.	
login-module	Defines the details of the login module that should be used for authentication.	The flag attribute controls how a login module participates in the overall authentication procedure: Required means the login module is required to succeed. Irrespective of whether it succeeds or fails, the authentication continues to proceed down the login module list.

continues

Element	Function	Attributes
		`Requisite` means the login module is required to succeed. If it succeeds, authentication continues down the login module list. If it fails, control immediately returns to the application.
		`Sufficient` means the login module isn't required to succeed. If it does succeed, control immediately returns to the application. If it fails, authentication continues down the login module list.
		`Optional` means the login module isn't required to succeed. If it succeeds or fails, authentication continues to proceed down the login module list.
		The overall authentication succeeds only if all required and requisite login modules succeed. If a sufficient login module is configured and it succeeds, only the required and requisite login modules *prior* to that sufficient login module need to have succeeded for the success of the overall authentication. If no required or requisite login modules are configured for an application, then at least *one* sufficient or optional login module must succeed.
		`code` is a mandatory attribute used to define the name of the class that implements the JAAS `LoginModule` interface.

Element	Function	Attributes
module-option	Used to define any options that are specific to the configured login module. For example, it can be used for defining the datasource JNDI name, user ID, password, and so on for a database login module. The value of the text content defines the value of the option and the value of the name attribute defines the name of the option.	The name attribute is used to define the name of the module option.

The following snippet shows how the login configuration explained in the previous section can be defined using the XML structure:

```
<policy>
  <application-policy name="identityModule">
    <authentication>
      <login-module
        flag="true"
        code="org.jboss.security.auth.spi.IdentityLoginModule">
        <module-option name="principal">Meeraj</module-option>
        <module-option name="roles">admin,author</module-option>
      </login-module>
    </authentication>
</policy>
```

You'll look at these options in more detail the following sections.

7.3.4 Prebuilt Login Modules

JBoss comes with a set of prebuilt login modules as well as some abstract login module implementations, which can be used for writing your own custom login module. The important prebuilt login modules that come with JBoss are as follows:

- ❑ Identity login module
- ❑ Users roles login module
- ❑ LDAP login module
- ❑ Database login module
- ❑ Client login module

77

In this section, you'll see how to configure each of these login modules in detail.

7.3.4.1 Identity Login Module

The identity login module is primitive and can be used for testing the security behavior of your application. The implementation class is `org.jboss.security.auth.spi.Identity-LoginModule`. The users and roles information are stored in the login module configuration itself. This module supports the following module options:

Module Option	Function
principal	Defines the value against which the identities of all subjects are authenticated.
roles	Specifies a list of comma-separated roles to which the principals are assigned.
password-stacking	If the value of this option is set to `true`, the module will look for a property by the name `javax.security.auth.login.name` in its shared state map. If found, it'll use that value for authenticating the user. If not, it'll store the value specified by the principal option in the shared state map against the same name. Login modules use shared state for sharing information.

An example of configuring identity login modules is as follows:

```
<policy>
  <application-policy name="myIdentityModule">
    <authentication>
      <login-module
        flag="true"
        code="org.jboss.security.auth.spi.IdentityLoginModule">
        <module-option name="principal">Meeraj</module-option>
        <module-option name="roles">admin,author</module-option>
      </login-module>
    </authentication>
  </policy>
```

This example defines a login module that will authenticate a user only if the user name is `Meeraj` and assigns the roles `admin` and `author` to the authenticated user.

7.3.4.2 Users Roles Login Module

The users roles login module is based on two properties files that store the users and roles information. The user names and passwords are stored in a file called `users.properties`, and the roles assigned to users are stored in `roles.properties`.

These files can be placed in any location available to the thread context classloader. This means you can place the files in the system or server classpath, including deployment units, configuration directory, and so on.

The code attribute is `org.jboss.security.auth.spi.UsersRolesLoginModule`, which supports the following module options:

Module option	Function
unauthenticated-identity	This specifies the identity for requests without any authentication information. This can be used for getting the name of the authenticated principal in unsecured EJB methods and servlet URIs.
password-stacking	If the value of this option is set to `true`, the module will look in its shared state map for a property by the name `javax.security.auth.login.name`. If found, it'll use that value for authenticating the user. If not found, it'll store the value specified by the principal option in the shared state map against the same name. Login modules use shared state for sharing information amongst them.
hashAlgorithm	This is the message digest algorithm to be used to hash the password. If hashing is enabled, the passwords stored in the properties file should be hashed. The password obtained from the caller is hashed before they are compared to those stored in the properties file. Unless specified, hashing isn't used. The valid hashing algorithms are MD5, SHA-1, and so on.
hashEncoding	This defines the string format for the hashed password and should be either `hex` or `base64`. The default is `base64`. This is only used if a hash algorithm is specified.
hashCharset	This defines the character set to transform the hashed password to a byte array. If not specified, this uses the platform's default character set.
usersProperties	This defines the name of the file that contains the users-to-passwords mapping, and the default value is `users.properties`.
rolesProperties	This defines the name of the file that contains the users-to-roles mapping, and the default value is `roles.properties`.

7.3.4.2.1 Properties File Format

The properties file that stores the users-to-passwords mapping stores it in the format `user_name=password` as follows:

```
Meeraj=batoutofhell
Waheeda=barkatthemoon
Fiza=hitthelights
```

The roles properties file stores the users-to-roles mapping in the format `user_name=role1,role2,....` The users-to-roles mapping can optionally use a role group value. The role group defines a named group of roles assigned to the user. The JAAS security manager expects the standard `Roles` role group to define the permissions defined for the user. An example is as follows:

```
meeraj=admin,author
meeraj.Roles=admin,author
```

An example of using the Users Roles login module is as follows:

```
<policy>
  <application-policy name="myUsersRolesModule">
    <authentication>
      <login-module
        flag="true"
        code="org.jboss.security.auth.spi.UsersRolesLoginModule">
        <module-option name="hashAlgorithm">MD5</module-option>
      </login-module>
    </authentication>
  </policy>
```

This login module reads the user and role mapping information from the default `users.properties` and `roles.properties` file to perform authentication/authorization. The passwords are hashed using MD5 algorithm.

7.3.4.3 Database Login Module

The database login module authenticates the users and roles against the security information stored in a Java Database Connectivity (JDBC)–compliant database. The login module implementation class used is `org.jboss.security.auth.spi.DatabaseServerLoginModule`. This login module uses SQL to get the users-to-passwords mapping and users-to-roles mapping information.

The query for the users-to-passwords mapping should return a result set of the following format:

```
Principal          Password
********************************
Meeraj             nightcrawler
```

The names of the columns aren't important. However, the number and order of columns are important. The SQL for returning user information should return two columns representing the user names and passwords respectively. The query for the users-to-roles mapping should return the result set in the following format:

```
Principal            Role        RoleGroup
***********************************************
Meeraj               admin       Roles
Meeraj               author      Roles
```

Please note that for the JAAS security manager, the roles assigned to the user should be defined in rows for which the RoleGroup value is Roles. The names of the columns aren't important, but the number and order of columns are. The SQL for returning roles mapping should return three columns representing user name, role, and role group, respectively.

A simple database table creation script for storing users-to-passwords mapping may look like this:

```
CREATE TABLE users (
   user_id VARCHAR(30) NOT NULL PRIMARY KEY,
   password VARCHAR(30) NOT NULL)
```

The query for getting the users-to-passwords information may look like this:

```
SELECT user_id, password FROM users WHERE user_id = ?
```

A simple database table creation script for storing users-to-roles mapping may look like list:

```
CREATE TABLE roles (
   user_id VARCHAR(30) NOT NULL,
   role VARCHAR(30) NOT NULL,
   role_group VARCHAR(30) NOT NULL)
```

The query for getting the users-to-roles information may look like this:

```
SELECT user_id, roles, role_group FROM roles WHERE user_id = ?
```

The database server login module supports the following module options in addition to unauthenticated-identity, password-stacking, hashAlgorithm, hashEncoding, and hashCharset options, as discussed in section 7.3.4.2, "User Roles Login Module:"

Module Option	Function
dsJndiName	The JNDI name of the datasource used to get connections to the database that stores the security information. The default value is java:/DefaultDS.
principalsQuery	Defines the query used for getting the principals-to-passwords mapping information. This query expects the subject identity as known in the operational environment as an input argument.
rolesQuery	Defines the query used for getting the principals-to-roles mapping information. This query expects the subject identity as known in the operational environment as an input argument.

An example of using the database login module is as follows:

```
<policy>
  <application-policy name="myDatabaseModule">
    <authentication>
      <login-module
        flag="true"
        code="org.jboss.security.auth.spi.DatabaseServerLoginModule">
        <module-option name="dsJndiName">java:/MyDS</module-option>
        <module-option name="principalsQuery">
          SELECT * FROM users WHERE user_id = ?
        </module-option>
        <module-option name="rolesQuery">
          SELECT * FROM roles WHERE user_id = ?
        </module-option>
      </login-module>
    </authentication>
  </application-policy>
</policy>
```

This example defines a login module that will read the users and roles mapping information from database tables.

7.3.4.4 LDAP Login Module

The LDAP login module retrieves the security information from an LDAP directory server. The login module implementation class used is org.jboss.security.auth.spi-.LDAP-LoginModule. The LDAP login module supports the following module options in addition to unauthenticated-identity, password-stacking, hashAlgorithm, hashEncoding, and hashCharset options as described in section 7.3.4.2, "User Roles Login Module:"

Module Option	Function
`java.naming.factory.initial`	The JNDI initial context factory used to connect to the LDAP server.
`java.naming.provider.url`	The JNDI provider URL used to connect to the LDAP server.
`java.naming.security.authentication`	The security level to use to connect to the LDAP server. The allowed values are `none` (for using no authentication, binding anonymously) and `simple` (for weak authentication, using a clear text password).
`java.naming.security.protocol`	Optionally used to define the wire protocol for secure access to the LDAP server.
`java.naming.security.principal`	The principal used to connect to the LDAP server.
`java.naming.security.credentials`	The credentials used to connect to the LDAP server.
`principalDNPrefix`	To specify a string that should be prefixed to the passed user name to construct the fully distinguished LDAP name of the user.
`principalDNSuffix`	To specify a string that should be suffixed to the passed user name to construct the fully distinguished LDAP name of the user.
`useObjectCredential`	A flag is used to define whether JBoss should use an opaque object for the password or a plain char array.
`rolesCtxDN`	To specify the distinguished name of the context that's used to store the users-to-roles mapping.
`roleAttributeId`	To specify the name of the attribute that contains the user's roles. The default value is `roles`.
`uidAttributeID`	To specify the attribute name used to identify the object containing the roles for a user ID.
`matchOnUserDN`	If this flag is `true`, the search for user roles should match the users fully distinguished name.

An example of using the LDAP login module for getting users and roles mapping information is as follows:

```
<policy>
  <application-policy name="myLDAPModule">
    <authentication>
      <login-module
        flag="true"
        code="org.jboss.security.auth.spi.LDAPLoginModule">
        <module-option name="java.naming.factory.initial">
          com.sun.jndi.ldap.LdapCtxFactory
        </module-option>
        <module-option name="java.naming.provider.url">
          ldap://Scooby-doo:1389
        </module-option>
        <module-option name="java.naming.security.authentication">
          simple
        </module-option>
        <module-option name="principalDNPrefix">
          uid=
        </module-option>
        <module-option name="uidAttributeID">
          user_id
        </module-option>
        <module-option name="roleAttributeID">
          role
        </module-option>
        <module-option name="principalDNSuffix">
          ou=I Solutions, o=EDS
        </module-option>
        <module-option name="rolexCtxDN">
          cn=Roles, ou=Roles, o=EDS
        </module-option>
      </login-module>
    </authentication>
  </application-policy>
</policy>
```

In the previous example, users-to-roles mapping will be stored in a context identified by the DN "cn=Roles, ou-Roles, o=EDS" under the attribute named role. The login module uses the JNDI properties specified as the module option to connect to the LDAP server. The LDAP module will set the JNDI principal property by concatenating the values specified for principalDNPrefix and principalDNSuffix around the subject ID passed to the login module. In this case, if the passed subject identity is meeraj, the principal that's set will be "uid=meeraj,ou=I Solutions, o=EDS". The JNDI credentials property will be set to the password passed to the login module. The login to succeed the passed password should match the userPassword attribute stored in the principal context.

To perform authorization, the login module will get the list of attributes by the name `role` in the subcontexts with an attribute named `user_id` matching the subject identity passed in any subcontexts of the roles context. An example of the context organization is as follows:

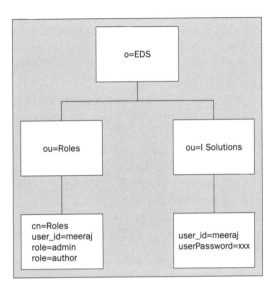

7.3.4.5 Client Login Modules

JBoss EJB clients can use: client modules for authenticating themselves. An example of the client login module configuration is as follows:

```
<policy>
  <application-policy name="myClientModule">
    <authentication>
      <login-module
        flag="true"
        code=" org.jboss.security.auth.spi.ClientLoginModule">
      </login-module>
    </authentication>
  </policy>
```

This login module doesn't perform any authentication. It simply copies the authentication information to the client-side EJB invocation layer, which sends it to the server during EJB invocation. This login module supports the following module options:

Module Option	Function
password-stacking	If the value of this option is set to true, the module will look in its shared state map for a property by the name javax.security.auth.login.name. If found, it'll use that value for authenticating the user. If not found, it'll store the value specified by the principal option in the shared state map against the same name. Login modules use shared state for sharing information amongst them.
multi-threaded	If this flag is set to true, each thread will have its own copy of principal and credentials information.

The \client directory under JBoss installation contains a sample login config file called auth.conf based on the standard JAAS configuration format that can be used for client login. The following snippet shows the excerpt from this file for configuring client login module:

```
other {

    // JBoss LoginModule
    org.jboss.security.ClientLoginModule required
        ;
};
```

To use the client login module in your applications, you need to perform the following steps:

1. Write an implementation of the JAAS CallbackHandler interface:

```
public class MyCallbackHandler implements CallbackHandler {

    private String userId;
    private char[] passwd;

    public MyCallbackHandler(String arg0, String arg1) {
        userId = arg0;
        passwd = arg1.toCharArray();
    }

    public void handle(Callback[] callbacks)
        throws IOException, UnsupportedCallbackException {

        for(int i = 0; i < callbacks.length; i++) {
            if(callbacks[i] instanceof NameCallback) {
                ((NameCallback)callbacks[i]).setName(userId);
            } else if(callbacks[i] instanceof PasswordCallback) {
                ((PasswordCallback)callbacks[i]).setPassword(passwd);
            }
        }
    }
}
```

2. In the client code, set the path to the JBoss login configuration file should be set as the system property `java.security.auth.login.config`:

```
System.setProperty("java.security.auth.login.config", c:\\auth.conf");
```

3. Create a JAAS `login()` context by passing an instance of your callback handler and the name of the login module to use:

```
MyCallbackHandler handler = new MyCallbackHandler("meeraj",
                                                  password");
```

4. Call the `login()` method on the login context:

```
ctx.login();
```

7.3.5 Custom Login Modules

To write custom login modules that can work with the JAAS security manager, you need to understand how the JAAS security manager identifies subject identities and roles. The JAAS security manager uses the `javax.security.auth.Subject` class to store subject identities and roles. JAAS security manager expects user identities to be stored using `java.security.Principal` instances in the set of principals for the `Subject`. JBoss provides an implementation of `java.security.Principal`, called `org.jboss.security.SimplePrincipal`.

The roles assigned to a user are also stored as set of principals. They're grouped as a set of `java.security.acl.Group` instances. This interface extends the `Principal` interface and models an aggregation of principals. The JAAS security manager expects a group called `Roles` that contains the list of roles assigned to the user.

JBoss provides two abstract login modules that provide the implementation of the subject usage pattern. You can extend these classes to write a custom login module. These are the following:

`AbstractServerLoginModule`

`UserNamePasswordLoginModule`

7.3.5.1 AbstractServerLoginModule

The `AbstractServerLoginModule` class is the base class of all the JBoss login modules and implements the JAAS SPI interface `LoginModule`. If you're using this as your base class, you need to override and provide implementation to the following methods:

```
public void initialize(Subject subject,
                       CallbackHandler handler,
                       Map sharedSate,
                       Map options);
```

87

This method initializes the login module. Normally you would call `super.initialize()` and extract any module options you've specified for your module in the login module configuration from the options map. For example, in the database login module you'd extract the module options such as datasource JNDI name.

```
public boolean login();
```

This method will implement the logic for verifying the subject's identity. The superclass provides convenience methods for getting subject identity in the operational environment and the credentials that are passed. This method should look for the following properties in the shared state map if the `useFirstPass` option is set:

❑   `javax.security.auth.login.name` for the subject identity that's passed

❑   `javax.security.auth.login.password` for the credentials that are passed

```
abstract protected Principal getIdentity();
```

This method should return the subject identity in the underlying security information store corresponding the identity that's passed in.

```
abstract protected Group[] getRoleSets();
```

This method should return the groups that correspond to the roles that are assigned to the users. The JAAS security manager expects a group called `Roles` that contains all the roles assigned to the user.

7.3.5.2 UserNamePasswordLoginModule

The `UserNamePasswordLoginModule` class extends the `AbstractServerLoginModule` and provides convenience methods that return user identity as a string and password as a char array. If you're using this class as your base class, you need to override and provide implementation to the following methods:

```
public void initialize(Subject subject,
                       CallbackHandler handler,
                       Map sharedSate,
                       Map options);
```

This method initializes the login module. Normally you'd call `super.initialize()` and extract any module options you've specified for your module in the login module configuration from the options map. For example, in the database login module you'd extract the module options such as datasource JNDI name:

```
abstract protected String getUsersPassword();
```

This method should return the password of the subject identity in the underlying security information store:

```
abstract protected Group[] getRoleSets();
```

This method should return the groups that correspond to the roles that are assigned to the users. The JAAS security manager expects a group called `Roles` that contains all the roles assigned to the user.

7.3.5.3 Writing a Login Module

In this example, you look at a `UsersRolesLoginModule` class, which extends the `UsernamePasswordLoginModule`, to see how to write custom login modules:

```
package org.jboss.security.auth.spi;

import java.io.InputStream;
import java.io.IOException;
import java.net.URL;
import java.util.*;

import java.security.acl.Group;
import javax.security.auth.Subject;
import javax.security.auth.callback.*;
import javax.security.auth.login.*;
import javax.security.auth.spi.LoginModule;

import org.jboss.security.*;
import org.jboss.security.auth.spi.UsernamePasswordLoginModule;

public class UsersRolesLoginModule
extends UsernamePasswordLoginModule {
```

The instance variables store the users-to-passwords and users-to-roles mapping:

```
private String usersRsrcName = "users.properties";
private String rolesRsrcName = "roles.properties";
private Properties users;
private Properties roles;
```

The `initialize()` method calls the same on the superclass and parses the module options. It also loads the security information stored in the files:

```
public void initialize(Subject subject,
    CallbackHandler callbackHandler, Map sharedState, Map options) {

  super.initialize(subject, callbackHandler, sharedState, options);
  try {
    String option = (String) options.get("usersProperties");
    if(option != null) usersRsrcName = option;
```

```
        option = (String) options.get("rolesProperties");
        if(option != null) rolesRsrcName = option;

        loadUsers();
        loadRoles();
    } catch(Exception e) {
        super.log.error("Failed to load users/passwords/role files", e);
    }

}
```

The `login()` method calls the same method on the superclass:

```
public boolean login() throws LoginException {

    if(users == null) {
        throw new LoginException("Missing users.properties file.");
    }
    if(roles == null) {
        throw new LoginException("Missing roles.properties file.");
    }
    return super.login();

}
```

The following method iterates through the roles defined for the users and returns the roles as an array of groups. Each group in the array is a named role set:

```
protected Group[] getRoleSets() throws LoginException {

    String targetUser = getUsername();
    Enumeration users = roles.propertyNames();
```

This group is important for the JAAS security manager because it should contain all the roles that are allowed to the user:

```
    SimpleGroup rolesGroup = new SimpleGroup("Roles");

    ArrayList groups = new ArrayList();
    groups.add(rolesGroup);
    while(users.hasMoreElements() && targetUser != null) {

        String user = (String) users.nextElement();
        String value = roles.getProperty(user);

        int index = user.indexOf('.');
        boolean isRoleGroup = false;
        boolean userMatch = false;

        if(index > 0 && targetUser.regionMatches(0, user, 0, index)
            == true) {
            isRoleGroup = true;
```

```
      } else {
        userMatch = targetUser.equals(user);
      }
      if(isRoleGroup == true ) {
        String groupName = user.substring(index+1);
        if( groupName.equals("Roles")) {
          parseGroupMembers(rolesGroup, value);
        } else {
          SimpleGroup group = new SimpleGroup(groupName);
          parseGroupMembers(group, value);
          groups.add(group);
        }
      } else if(userMatch == true) {
        parseGroupMembers(rolesGroup, value);
      }
    }
    Group[] roleSets = new Group[groups.size()];
    groups.toArray(roleSets);

    return roleSets;
  }
```

The following method returns the user's password. This method is used from the superclass for performing the login:

```
protected String getUsersPassword() {

  String username = getUsername();
  String password = null;
  if(username != null) {
    password = users.getProperty(username , null);
  }
  return password;
}
```

A utility method for parsing the roles is as follows:

```
private void parseGroupMembers(Group group, String value) {

  StringTokenizer tokenizer = new StringTokenizer(value, ",");
  while(tokenizer.hasMoreTokens()) {
    String token = tokenizer.nextToken();
    SimplePrincipal p = new SimplePrincipal(token);
    group.addMember(p);
  }
}
```

The next three methods are utility methods for loading the security information:

```
private void loadUsers() throws IOException {
  users = loadProperties(usersRsrcName);
}
```

```
private void loadRoles() throws IOException {
  roles = loadProperties(rolesRsrcName);
}

private Properties loadProperties(String propertiesName)
    throws IOException {

  Properties bundle = null;
  ClassLoader loader =
  Thread.currentThread().getContextClassLoader();

  URL url = loader.getResource(propertiesName);
  if(url == null) {
      throw new IOException("Properties file " + propertiesName +
      " not found");
  }
  super.log.trace("Properties file=" + url);
  InputStream is = url.openStream();
  if(is != null) {
    bundle = new Properties();
    bundle.load(is);
  } else {
    throw new IOException("Properties file " +
      propertiesName + " not avilable");
  }
  return bundle;
}
}
```

To use your login module within JBoss, you need to first make the login module class available to the classloader. An easy way to do this is to package this into a Java Archive (JAR) and copy to the \lib directory of the configuration set you use. Once you've done that, you can use it in login-config.xml by specifying the class name of your login module as the value for the class attribute for the login module you're configuring.

7.3.6 JAAS Security Domain

The JAAS security domain extends the JAAS security manager that provides, in addition to the functionality already provided by the JAAS security manager, support for Secure Sockets Layer (SSL) and cryptographic functionalities. You need to use the JAAS security domain if you want to set up SSL for accessing the JBoss embedded web container or invoke EJBs over SSL. The JAAS security domain supports the following MBeans:

❑ KeyStoreType
   The type of the keystore that's used.

❑ KeyStoreURL
   The location of the keystore that should be used.

❑ `KeyStorePass`
The keystore password.

❑ `LoadSunJSEProvider`
A flag to indicate whether the Sun JSSE provider should be loaded.

❑ `ManagerServiceName`
To set the object name of the security manager service MBean. The default value is `jboss.security:service=JaasSecurityManager`.

Configuring the JAAS security domain is covered in section 11.2.3.3, "Enabling SSL on Jetty" and section 12.1.8, "Enabling SSL on Tomcat."

7.4 Security Proxies

Security proxies provide a mechanism of externalizing custom security code from the business components on a per-method basis. Security proxy works alongside the security proxy interceptor. In the JBoss-specific EJB deployment descriptor, you can specify a security proxy class that will implement the custom security logic for that EJB. The interceptor architecture will use the proxy to execute the custom security code before invoking the bean methods. These classes are required to implement the `org.jboss.security.SecurityProxy` interface. The interface defines the following methods:

```
public void init(Class beanHome,
                 Class beanRemote,
                 Object securityMgr)
   throws InstantiationException;
```

You can use this method to perform any initialization such as caching method references for the home and remote classes:

```
public void setEJBContext(EJBContext ctx);
```

This method is called prior to any method invocation to set the current EJB context:

```
public void invokeHome(Method m, Object[] args)
   throws SecurityException;
```

This method is called to allow the security proxy to perform any custom security checks required for the EJB home interface method:

```
public void invoke(Method m, Object[] args, Object bean)
   throws SecurityException;
```

93

This method is called to allow the security proxy to perform any custom security checks required for the EJB remote interface method:

You can use the `security-proxy` element in the JBoss EJB deployment descriptor for configuring a security proxy with a bean.

> **Security proxies are covered in further detail in section 17.5.3, "Security Proxy."**

7.5 Enabling SSL

JBoss allows you to use Remote Method Invocation (RMI) over SSL for invoking EJBs and the web container allows SSL for secure access to web components. JBoss uses **Java Secure Socket Extension (JSSE)** for enabling SSL-based invocation. To enable SSL-based invocation, you need to perform the following steps:

1. Install JSSE.

   If you're using Java Development Kit (JDK) 1.4, you don't need to do this because JSSE bundles with JDK. If you're using an earlier version, follow the following steps explained.

   You can download JSSE from the Javasoft web site (http://www.javasoft.com/products/jsse/). The latest version is 1.0.3. Please follow the following steps to install JSSE:

   ❑ Unpack the downloaded file to your local drive. This will create a directory called `\jsse1.0.3` that will contain a `\lib` directory. The `\lib` directory will contain the files `jcert.jar`, `jnet.jar`, and `jsse.jar`.

   ❑ Install these files as installed extensions. For this, copy these files to the `\lib\ext` directory of your Java Runtime Environment (JRE).

   ❑ Register the JSSE provider in the `java.security` file in the `\lib\security` directory of your JRE by adding the following entry. Depending on the number of registered providers, the number following the string `security.provider` will vary.

```
security.provider.3=com.sun.net.ssl.internal.ssl.Provider
```

2. Install a keystore entry for the key pair to use.

Now you need to generate the key pair. For testing, you'll use a self-signed certificate. In production, you may need to get your certificate signed by a Certificate Authority (CA) such as VeriSign or RSA. To do this, use the following command:

```
keytool -genkey -keyalg RSA -storepass password -keypass password
        -keystore ssl.keystore
```

This will create a new keystore using the RSA key algorithm by the name ssl.keystore with the store password and the default key password as password. Now create a directory called \ssl under the JBoss \bin directory and copy the keystore to the newly created directory.

Using SSL with the EJB and web containers is covered more specifically in section 11.2.3.3, "Enabling SSL on Jetty" and section 12.1.8, "Enabling SSL on Tomcat."

Configuring JCA and Datasources

The Java Connector Architecture (JCA) is a Java 2 Enterprise Edition (J2EE) Application Programming Interface (API) for enabling J2EE applications to interface with external resource managers, such as databases, legacy mainframe systems, Enterprise Resource Planning (ERP) systems, and so on. **JBossCX** is a JCA implementation that comes with JBoss. Internally JBoss uses the JCA implementation for connecting to Java Database Connectivity (JDBC) databases.

JCA is based on resource adapters that are used for connecting to external resource managers. Resource managers provide standard resource adapters that are used to connect them. These resource adapters run within any application server that supports JCA to use the various services provided by the applications, such as resource pooling, transactions, and security.

The following diagram depicts an overview of JCA:

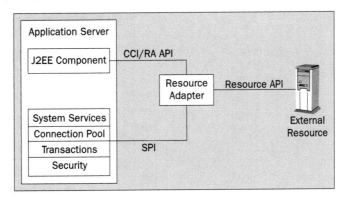

The resource adapter uses a resource-specific API to communicate to the external resource manager. J2EE components can communicate with the external resource through the resource adapter. For this they can either use the resource adapter–specific API or the loosely typed Common Client Interface (CCI). Visual development tools provided by the resource manager normally use CCI. In most cases, application developers will use a resource-specific API for communicating with the resource manager.

For example, JBoss provides JCA adapters for communicating with JDBC databases. In this case, rather than using CCI, you'll use JDBC to communicate with the database.

JCA resource adapters are packaged as Java Archive (JAR) files with `.rar` extensions. They contain a file called `ra.xml` in the `\META-INF` directory that describes the resource adapter. The resource adapter deployment descriptor provides information on handling connection pooling, security, transactions, and so on.

8.1 JCA in JBossCX

JBossCX implements the application server side of JCA. The JBossCX implementation uses several MBean components for enabling the use of JCA resource adapters within the JBoss environment. These MBean components expose the connection factory that's used to create connections to the resource manager in the Java Naming Directory Interface (JNDI) namespace. The location in the JNDI namespace is defined as one of the MBean attributes.

Before you deploy the MBean services used to expose the resource adapter connection factory in the JNDI namespace, you need to make sure that the Resource Archive (RAR) representing the resource adapter is deployed within JBoss. The MBean services get relevant information on the managed connection factory and other details from the RAR deployment descriptor of the deployed resource adapter.

The following diagram depicts the main MBeans used to create the resource adapter connection factory in the JNDI namespace and their dependencies:

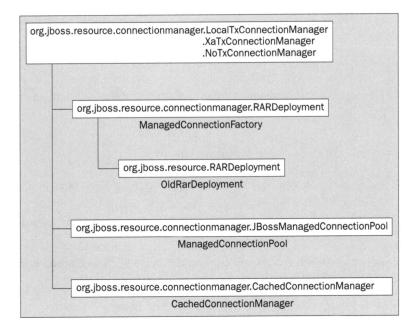

8.1.1 The Connection Manager MBean

The connection manager MBean is the main MBean that decides the level of transaction support you require from the JCA resource adapter. JBoss provides three connection managers that extend `org.jboss.resource.connection-manager.BaseConnectionManager2`. These connection managers are (all located in the `org.jboss.resource.connectionmanager` package):

- `NoTxConnectionManager`
  Use this if your connection factory doesn't support transactions.

- `LocalTxConnectionManager`
  Use this if your connection factory supports only local transactions.

- `XATxConnectionManager`
  Use this if your connection factory supports distributed transactions.

The following example shows a connection manager MBean definition that supports local transactions:

```
<mbean
   code=
   "org.jboss.resource.connectionmanager.LocalTxConnectionManager"
   name="jboss.jca:service=LocalTxCM,name=OracleDS">
</mbean>
```

This MBean mainly depends on the following MBeans:

❑ Managed connection factory (see section 8.1.1.1, "The Managed Connection Factory MBean")

❑ Managed connection pool (see sect section 8.1.1.2, "The Managed Connection Pool MBean")

❑ Cached connection manager (see section 8.1.1.3, "The Cached Connection Manager MBean")

8.1.1.1 The Managed Connection Factory MBean

The managed connection factory MBean is responsible for creating an instance of the connection factory and exposing it in the JNDI namespace by the specified JNDI name. Normally this MBean is defined as an embedded MBean of the connection manager MBean as follows:

```
<mbean
   code="org.jboss.resource.connectionmanager.
        LocalTxConnectionManager"
   name="jboss.jca:service=LocalTxCM,name=OracleDS">
   ...
   <depends
     optional-attribute-name="ManagedConnectionFactoryName">
     <mbean
       code="org.jboss.resource.connectionmanager.RARDeployment"
       name="jboss.jca:service=LocalTxDS,name=OracleDS">
       ...
     </mbean>
   </depends>

</mbean>
```

This MBean gathers information about the resource adapter from the actual RAR that's deployed. Each time a RAR is deployed, the RAR deployer starts an MBean that exposes an MBean of type `org.jboss.resource.connectionmanager.RARDeployment` that encapsulates the deployment descriptor information present in `ra.xml`. The object name of this MBean takes the format `jboss.jca:service=RARDeployment,name=<Display Name>`, where `<Display Name>` represents the display name of the resource adapter specified in the RAR deployment descriptor.

The managed connection factory MBean should use the `depends` element with the `optional-attribute-name` attribute to define the object name of the MBean that encapsulates the RAR deployment descriptor as follows. The value of the `optional-attribute-name` attribute should be `OldRarDeployment`:

```
<mbean
    code="org.jboss.resource.connectionmanager.RARDeployment"
    name="jboss.jca:service=LocalTxDS,name=OracleDS">
    <depends optional-attribute-name="OldRarDeployment">
        jboss.jca:service=RARDeployment,name=JBoss LocalTransaction
        JDBC Wrapper
    </depends>
    . . .
</mbean>
```

The previous MBean supports two MBean attributes:

❑   The first one called `JndiName` specifies the JNDI name to which the resource manager connection factory is bound.

❑   The second called `ManagedConnectionFactoryProperties` is an XML fragment required to specify the configuration information required for the connection factory.

The XML fragment for the `ManagedConnectionFactoryProperties` attribute has the following format:

```
<properties>
    <config-property name="name" type="type"></config-property>
    <config-property name="name" type="type"></config-property>
    . . .
<properties>
```

The root element is `properties`, which can contain zero or more `config-property` elements. Each `config-property` element has a `name` attribute identifying the name of the property and a `type` attribute specifying the type of the property. The text content of this element defines the value of the property. The properties are passed to the resource manager connection factory by the managed connection factory MBean.

The connection factory properties for a local transaction connection factory are as follows:

❑   `ConnectionURL`

❑   `DriverClass`

❑   `UserName`

❑   `Password`

For an XA connection factory, the properties expected are as follows:

❑   `XADataSourceProperties`

❑   `XADataSourceClass`

❑   `UserName`

❑   `Password`

The following example shows the properties required to create a local transaction–based connection to an Oracle database:

```
<mbean
    code="org.jboss.resource.connectionmanager.RARDeployment"
    name="jboss.jca:service=LocalTxDS,name=OracleDS">
    ...
    <attribute name="JndiName">OracleDS</attribute>

    <attribute name="ManagedConnectionFactoryProperties">
      <properties>
        <config-property name="ConnectionURL" type="java.lang.String">
          jdbc:oracle:thin:@youroraclehost:1521:yoursid
        </config-property>
        <config-property name="DriverClass" type="java.lang.String">
          oracle.jdbc.driver.OracleDriver
        </config-property>
        <config-property name="UserName" type="java.lang.String">
          megadeath
        </config-property>
        <config-property name="Password" type="java.lang.String">
          euthanasia
        </config-property>
      </properties>
    </attribute>

</mbean>
```

8.1.1.2 The Managed Connection Pool MBean

The managed connection pool MBean is responsible for providing connection pooling functionality. JBoss provides a managed connection pool implemented by the class

102

`org.jboss.resource.connectionmanager.JbossManagedConnectionPool.`
This MBean supports the following attributes:

Attribute	Function
MinSize	Minimum size of the pool.
MaxSize	Maximum size of the pool.
BlockingTimeoutMillis	Indicates the maximum time to block while waiting for a connection before throwing an exception.
IdleTimeoutMinutes	Indicates the maximum time a connection may be idle before being closed.
Criteria	Indicates whether to use container-managed security for this connection. The possible values are as follows:
	❏ ByContainerAndApplication
	❏ ByContainer
	❏ ByApplication
	❏ ByNothing

The managed connection pool MBean is defined as an embedded MBean within the connection manager MBean using the `depends` element with the `optional-attribute-name` attribute set to `ManagedConnectionPool`:

```
<mbean
    code="org.jboss.resource.connectionmanager.LocalTxConnectionManager"
    name="jboss.jca:service=LocalTxCM,name=OracleDS">
    ...
    <depends optional-attribute-name="ManagedConnectionPool">
      <mbean
        code="org.jboss.resource.connectionmanager.
            JBossManagedConnectionPool"
        name="jboss.jca:service=LocalTxPool,name=OracleDS">

        <attribute name="MinSize">0</attribute>
        <attribute name="MaxSize">50</attribute>
        <attribute name="BlockingTimeoutMillis">5000</attribute>
        <attribute name="IdleTimeoutMinutes">15</attribute>
      </mbean>
    </depends>
    ...
</mbean>
```

8.1.1.3 The Cached Connection Manager MBean

The connection manager uses this for handling connections across transaction and method boundaries. The connection manager uses the optional attribute name `CachedConnectionManager` to get a reference to the object name of the cached connection manager as an MBean attribute. The cached connection manager MBean is normally defined in the `transaction-service.xml` file, which is defined in the `\deploy` directory of the configuration set:

```
<mbean
    code="org.jboss.resource.connectionmanager.CachedConnectionManager"
    name="jboss.jca:service=CachedConnectionManager">
    <!--SpecCompliant false means JBoss will close connections left
        open when you return from a method call and generate a loud
        warning. SpecCompliant true means JBoss will disconnect
        connection handles left open on return from a method call
        and reconnect them with an appropriate (security, tx)
        connection on the next call to the same object.-->
    <attribute name="SpecCompliant">false</attribute>
</mbean>
```

8.1.1.4 Other Dependencies and Attributes

The connection manager may also define the following attributes and dependencies:

❏   JaasSecurityManagerService
    This is defined as a `depends` element with the `optional-attribute-name` attribute. This refers to the object name of the Java Authentication and Authorization Service (JAAS) security manager MBean.

❏   TransactionManager
    This is defined as a plain MBean attribute and refers to the JNDI name of the transaction manager.

❏   RARDeployer
    This is defined as a `depends` element that refers to the object name of the RAR deployer MBean. This is actually a hack to get the RAR deployer MBean started and all the RARs deployed before the MBeans used for exposing the RAR connection factory in the JNDI namespace and providing connection pooling to the resource manager are started.

The following code is an example of these three dependencies:

```
<mbean
    code="org.jboss.resource.connectionmanager.LocalTxConnectionManager"
    name="jboss.jca:service=LocalTxCM,name=OracleDS">
    ...
    <depends optional-attribute-name="JaasSecurityManagerService">
```

```
      jboss.security:service=JaasSecurityManager
  </depends>

  <attribute name="TransactionManager">
    java:/TransactionManager
  </attribute>

  <depends>jboss.jca:service=RARDeployer</depends>

</mbean>
```

8.2 JBossCX and Datasources

JBoss uses JCA to interface with relational databases. For databases that support JCA, JBoss directly uses the resource adapters provided by the database. However, for databases that don't support JCA, JBoss provides two resource adapters that are present in the \deploy directory of the default configuration set:

❑ jboss-local-jdbc.rar
   This resource adapter should be used for configuring datasources that support only local transactions.

❑ jboss-xa.rar
   This should be used for configuring datasources that support distributed transactions.

One thing you need to keep in mind about these resource adapters is their display names in the resource deployment descriptor because you need this when you configure the managed connection factory MBean. The display name for the local RAR is JBoss LocalTransaction JDBC Wrapper and that for the XA RAR is Minerva JDBC XATransaction ResourceAdapter.

To configure a datasource, you need to configure the MBeans explained in the previous sections. JBoss provides example MBean configurations for many mainstream databases in the \docs\examples\jca\ directory of the JBoss installation. These examples include the following:

❑ asapxcess-jb3.2-ds.xml
   Datasources for aSAPXcess SAP

❑ cicsr9s-service.xml
   JCA-compliant adapter for CICS ECI

105

❑ `db2-ds.xml`
    Datasources supporting local transactions for DB2

❑ `db2-xa-ds.xml`
    Datasources supporting distributed transactions for DB2

❑ `facets-ds.xml`
    Connection factory for GemStone Facets

❑ `fastobjects-jboss32-ds.xml`
    Connection factory for FastObjects t7 resource adapter

❑ `firebird-ds.xml`
    Firebird provides a JCA-compliant adapter

❑ `generic-ds.xml`
    A sample configuration showing all the possible options

❑ `hsqldb-ds.xml`
    Datasources supporting local transactions for the Hypersonic SQL database

❑ `informix-ds.xml`
    Datasources supporting local transactions for Informix

❑ `informix-xa-ds.xml`
    Datasources supporting distributed transactions for Informix

❑ `jdatastore-ds.xml`
    Datasources supporting local transactions for Borland JDataStore

❑ `lido-versant-service.xml`
    LIDO provides a JCA-compliant adapter

❑ `msaccess-ds.xml`
    Datasources supporting local transactions for Microsoft Access

❑ `mssql-ds.xml`
    Datasources supporting local transactions for Microsoft SQL Server

❑ `mssql-xa-ds.xml`
    Datasources supporting distributed transactions for Microsoft SQL Server

❑ `oracle-ds.xml`
    Datasources supporting local transactions for Oracle

❑ `oracle-xa-ds.xml`
    Datasources supporting distributed transactions for Oracle

❑   `postgres-ds.xml`
Datasources supporting local transactions for PostgreSQL

❑   `sapdb-ds.xml`
Datasources supporting local transactions for SAP DB

❑   `sapr3-ds.xml`
Connection manager for SAP R/3

❑   `solid-ds.xml`
Datasources supporting local transactions for Solid

❑   `sybase-ds.xml`
Datasources supporting local transactions for Sybase SQL Server

8.2.1 Configuring Datasources

Configuring datasources within JBoss involves the same steps as configuring any JCA resource adapter connection factory explained in section 8.1.1, "The Connection Manager MBean." This section summarizes the steps involved once again whilst constructing a datasource to connect to an Oracle database using local transactions for the PetStore application:

1. Configure the connection manager MBean. This is normally defined as the root MBean of a SAR deployment descriptor. The code for this MBean should be one of `NoTxConnectionManager`, `LocalTxConnectionManager`, or `XaTxConnection-Manager` depending on the level of transaction support you need:

```
<mbean
   code="org.jboss.resource.connectionmanager.
         LocalTxConnectionManager"
   name="jboss.jca:service=LocalTxCM,name=jdbc/petstore/PetStoreDB">
```

2. Define an embedded MBean within the connection manager MBean using the depends element to define the connection factory MBean. The depends element should have an `optional-attribute-name` attribute with value set to `ManagedConnectionFactoryName`:

```
<depends optional-attribute-name="ManagedConnectionFactoryName">
  <mbean
     code="org.jboss.resource.connectionmanager.RARDeployment"
     name="jboss.jca:service=LocalTxDS,
           name=jdbc/petstore/PetStoreDB">
```

107

3. Use the `ManagedConnectionFactoryProperties` MBean attribute of the connection factory MBean to define an XML fragment containing the configuration information for the connection factory. The local JDBC/JCA wrapper provided by JBoss expects `DriverClass`, `ConnectionURL`, `UserName`, and `Password` whereas the XA JDBC/JCA wrapper provided by JBoss expects `XADataSourceProperties`, `XADataSourceClass`, `UserName`, and `Password`:

```
<attribute name="ManagedConnectionFactoryProperties">
  <properties>
    <config-property name="ConnectionURL"
                     type="java.lang.String">
     jdbc:oracle:thin:@youroraclehost:1521:yoursid
    </config-property>
    <config-property name="DriverClass"
                     type="java.lang.String">
      oracle.jdbc.driver.OracleDriver
    </config-property>
    <config-property name="UserName" type="java.lang.String">
      megadeath
    </config-property>
    <config-property name="Password" type="java.lang.String">
      euthanasia
    </config-property>
  </properties>
</attribute>
```

> **Of course, the driver class needs to be loaded onto the JBoss classpath. See section 5.2, "Setting the Classpath," for how to do this.**

4. Use the `JndiName` MBean attribute of the connection factory MBean to define the JNDI name used look up the datasource:

```
<attribute name="JndiName">
  jdbc/petstore/PetStoreDB
</attribute>
```

5. Define an embedded MBean within the connection factory MBean using the `depends` element to define the RAR deployment MBean that encapsulates the RAR deployment information. For the local JDBC/JCA wrapper, this content should be `jboss.jca:service=RARDeployment,name=JBoss LocalTransaction JDBC Wrapper`, and for XA JDBC-JCA wrapper it should be `jboss.jca:service=RARDeployment,name=Minerva JDBC XATransaction ResourceAdapter`:

```
<depends optional-attribute-name="OldRarDeployment">
  jboss.jca:service=RARDeployment,
  name=JBoss LocalTransaction JDBC Wrapper
</depends>
```

6. Define an embedded MBean within the connection manager MBean using the depends element to define the connection factory MBean. The depends element should have an optional-attribute-name attribute with value set to ManagedConnectionPool. Use the embedded MBean's attributes to define pool initial size, maximum size, and so on:

```
<depends optional-attribute-name="ManagedConnectionPool">
  <mbean
    code="org.jboss.resource.connectionmanager.
        JBossManagedConnectionPool"
    name="jboss.jca:service=LocalTxPool,
        name=jdbc/petstore/PetStoreDB">

    <attribute name="MinSize">1</attribute>
    <attribute name="MaxSize">50</attribute>
    <attribute name="BlockingTimeoutMillis">5000</attribute>
    <attribute name="IdleTimeoutMinutes">15</attribute>
    <attribute name="Criteria">ByContainer</attribute>
  </mbean>
</depends>
```

7. Define a depends element within the connection manager MBean with content as the object name of the cached connection manager MBean. The depends element should have an optional-attribute-name attribute with value set to CachedConnectionManager:

```
<depends optional-attribute-name="CachedConnectionManager">
  jboss.jca:service=CachedConnectionManager
</depends>
```

8. Define a depends element within the connection manager MBean with content as the object name of the JAAS security manager MBean:

```
<depends optional-attribute-name="JaasSecurityManagerService">
  jboss.security:service=JaasSecurityManager
</depends>
```

9. Define an `attribute` element within the connection manager MBean with content pointing to the JNDI name of the transaction manager:

```
<attribute name="TransactionManager">
  java:/TransactionManager
</attribute>
```

10. Define a `depends` element within the connection manager MBean with content as the object name of the RAR deployer to force the RAR deployer to deploy all the RAR components:

```
<depends>jboss.jca:service=RARDeployer</depends>
```

8.2.2 Using Container-Managed Resource Security

When you connect to a resource manager from your application, you can either manage the security in the application or let the container handle the security. Examples for this are the `getConnection()` and `getConnection(user, passwd)` methods on the `javax.sql.DataSource` class. If you use the first method, the *container* should manage the security, and in the second instance the *application* manages security.

When you configure datasources in JBoss, it can manage the security for you. To enable this, follow these steps:

1. Set the `Criteria` attribute of your connection pool to `ByContainer`:

```
<mbean
   code="org.jboss.resource.connectionmanager.
         JBossManagedConnectionPool"
   name="jboss.jca:service=LocalTxPool,
         name=jdbc/petstore/PetStoreDB">

   <attribute name="MinSize">1</attribute>
   <attribute name="MaxSize">50</attribute>
   <attribute name="BlockingTimeoutMillis">5000</attribute>
   <attribute name="IdleTimeoutMinutes">15</attribute>
   <attribute name="Criteria">ByContainer</attribute>
</mbean>
```

2. Next, you'll have to configure a login module that's an instance of the `org.jboss.resouce.security.AbstractPasswordCredentialLoginModule` class. This login module expects a module option called `managedConnectionFactoryName`, which should be set to the connection manager object name. JBoss provides two subclasses of the aforementioned login module. They are as follows:

❏ `ConfiguredIdentityLoginModule`
This will use the principal and credentials specified as the module options for connecting to the resource manager.

❏ `CallerIdentityLoginModule`
This login module will use the principal and credentials of the user authenticated by the application for connecting to the resource manager.

You can configure the login module embedded either in the connection manager MBean or in the `login-config.xml` file. The following uses the embedded MBean:

```
<mbean
    code="org.jboss.resource.connectionmanager.
        LocalTxConnectionManager"
    name="jboss.jca:service=LocalTxCM,name=jdbc/petstore/PetStoreDB">
    ...
    <application-policy name="DbRealm">
      <authentication>
        <login-module
          code="org.jboss.resource.security.
              ConfiguredIdentityLoginModule"
        flag="required">
        <module-option name="principal">dba</module-option>
        <module-option name="userName">sql</module-option>
        <module-option name="password">sql</module-option>
        <module-option name="managedConnectionFactoryName">
          jboss.jca:service=LocalTxCM,name=jdbc/petstore/PetStoreDB
        </module-option>
      </login-module>
    </authentication>
  </application-policy>
    ...
</mbean>
```

Please refer to section 7.3.3.3, "Login Configuration," for a guideline to the elements configured previously.

The module option `managedConnectionFactoryName` should match the object name of the connection manager. You can also define the login module inside the `login-config.xml` file, as discussed in section 7.3.3.3, "Login Configuration."

3. Next, you need to specify the name of the login module as the value for the `SecurityDomainJndiName` of the connection manager:

```
<mbean
    code="org.jboss.resource.connectionmanager.
        LocalTxConnectionManager"
    name="jboss.jca:service=LocalTxCM,name=jdbc/petstore/PetStoreDB">
    ...
    <attribute name="SecurityDomainJndiName">DbRealm</attribute>
</mbean>
```

The MBean attribute `SecurityDomainJndiName` should match the login module that should be used for authentication.

In the previous example, the container passes the user name and password specified by the configured identity login module for getting connections from the database.

Configuring JBossMQ

In this chapter, you'll look at how to configure JBossMQ, a fully compliant Java Message Service (JMS) 1.0.2 implementation from JBoss for building message-oriented enterprise-class applications. JBossMQ supports both point-to-point and publish/subscribe messaging. To begin with, let's look at the JBossMQ architecture.

9.1 JBossMQ Architecture

JBossMQ comprises multiple submodules as depicted in the following diagram:

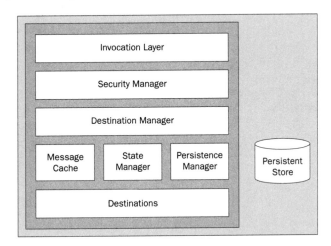

The submodules of JBossMQ are as follows:

- **Invocation Layer**
  The invocation layer handles the communication between JBossMQ and messaging clients for sending and receiving JMS messages.

- **Security Manager**
  The security manager controls access to the JMS destinations defined with JBossMQ.

- **Destination Manager**
  The destination manager is responsible for managing destinations, message cache, state manager, and persistence manager.

- **Message Cache**
  JMS messages within JBossMQ are stored in memory caches for performance enhancement.

- **State Manager**
  JBossMQ uses the state manager to keep track of users and their durable subscriptions.

- **Persistence Manager**
  JBossMQ uses the persistence manager to persist the JMS messages that are marked as persistent to a **persistent store**.

- **Destinations**
  Destinations are the topics and queues to which JMS messages are sent and consumed.

9.2 Invocation Layer

The invocation layer controls the communication between JBossMQ and the messaging clients. JBossMQ currently supports four different types of invocation layers. Connection factories for all the four types of invocation layers are created and bound in the Java Naming and Directory Interface (JNDI) namespace under different names. The clients using a particular type of invocation layer need to look up and use the connection factory associated with that invocation layer.

The invocation layers supported by JBossMQ are as follows:

❑ **RMI Invocation Layer**
The Remote Method Invocation (RMI) invocation layer uses the Java RMI protocol for handling the communication. The RMI invocation layer uses Transmission Control Protocol/Internet Protocol (TCP/IP) sockets to connect the server to the client, which can cause problems by stopping the clients in a restricted environment from opening server sockets. The RMI invocation layer is useful in scenarios where the JMS clients and JBoss run in an intranet environment.

❑ **Optimized Invocation Layer**
The Optimized Invocation Layer (OIL) uses a custom TCP/IP protocol for handling communication to enhance performance. However, this invocation layer is restricted in ways similar to the RMI invocation layer.

❑ **Unified Invocation Layer**
The Unified Invocation Layer (UIL) allows clients sitting within a firewall to send and receive JMS messages. However, this invocation layer is slower than the OIL.

❑ **JVM Invocation Layer**
The Java Virtual Machine (JVM) invocation layer is used when both the client and the server reside within the same VM. It doesn't have the overhead associated with TCP/IP socket-based communication.

All the four invocation layers use a full duplex channel for communication. This enables the clients to simultaneously send and receive messages. Invocation layers are configured as MBean services either in a single `jbossmq-service.xml` file or as separate `-service.xml` files, all of which are available in the `\deploy\jms` directory of the configuration set you use.

9.2.1 RMI Invocation Layer

The RMI invocation layer is implemented using an MBean service. Here's the MBean definition:

```
<mbean
  code="org.jboss.mq.il.rmi.RMIServerILService"
  name="jboss.mq:service=InvocationLayer,type=RMI">
```

This MBean supports the following configurable attributes:

Attribute	Function
Invoker	The object name of the Mbean that passes the client requests to the JBossMQ destination manager.
ConnectionFactoryJNDIRef	The JNDI name to which the RMI invocation layer will bind its connection factory.
XAConnectionFactoryJNDIRef	The JNDI name to which the RMI invocation layer will bind its XA connection factory.
PingPeriod	The interval, in milliseconds, which the client should ping the server to ensure that the connection isn't lost. The value zero is used for disabling pinging.

The following snippet shows the MBean definition for the RMI invocation layer:

```
<mbean
    code="org.jboss.mq.il.rmi.RMIServerILService"
    name="jboss.mq:service=InvocationLayer,type=RMI">
    <depends optional-attribute-name="Invoker">
        jboss.mq:service=Invoker
    </depends>
    <attribute name="ConnectionFactoryJNDIRef">
        RMIConnectionFactory
    </attribute>
    <attribute name="XAConnectionFactoryJNDIRef">
        RMIXAConnectionFactory
    </attribute>
    <attribute name="PingPeriod">60000</attribute>
</mbean>
```

JBoss comes preconfigured with the RMI invocation layer in the jbossmq-service.xml file, which is in the \deploy\jms directory of the default configuration set. Clients intending to use the RMI invocation layer should name RMIConnectionFactory or RMIXAConnectionFactory to look up the JMS connection factory depending on whether they need XA transaction support.

9.2.2 Optimized Invocation Layer

The optimized invocation layer is implemented using an MBean service. The MBean definition is as follows:

```
<mbean
    code="org.jboss.mq.il.oil.OILServerILService"
    name="jboss.mq:service=InvocationLayer,type=OIL">
```

In addition to the attributes supported by the RMI invocation layer, this MBean supports the following configurable attributes:

Attribute	Function
ServerBindPort	The attribute used for defining the listen port on the server.
BindAddress	The attribute used to define the listen address on the server.
EnableTcpNoDelay	This flag indicates whether the TcpNoDelay option should be used. If it's set to true, TCP/IP packets will not be buffered.

The following snippet shows the MBean definition for the OIL:

```
<mbean
    code="org.jboss.mq.il.oil.OILServerILService"
    name="jboss.mq:service=InvocationLayer,type=OIL">
    <depends optional-attribute-name="Invoker">
      jboss.mq:service=Invoker
    </depends>
    <attribute name="ConnectionFactoryJNDIRef">
      ConnectionFactory
    </attribute>
    <attribute name="XAConnectionFactoryJNDIRef">
      XAConnectionFactory
    </attribute>
    <attribute name="ServerBindPort">8090</attribute>
    <attribute name="PingPeriod">60000</attribute>
    <attribute name="EnableTcpNoDelay">true</attribute>
</mbean>
```

JBoss comes preconfigured with the optimized invocation layer in the jbossmq-service.xml file in the \deploy\jms directory of the default configuration set. Clients intending to use the optimized invocation layer should use the JNDI name ConnectionFactory or XAConnectionFactory to look up the JMS connection factory depending on whether they need XA transaction support.

9.2.3 Unified Invocation Layer

The UIL is also configured as an MBean and supports all the attributes supported by the MBean for OIL.

The following snippet shows an MBean definition for the UIL:

```
<mbean code="org.jboss.mq.il.uil2.UILServerILService"
       name="jboss.mq:service=InvocationLayer,type=UIL2">
    <depends optional-attribute-name="Invoker">
       jboss.mq:service=Invoker
    </depends>
    <attribute name="ConnectionFactoryJNDIRef">
       UIL2ConnectionFactory
    </attribute>
    <attribute name="XAConnectionFactoryJNDIRef">
       UIL2XAConnectionFactory
    </attribute>
    <attribute name="ServerBindPort">8093</attribute>
    <attribute name="PingPeriod">60000</attribute>
    <attribute name="EnableTcpNoDelay">true</attribute>
    <attribute name="ReadTimeout">70000</attribute>
    <attribute name="BufferSize">2048</attribute>
    <attribute name="ChunkSize">1000000</attribute>
</mbean>>
```

JBoss comes preconfigured with the unified invocation layer in the `jbossmq-service.xml` file, which is in the `\deploy\jms` directory of the `default` configuration set. Clients intending to use the unified invocation layer should use the JNDI name `UILConnection-Factory` or `UILXAConnectionFactory` to look up the JMS connection factory depending on whether they need XA transaction support.

9.2.4 JVM Invocation Layer

The JVM invocation layer is also implemented as an MBean and supports all the attributes supported by the RMI invocation layer.

The following snippet shows the MBean definition for the JVM invocation layer:

```
<mbean
    code="org.jboss.mq.il.jvm.JVMServerILService"
    name="jboss.mq:service=InvocationLayer,type=JVM">
    <depends optional-attribute-name="Invoker">
       jboss.mq:service=Invoker
    </depends>
    <attribute name="ConnectionFactoryJNDIRef">
       java:/ConnectionFactory
    </attribute>
    <attribute name="XAConnectionFactoryJNDIRef">
       java:/XAConnectionFactory
    </attribute>
    <attribute name="PingPeriod">0</attribute>
</mbean>
```

Note that the ping period is set to zero for the JVM invocation layer because the JMS client and the provider both run in the same VM. JBoss comes preconfigured with the JVM invocation layer in the `jbossmq-service.xml` file, which is in the `\deploy\jms` directory of the `default` configuration set. Clients intending to use the JVM invocation layer should use the JNDI name `java:/ConnectionFactory` or `java:/XAConnectionFactory` to look up the JMS connection factory depending on whether they need XA transaction support.

9.3 Destination Manager

The destination manager is responsible for keeping track of all the destinations and managing the message cache, the state manager, and the persistence manager. The destination manager is configured in the `jbossmq-service.xml` file as an MBean service. The MBean definition is as follows:

```
<mbean
    code="org.jboss.mq.server.jmx.DestinationManager"
    name="jboss.mq:service=DestinationManager">
```

The service supports the following attributes:

Attribute	Function
PersistenceManager	The object name of the MBean that configures the persistence manager
StateManager	The object name of the MBean that configures the state manager

The following snippet shows an example of the destination manager MBean configuration:

```
<mbean
    code="org.jboss.mq.server.jmx.DestinationManager"
    name="jboss.mq:service=DestinationManager">
    <depends optional-attribute-name="PersistenceManager">
      jboss.mq:service=PersistenceManager
    </depends>
    <depends optional-attribute-name="StateManager">
      jboss.mq:service=StateManager
    </depends>
</mbean>
```

The destination manager is part of an interceptor chain that passes the message from the invocation layer through to the destinations. The destination manager is required to be the last interceptor in that chain.

119

The following diagram depicts the interceptor chain that's preconfigured in the file `jbossmq-service.xml`:

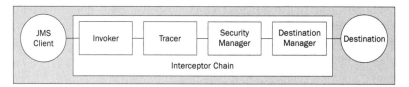

The interceptor chain shown previously contains the following components:

❑ **Invoker**
The invoker passes the invocation layer requests to the destination manager through the interceptor chain.

❑ **Tracer**
The tracer traces all the requests that go through the interceptor chain. To improve performance, you may remove this interceptor from the chain.

❑ **Security Manager**
The security manager controls access to the destinations. If you don't want to secure your destinations, you may remove this interceptor from the chain to improve performance.

❑ **Destination Manager**
The destination manager is responsible for keeping track of all the destinations, and managing the message cache, the state manager, and the persistence manager.

The following listing shows how the interceptor chain is configured in the `jbossmq-service.xml` file:

```
<mbean
  code="org.jboss.mq.server.jmx.Invoker"
  name="jboss.mq:service=Invoker">
  <depends
    optional-attribute-name="NextInterceptor">
    jboss.mq:service=TracingInterceptor
  </depends>
</mbean>

<mbean
  code="org.jboss.mq.server.jmx.InterceptorLoader"
  name="jboss.mq:service=TracingInterceptor">
  <attribute
    name="InterceptorClass">
    org.jboss.mq.server.TracingInterceptor
  </attribute>
  <depends
```

```
      optional-attribute-name="NextInterceptor">
      jboss.mq:service=SecurityManager
   </depends>
</mbean>

<mbean
   code="org.jboss.mq.security.SecurityManager"
   name="jboss.mq:service=SecurityManager">
   <depends
     optional-attribute-name="NextInterceptor">
     jboss.mq:service=DestinationManager
   </depends>
</mbean>

<mbean
   code="org.jboss.mq.server.jmx.DestinationManager"
   name="jboss.mq:service=DestinationManager">
   <depends
     optional-attribute-name="PersistenceManager">
     jboss.mq:service=PersistenceManager
   </depends>
   <depends
     optional-attribute-name="StateManager">
     jboss.mq:service=StateManager
   </depends>
</mbean>
```

Each interceptor defines the next interceptor in the chain by referring to the next interceptor's JMX object name as a depended MBean.

9.4 Message Cache

JBossMQ uses an in-memory cache to store the messages that are created. However, when the JVM runs short of resources, JBossMQ may decide to swap the messages in the cache to a persistent storage, based on a least recently used algorithm. The two MBeans (MessageCache and CacheStore), explained as follows, control the behavior of the message cache.

The first MBean, MessageCache, decides where to put JBossMQ messages waiting to be consumed by a client. Once the JVM memory usage hits the high memory mark, the old messages in the cache will start getting stored in a persistent store. As memory usage gets closer to the MaxMemoryMark, the number of messages kept in the memory cache approaches zero. The MBean's definition is as follows:

```
<mbean
   code="org.jboss.mq.server.MessageCache"
   name="jboss.mq:service=MessageCache">
```

The `MessageCache` MBean supports the following attributes:

Attribute	Function
CacheStore	Defines the object name of the MBean that configures the persistent store to which the messages are written.
HighMemoryMark	The JVM heap, in megabytes, that should be used before the messages are swapped to secondary storage. The default value when not specified is 16 megabytes (MB).
MaxMemoryMark	The maximum amount of JVM heap that the message cache can use in megabytes. The default value when not specified is 32MB.

The following snippet shows the message cache MBean definition configured in the `jbossmq-service.xml` file, or you may find it in a preconfigured `hsqldb-jdbc2-service.xml` file:

```
<mbean
  code="org.jboss.mq.server.MessageCache"
  name="jboss.mq:service=MessageCache">
  <attribute name="HighMemoryMark">50</attribute>
  <attribute name="MaxMemoryMark">60</attribute>
  <depends optional-attribute-name="CacheStore">
    jboss.mq:service=PersistenceManager
  </depends>
</mbean>
```

The second MBean that controls the behavior of the message cache, the `CacheStore` MBean, decides where to store JBossMQ messages that the `MessageCache` has decided to move to the secondary storage. This MBean has the following definition, stored in the `jbossmq-service.xml` file:

```
<mbean
  code="org.jboss.mq.pm.file.CacheStore"
  name="jboss.mq:service=CacheStore">
  <attribute name="DataDirectory">tmp/jbossmq</attribute>
</mbean>
```

It supports only one attribute, `DataDirectory`, which specifies the directory to which the messages are stored.

9.5 State Manager

The state manager is responsible for keeping track of the users who access the JBossMQ server and their durable subscriptions. The state manager is configured in the jbossmq-service.xml file as an MBean service. The service supports a single attribute called StateFile, which stores the users and durable subscriptions. The following example shows the state manager MBean configuration:

```
<mbean
  code="org.jboss.mq.sm.file.DynamicStateManager"
  name="jboss.mq:service=StateManager">
  <attribute name="StateFile">jbossmq-state.xml</attribute>
</mbean>
```

The state file is stored in Extensible Markup Language (XML) format in the \conf directory with the following format:

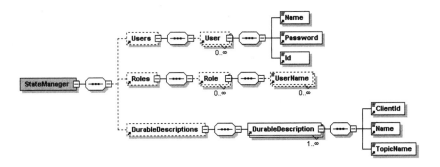

The XML contains three main elements:

❑ Users:
Contains zero or more User elements used to define the user name, password, and ID. The User element contains the following subelements:

- Name
  Used to specify the name of the user

- Password
  Used to define the password of the user

- Id
  The client ID assigned for JMS connections. The client ID is used for setting durable subscriptions

❑ Roles
Contains zero or more Role elements. Each Role element has a name attribute identifying the role name and zero or more UserName elements defining the users that have this role. The UserName element content should be one of the users defined within the User element.

❑ DurableSubscriptions
This element may contain one or more DurableSubscription elements representing the durable subscription properties. This element contains the following subelements:

- ClientID
  Used to specify the client ID used for durable subscriptions

- Name
  Used to define the durable subscription name

- TopicName
  Used to specify the topic for which the durable subscription is defined

The following snippet shows an example of the state file:

```xml
<?xml version="1.0" encoding="UTF-8"?>
<StateManager>
  <Users>
    <User>
      <Name>meeraj</Name>
      <Password>hitthelights</Password>
      <Id>DurableSubscriberExample</Id>
    </User>
    <User>
      <Name>guest</Name>
      <Password>guest</Password>
    </User>
    <User>
      <Name>nobody</Name>
      <Password>nobody</Password>
    </User>
  </Users>
  <Roles>
    <Role name="guest">
      <UserName>guest</UserName>
      <UserName>meeraj</UserName>
    </Role>
    <Role name="subscriber">
      <UserName>meeraj</UserName>
    </Role>
    <Role name="publisher">
      <UserName>meeraj</UserName>
      <UserName>dynsub</UserName>
```

```
        </Role>
        <Role name="durpublisher">
          <UserName>meeraj</UserName>
          <UserName>dynsub</UserName>
        </Role>
        <Role name="noacc">
          <UserName>nobody</UserName>
        </Role>
      </Roles>
      <DurableSubscriptions>
        <DurableSubscription>
          <ClientID>DurableSubscriberExample</ClientID>
          <Name>myDurableSub</Name>
          <TopicName>TestTopic</TopicName>
        <DurableSubscription>
      </DurableSubscriptions>
    </StateManager>
```

9.6 Persistence Manager

The persistence manager is responsible for storing persistent messages to a secondary storage device. JBossMQ supports three different types of persistence managers:

❑ **File Persistence Manager**
  This persistence manager stores persistent messages in a file system. It creates one directory per destination for storing persistent messages. Each message is stored as a file in the directory that corresponds to its respective destination.

❑ **Rolling Logged Persistence Manager**
  This is similar to the file persistence manager, but it stores multiple messages in a single file. This file is rolled every day.

❑ **JDBC2 Persistence Manager**
  This stores persistent messages in a Java Database Connectivity (JDBC) database.

Persistence managers are normally configured in the jbossmq-service.xml file, and you can only define one persistence manager.

9.6.1 File Persistence Manager

The MBean for configuring the file persistence manager has the following definition:

```
<mbean
  code="org.jboss.mq.pm.file.PersistenceManager"
  name="jboss.mq:service=PersistenceManager">
```

125

It supports the following attributes:

Attribute	Function
MessageCache	The object name of the message cache to use
DataDirectory	The directory used to store the persistent messages

The following snippet shows an example configuration of the file persistence manager MBean:

```
<mbean
   code="org.jboss.mq.pm.file.PersistenceManager"
   name="jboss.mq:service=PersistenceManager">
   <attribute name="DataDirectory">db/jbossmq/file</attribute>
   <depends optional-attribute-name="MessageCache">
     jboss.mq:service=MessageCache
   </depends>
</mbean>
```

9.6.2 Rolling Logged Persistence Manager

The rolling logged persistence manager supports the same attributes as the file persistence manager. The following snippet shows an example configuration of the rolling logged persistence manager MBean:

```
<mbean
   code="org.jboss.mq.pm.rollinglogged.PersistenceManager"
   name="jboss.mq:service=PersistenceManager">
   <attribute name="DataDirectory">db/jbossmq/file</attribute>
   <depends optional-attribute-name="MessageCache">
     jboss.mq:service=MessageCache
   </depends>
</mbean>
```

9.6.3 JDBC2 Persistence Manager

The JDBC2 persistence manager MBean has the following definition:

```
<mbean
   code="org.jboss.mq.pm.jdbc2.PersistenceManager"
   name="jboss.mq:service=PersistenceManager">
```

This MBean supports the following attributes:

Attribute	Function
MessageCache	The object name of the message cache.
ConnectionManager	The persistence manager now uses the connection manager MBean to get the JNDI name of the datasource that's associated with the connection manager. The JNDI name is then used to look up the datasource and subsequently get a connection to the persistent store.
SqlProperties	Defines the SQL statements for creating, selecting from and inserting into tables that store persistent messages, and handling JMS transactions. The JDBC-based persistence manager uses two tables, JMS_MESSAGES for storing messages and JMS_TRANSACTIONS for keeping track of transactions.

The following snippet shows an example configuration of the JDBC2 persistence manager MBean:

```
<mbean
    code="org.jboss.mq.pm.jdbc2.PersistenceManager"
    name="jboss.mq:service=PersistenceManager">
    <depends optional-attribute-name="MessageCache">
        jboss.mq:service=MessageCache
    </depends>
    <depends optional-attribute-name="ConnectionManager">
        jboss.jca:service=LocalTxCM,name=DefaultDS
    </depends>
    <attribute name="SqlProperties">
    BLOB_TYPE=OBJECT_BLOB
    INSERT_TX = INSERT INTO JMS_TRANSACTIONS (TXID) values(?)
    INSERT_MESSAGE = INSERT INTO JMS_MESSAGES (MESSAGEID, \
        DESTINATION, MESSAGEBLOB, TXID, TXOP) VALUES(?,?,?,?,?)
    SELECT_ALL_UNCOMMITED_TXS = SELECT TXID FROM JMS_TRANSACTIONS
    SELECT_MAX_TX = SELECT MAX(TXID) FROM JMS_MESSAGES
    SELECT_MESSAGES_IN_DEST = SELECT MESSAGEID, MESSAGEBLOB \
        FROM JMS_MESSAGES WHERE DESTINATION=?
    SELECT_MESSAGE = SELECT MESSAGEID, MESSAGEBLOB FROM \
    JMS_MESSAGES WHERE MESSAGEID=? AND DESTINATION=?
    MARK_MESSAGE = UPDATE JMS_MESSAGES SET (TXID, TXOP) \
        VALUES(?,?) WHERE MESSAGEID=? AND DESTINATION=?
    DELETE_ALL_MESSAGE_WITH_TX = DELETE FROM JMS_MESSAGES \
        WHERE TXID=?
    DELETE_TX = DELETE FROM JMS_TRANSACTIONS WHERE TXID = ?
    DELETE_MARKED_MESSAGES = DELETE FROM JMS_MESSAGES WHERE \
        TXID=? AND TXOP=?
    DELETE_MESSAGE = DELETE FROM JMS_MESSAGES WHERE MESSAGEID=? \
        AND DESTINATION=?
    CREATE_MESSAGE_TABLE = CREATE TABLE JMS_MESSAGES \
        ( MESSAGEID INTEGER NOT NULL, \
        DESTINATION VARCHAR(50) NOT NULL, TXID INTEGER, TXOP CHAR(1), \
        MESSAGEBLOB OBJECT, PRIMARY KEY (MESSAGEID, DESTINATION) )
```

```
            CREATE_TX_TABLE = CREATE TABLE JMS_TRANSACTIONS ( TXID INTEGER )
        </attribute>
    </mbean>
```

9.7 Destinations

Destinations are also configured as MBeans, normally in the `jbossmq-destinations-service.xml` file in the `\deploy\jms` directory of the configuration set. The MBean has the following definition for defining queues:

```
<mbean
    code="org.jboss.mq.server.jmx.Queue"
    name="jboss.mq.destination:service=Queue,name=queue">
```

While defining topics, this MBean has the following definition:

```
<mbean
    code="org.jboss.mq.server.jmx.Topic"
    name="jboss.mq.destination:service=Topic,name=testDurableTopic">
```

It supports the following attributes:

Attribute	Function
DestinationManager	The object name of the destination manager used.
SecurityManager	The JNDI name of the security manager used to control access to the destinations.
SecurityConf	Contains an XML element that defines the roles required to read, write, and create destinations.
JNDIName	Defines the JNDI name of the destination. If the JNDI name is not specified, the JNDI name defaults to queue|topic/queue-name|topic-name, where queue-name|topic-name identifies the name attribute of the object name of the MBean.

The format of the `SecurityConf` XML fragment is as follows:

```
<security>
    <role name="name" read="true/false" write="true/false"
        create="true/false"></role>
    <role name="name" read="true/false" write="true/false"
        create="true/false"></role>
    ...
</security>
```

The root element is `security`, which defines the roles required for reading from, writing to, and creating durable subscriptions to the destination. Roles and the permissions available for each role are defined using zero or more `role` child elements of the `security` element. The `role` element contains the attributes `name` that specifies the role, and `read`, `write`, and `create` can take either `true` or `false` to indicate that the user, having the role identified by the `name` attribute, can read, write, and create durable subscriptions to the destination, respectively. The default value for read, write, and create when not specified is `false`.

The following snippet shows an example of a queue definition:

```
<mbean
    code="org.jboss.mq.server.jmx.Queue"
    name="jboss.mq.destination:service=Queue,name=queue">
    <depends optional-attribute-name="DestinationManager">
        jboss.mq:service=DestinationManager
    </depends>
    <depends optional-attribute-name="SecurityManager">
        jboss.mq:service=SecurityManager
    </depends>
    <attribute name="SecurityConf">
        <security>
            <role name="guest" read="true" write="false"/>
            <role name="publisher" read="true" write="true"/>
            <role name="noacc" read="false" write="false" create="false"/>
        </security>
    </attribute>
    <attribute name="JNDIName">
        opc/MailOrderApprovalQueue
    </attribute>
</mbean>
```

The previous example defines a queue that can be accessed by the `opc/MailOrderApprovalQueue` JNDI name. Users with `guest` role can read from the queue and not write to it. Users with `publisher` role can read from and write to the queue.

The following snippet shows an example of a topic definition:

```
<mbean
    code="org.jboss.mq.server.jmx.Topic"
    name="jboss.mq.destination:service=Topic,name=testDurableTopic">
    <depends optional-attribute-name="DestinationManager">
        jboss.mq:service=DestinationManager
    </depends>
    <depends optional-attribute-name="SecurityManager">
        jboss.mq:service=SecurityManager
    </depends>
    <attribute name="SecurityConf">
```

129

```
    <security>
      <role name="guest" read="true" write="true"/>
      <role name="publisher" read="true" write="true" create="true"/>
    </security>
  </attribute>
  <attribute name="JNDIName">
    opc/InvoiceTopic
  </attribute>
</mbean>
```

The previous example defines a topic that can be accessed by the opc/
InvoiceTopic JNDI name. Users with guest role can read from and write to the topic.
Users with publisher role can read from, write to, and create durable subscriptions
to the queue.

9.8 Security Manager

You use the security manager to control access to the JMS destinations. The security
manager refers to the jbossmq-state.xml file to identify the user and the role
assigned to the user and the file in which the addressed destination is configured to
identify the roles required to read, write, and create the destination. The destinations
are normally configured in the jbossmq-destinations-service.xml file in the
\deploy\jms directory. You can remove the security manager from the interceptor
chain if you don't want to secure your destinations.

The MBean that configures the security manager is an intermediate interceptor in the
chain that passes the messages from the invocation layer. The NextInterceptor
attribute defines the object name of the MBean that acts as the next interceptor in the
chain. Normally, the next interceptor configured in the chain, after the security manager, is the destination manager. The following example shows the MBean definition
for the security manager in the jbossmq-service.xml file:

```
<mbean
  code="org.jboss.mq.security.SecurityManager"
  name="jboss.mq:service=SecurityManager">
  <depends optional-attribute-name="NextInterceptor">
    jboss.mq:service=DestinationManager
  </depends>
</mbean>
```

9.9 Administering JMS

Most of the JBossMQ subsystems are configured as MBean services and thus can be efficiently monitored and administered using the JMX console.

You can use the destination manager MBean to create and destroy destinations at runtime. To do this, click the destination manager MBean's object name (`service=DestinationManager`) under the `jboss.mq` domain in the JMX console. This will display the following window:

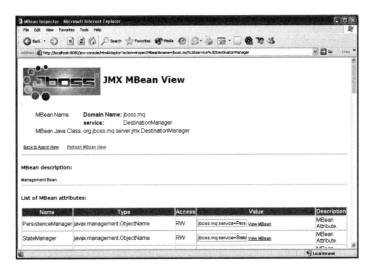

The destination manager MBean provides the operations to create and destroy queues and topics at runtime. Please note that the destinations added during runtime *aren't* available until after a server restart. The following operations are available for managing destinations at runtime:

- ❏ `createQueue(String name, String jndiName)`
  Creates a queue dynamically

- ❏ `destroyQueue(String name)`
  Removes a previously created queue

- ❏ `createTopic(String name, String jndiName)`
  Creates a topic dynamically

- ❏ `destroyTopic(String name)`
  Removes a previously created topic

You can use the message cache MBean for useful information regarding the message cache (such as the number of messages in the cache, the number of messages that have been swapped to the secondary storage, cache hits, cache misses, and so on) as follows:

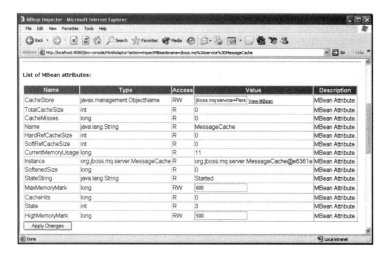

You can manage destinations by clicking the object name for the destination in the JMX console. The MBean object names for JMS destinations normally have the domain set to `jboss.mq.destination`. The following window shows the destinations that are configured within a JBoss server instance:

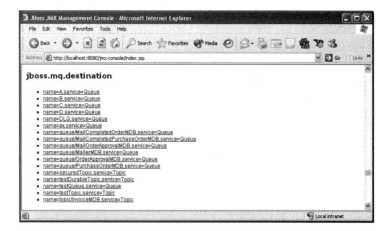

If you click the object name for the destination, `queue/MailerMDB`, for example, the JMX console will display the attributes for that destination:

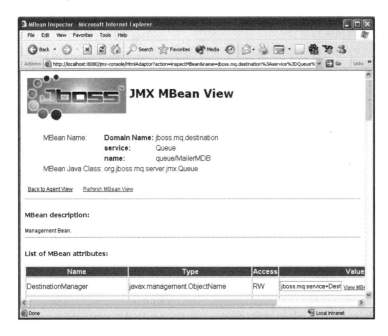

Both the MBean classes for queues and topics provide an MBean operation called `removeAllMessages()`, as shown in the following screenshot. This operation can be invoked from the JMX console to remove all the messages in the destination:

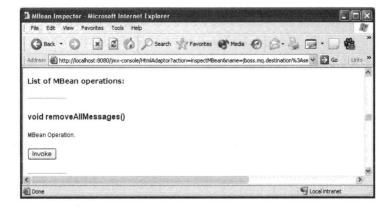

You can click the persistence manager's object name in the JMX console to set the properties for the persistence manager. By default you can find this under the domain jboss.mq with the attribute service=PersistenceManager. The following screen is for configuring the persistence manager:

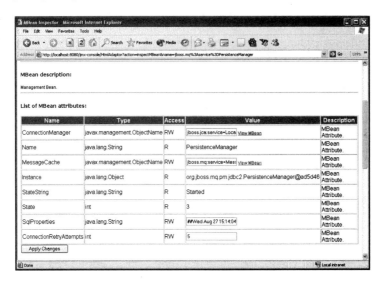

You can use this screen to set the connection manager for the JDBC persistence manager. If you were using the file persistence manager, the previous screen would display options to set the properties for the file persistence manager.

You can click the state manager's object name in the JMX console to set the properties for the state manager. By default, you can find this under the domain jboss.mq with the attribute service=StateManager. The following screen is for configuring the state manager:

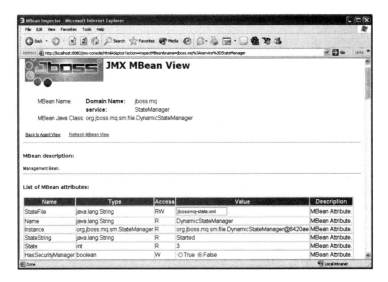

The state manager MBean allows you to set the file that stores the state information. The MBean also allows you to invoke the following operations:

❑ saveConfig()
Saves the current configuration to the backing state file. The default is jbossmq-state.xml. Note that you need to invoke this operation to persist any of the following operations you invoke on the state manager.

❑ addUser(String user, String passwd, String clientId)
Adds a new user.

❑ removeUser(String user)
Removes the user.

❑ addRole(String name)
Adds a new role.

❑ removeRole(String name)
Removes the role.

❑ addUserToRole(String user, String role)
Adds the specified user to the role.

❑ removeUserFromRole(String user, String role)
Removes the user from the role.

Configuring JavaMail

In this chapter, you'll look at how to configure JavaMail sessions in JBoss.

10.1 The Mail Service MBean

JBoss provides an MBean for configuring mail connection factories. This MBean is normally defined in the mail-service.xml file in the \deploy directory of your configuration set. The MBean definition is as follows:

```
<mbean
    code="org.jboss.mail.MailService"
    name="jboss:service=Mail">
```

The MBean supports the following attributes:

Attribute	Function
JNDIName	The Java Naming and Directory Interface (JNDI) name of the mail session that's configured.
User	The user ID for connecting to the mail server.
Password	The password for connecting to the mail server.

continues

Attribute	Function
Configuration	This attribute accepts an Extensible Markup Language (XML) element that defines the configuration information for connecting to the mail server and sending e-mails. This MBean accepts an XML structure of the following format: ``` <configuration> <property name="" value=""/> <property name="" value=""/> ... </configuration> ```

You use the `configuration` attribute for specifying the properties required by the mail session according to the JavaMail specification. The mail session properties are as follows:

- ❏ `mail.transport.protocol`
  This is the transport protocol to use.

- ❏ `mail.store.protocol`
  This is the store protocol to use.

- ❏ `mail.host`
  This is the default host for the transport and store protocols.

- ❏ `mail.user`
  Default user for both store and transport.

- ❏ `mail.from`
  User's return e-mail address.

- ❏ `mail.protocol.host`
  The host specific to the protocol. For example, to specify a Simple Mail Transfer Protocol (SMTP) host, you'd use `mail.smtp.host`.

- ❏ `mail.protocol.user`
  The user specific to the protocol. For example, to specify an SMTP user, you'd use `mail.smtp.user`.

- ❏ `mail.debug`
  The debug setting.

10.2 Configuring the Mail Service

To configure a mail service, follow these steps:

1. To configure a mail service, you need to configure the
`org.jboss.mail.MailService` MBean in the `mail-service.xml`
file of the `\deploy` directory of your configuration set.

First you add the JavaMail JAR files to the classpath:

```
<server>

<classpath
  codebase="lib"
  archives="mail.jar, activation.jar, mail-plugin.jar"/>
```

Then you define the MBean for the mail service:

```
<mbean
  code="org.jboss.mail.MailService"
  name="jboss:service=Mail">
</mbean>
```

2. Next you need to define the JNDI name by which the mail Session object is
looked up:

```
<mbean
  code="org.jboss.mail.MailService"
  name="jboss:service=Mail">
    <attribute name="JNDIName">java:/Mail</attribute>
</mbean>
```

3. Then you define the user name and password for the mail server:

```
<mbean
  code="org.jboss.mail.MailService"
  name="jboss:service=Mail">
    <attribute name="JNDIName">java:/Mail</attribute>
    <attribute name="User">fred</attribute>
    <attribute name="Password">flintstone</attribute>
</mbean>
```

4. Finally you define the configuration properties:

```
<mbean
  code="org.jboss.mail.MailService"
  name="jboss:service=Mail">
  ...
  <attribute name="Configuration">
    <configuration>
      <property name="mail.store.protocol"
                value="pop3"/>
      <property name="mail.transport.protocol"
                value="smtp"/>
      <property name="mail.user"
                value="meeraj@heaven.com"/>
      <property name="mail.pop3.host"
                value="myserver.pop3.com"/>
      <property name="mail.smtp.host"
                value="myserver.exchg.com"/>
      <property name="mail.from"
                value="meeraj@heaven.com"/>
      <property name="mail.debug"
                value="false"/>
    </configuration>
  </attribute>
</mbean>

</server>
```

The mail session configured previously can be looked up by the `java:/mail` JNDI name. However, in your Enterprise JavaBeans (EJBs) and web applications, you'll be using resource references to map the coded JNDI name of the mail sessions to the actual JNDI name.

140

11

Configuring Jetty

The core JBoss server doesn't come with a built-in web container. However, JBoss does provide an MBean that can be used for embedding a web container within the JBoss process. You can download the JBoss installation with either an embedded Tomcat or Jetty web server. In this chapter, you'll look at configuring Jetty with JBoss. You'll also look at how to run the JBoss/Jetty combination with Internet Information Services (IIS) and Apache front-end web servers. In fact, Jetty has a fully optimized web server suitable for the production environment. Hence, unless you have compelling reasons, you don't need to use a front-end web server with Jetty.

Integrating a web container involves the following three main steps:

- ❑ Handling Web Archive (WAR) deployment
- ❑ Mapping the web **Environment Naming Context (ENC)** Java Naming and Directory Interface (JNDI) namespace to the JBoss JNDI namespace
- ❑ Delegating authentication and authorization in the web tier to the JBoss security service

Using an embedded web container with JBoss provides numerous advantages over running an out-of-process web container with JBoss server:

- ❑ Optimized invocations for in–Virtual Machine (VM) Enterprise JavaBean (EJB) calls
- ❑ Integration with the JBoss JNDI naming context
- ❑ Integration with the JBoss security framework

❑ Administration by the JBoss Java Management Extensions (JMX) console

❑ Support for distributed sessions when running JBoss in a cluster

❑ Sharing classes across web and EJB modules using Enterprise Archive (EAR) deployment

To achieve the aforementioned purposes and to provide seamless integration with the JBoss core server, JBoss provides an abstract plug-in that the web container MBean services should extend. This plug-in is represented by the `org.jboss.web.AbstractWebContainer` class.

11.1 AbstractWebContainer

The `AbstractWebContainer` class provides consolidated JNDI and security contexts for the web applications that are deployed. Web containers embedded in JBoss are required to provide an MBean service that extends this class. This class uses the JBoss-specific web deployment descriptor, `jboss-web.xml`, for mapping the following properties defined within the standard deployment descriptor:

❑ Environment entries

❑ Resource references for datasources, Java Message Service (JMS) connection factories, Uniform Resource Locator (URL) factories, mail sessions, and so on

❑ Resource environment references for JMS destinations

❑ EJB references

❑ EJB local references

❑ Security constraints

The subclasses of the `AbstractWebContainer` class, provided by the web containers, are expected to perform the following tasks:

❑ Handle the deploying and undeploying of web applications

❑ Use the JBoss authentication manager and realm mapping classes to integrate with the JBossSX security framework

The `AbstractWebContainer` instance will parse the standard and JBoss-specific web deployment descriptors to create the necessary deployment information that's passed to the concrete subclass to deploy the web application. During this process, it will create lists of environment entries, resource references, resource environment references, and EJB local and remote references. These can be accessed by the concrete subclasses for creating the `java:comp/env` naming context for the web applications that are deployed.

This class also provides methods for linking environment entries, resource references, resource environment references, and EJB local and remote references in the `java:comp/env` context naming context to the JBoss JNDI naming context and the security constraints to the JBoss security domain.

> *In section 16.1, "The JBoss Web Deployment Descriptor," you'll take a closer look at the JBoss-specific web deployment descriptor. The main purposes of the JBoss-specific web deployment descriptor include defining the security domain for authentication and authorization, mapping the `java:comp/env` naming context to the JBoss JNDI naming context, and defining context paths and virtual hosts.*

11.2 Configuring Jetty

In this section, you'll learn about the various attributes that you can configure for the JBoss/Jetty embedded web container services.

Jetty is a Java web server and container compliant with the Servlet 2.3 and JavaServer Pages (JSP) 1.2 specifications. However, when you run Jetty as an embedded web container with JBoss, the only way you can serve static or dynamic web pages is to make them part of a J2EE web application and deploy the web application. More information about the Jetty web container is available at http://jetty.mortbay.com. When you install the standard JBoss 3.2.1 or below bundle, it comes configured with an embedded Jetty service. For version 3.2.2 or above, Tomcat becomes the default web server so there's a specific Jetty variant you need to install if you wish to use Jetty as your web server. The `org.jboss.jetty.JettyService` Jetty web container service extends the `AbstractWebContainer` class.

The Jetty service comes as a JBoss Service Archive (SAR) component with the standard distribution. The SAR component is available in exploded format in the `\jbossweb-jetty.sar` directory in the `\deploy` directory under the `default` configuration set. The SAR deployment descriptor, `jboss-service.xml`, which contains the MBean definition and the various configurable attributes for the MBean, is available in the `\META-INF` directory.

> *Section 13.3.6.2, "Configuring Jetty for HTTP Session Clustering," covers the embedded Jetty configuration to enable distributed sessions in detail.*

The definition of the Jetty service MBean is as follows:

```
<mbean
   code="org.jboss.jetty.JettyService"
   name="jboss.web:service=WebServer">
```

11.2.1 Unpacking WAR Files

Jetty normally unpacks WAR files for deploying. This is mostly necessary for compiling JSP files. You can turn off this default behavior by setting the UnpackWars attribute in the jboss-service.xml file for the Jetty service MBean:

```
<mbean
   code="org.jboss.jetty.JettyService"
   name="jboss.web:service=WebServer">
   ...
   <attribute name="UnpackWars">true</attribute>
   ...
</mbean>
```

11.2.2 Java 2 Classloading Behavior

Jetty normally uses the parent classloader to load classes before resorting to the WAR classloader. This is the standard Java 2 classloading behavior. However, the Servlet 2.3 specification requires the WAR classloader to first try loading the classes by looking into the \WEB-INF\classes and \WEB-INF\lib directories. To enable Servlet 2.3 classloading, you need to set the Java2ClassLoadingCompliance attribute in the jboss-service.xml file for the Jetty service MBean:

```
<mbean
   code="org.jboss.jetty.JettyService"
   name="jboss.web:service=WebServer">
   ...
   <attribute name="Java2ClassLoadingCompliance">true</attribute>
   ...
</mbean>
```

The default value is true.

11.2.3 Custom Jetty Service Configuration

You can provide custom configuration to the embedded Jetty service using the ConfigurationElement attribute for the Jetty service MBean. This MBean attribute accepts an Extensible Markup Language (XML) element as its content. You can use this element to configure a variety of services for the embedded Jetty web container.

The following diagram depicts the structure of the XML fragment passed to the
ConfigurationElement MBean attribute for the Jetty service MBean:

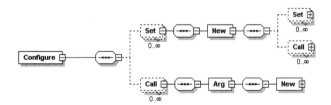

The Configure element may contain zero or more Call and/or Set elements. The
Call element will call the method specified by the name attribute on the instance
of the class specified by the class attribute of the Configure element. You can
specify the arguments for the method using nested Arg elements to the Call element.
The Arg elements can use the New element to create a new object that's passed as the
argument. For argument types of primitives and strings, you can use the content of
the Arg element. Call elements can be nested under New elements to call methods
on newly created objects.

The Set element will call the JavaBean-style mutator for the property specified by
the name attribute on the instance of the class specified by the class attribute of the
Configure element. You can specify the argument for the mutator using a nested
New element to the Set element or specifying it as the text content of the Set element. Set elements can be nested within Arg, New, and other Set elements. When a
Set element is nested, it'll try to set the property on the instance of the class specified
the class attribute of its immediate parent element.

The following snippet shows an example of Jetty service custom configuration using
the ConfigurationElement MBean attribute:

```
<attribute name="ConfigurationElement">

  <Configure class="org.mortbay.jetty.Server">
    <Call name="addListener">
      <Arg>
        <New class="org.mortbay.http.SocketListener">
          <Set name="Port">
            <SystemProperty name="jetty.port" default="8080"/>
          </Set>
          <Set name="MinThreads">10</Set>
          <Set name="MaxThreads">100</Set>
          <Set name="MaxIdleTimeMs">30000</Set>
          <Set name="LowResourcePersistTimeMs">5000</Set>
        </New>
      </Arg>
    </Call>
```

```
<Set name="DistributableSessionManagerPrototype">
  <New class="org.mortbay.j2ee.session.Manager">
   <Set name="scavengerPeriod">600</Set>
   <Set name="interceptorStack">
     <Array type="org.mortbay.j2ee.session.StateInterceptor">
       <Item>
        <New class=
            "org.mortbay.j2ee.session.ValidatingInterceptor"/>
       </Item>
       <Item>
        <New class=
            "org.mortbay.j2ee.session.TypeCheckingInterceptor"/>
       </Item>
       <Item>
        <New class=
            "org.mortbay.j2ee.session.BindingInterceptor"/>
       </Item>
       <Item>
        <New class=
            "org.mortbay.j2ee.session.PublishingInterceptor"/>
       </Item>
       <Item>
        <New class=
            "org.mortbay.j2ee.session.SubscribingInterceptor"/>
       </Item>
       <Item>
        <New class=
            "org.mortbay.j2ee.session.SynchronizingInterceptor"/>
       </Item>
     </Array>
   </Set>
  </New>
  </Set>

 </Configure>

</attribute>
```

> If your configuration gets too complex, it's recommended
> you use `jetty-web.xml`, which has the same content model as
> the element structure for the `Configure` element, rather than
> specifying all the configuration information in the SAR
> deployment descriptor.

Let's now look at the various properties that you can control using this extended configuration functionality.

11.2.3.1 HTTP Listener

Jetty uses the HTTP listener for accepting connections on the Hypertext Transfer Protocol (HTTP) listen port. Jetty uses the following XML element to configure the HTTP listener:

```
<attribute name="ConfigurationElement">
  <Configure class="org.mortbay.jetty.Server">

    <Call name="addListener">
      <Arg>
        <New class="org.mortbay.http.SocketListener">
          <Set name="Port">
            <SystemProperty name="jetty.port" default="8080"/>
          </Set>
          <Set name="Port">
              <SystemProperty name="jetty.port" default="8080"/>
          </Set>
          <Set name="MinThreads">10</Set>
          <Set name="MaxThreads">100</Set>
          <Set name="MaxIdleTimeMs">30000</Set>
          <Set name="LowResourcePersistTimeMs">5000</Set>
        </New>
      </Arg>
    </Call>
    ...
  </Configure>
</attribute>
```

The previous configuration element allows you to define the following properties:

Property	Description
HTTP Port	The default port on which Jetty listens for HTTP requests is 8080. This means that when accessing Jetty from the web browser, you need to specify the port address. You can change this to the default HTTP port number 80 if you don't want your clients to explicitly have to specify the port number.
	On a Unix system, however, the user running the process must have root privileges to listen on any port number less than 1024. This can also be specified as the system property jetty.port.
MinThreads	Specifies the minimum number of concurrent threads that are used for serving the requests. The default value is 5.

continues

147

Property	Description
MaxThreads	Specifies the maximum number of threads that are used for serving the requests. The default value is 255.
MaxIdleTimeMS	Specifies the maximum time, in milliseconds, that a thread can remain idle before expiring. The default value is 30000 (30 seconds).
MaxReadTimeMS	Specifies the maximum amount of time a thread can remain idle, in milliseconds, on serving a request. The default value is 10000 (10 seconds).
MaxStopTimeMS	Specifies the maximum time a thread is allowed to run, in milliseconds, before the Jetty service thread pool stops it. The default value is 5000 (5 seconds).
LowResourcePersist TimeMS	Specifies the time in milliseconds that idle threads are allowed to run when low on resources. The default value is 5000 (5 seconds).
ConfidentialPort	Specifies the port to which requests are redirected when a requested resource is configured in the web deployment descriptor to use confidential transport.
ConfidentialScheme	The protocol used for confidential transport. The default protocol is Secure Sockets Layer (SSL).
IntegralPort	Specifies the port to which requests are redirected when a requested resource is configured in the web deployment descriptor to use integral transport.
IntegralScheme	The protocol used for integral transport. The default protocol is SSL.
DefaultScheme	The protocol used for default transport. The default protocol is HTTP.

If you change the listen port to 80, you'll be able to access the Jetty web server without specifying a port number in the URL

11.2.3.2 HTTP Request Logs

The Jetty web container service normally writes the HTTP request log to the \log directory of the configuration set that's used. The log files are rolled daily and are stored in the format yyyy_mm_dd.request.log. You can configure the request logs using the following configuration element:

```
<attribute name="ConfigurationElement">
  <Configure class="org.mortbay.jetty.Server">
    ...
    <Set name="RequestLog">
      <New class="org.mortbay.http.NCSARequestLog">
        <Arg>
          <SystemProperty name="jboss.server.home.dir"/>
          <SystemProperty name="jetty.log" default="/log"/>
          /yyyy_mm_dd.request.log
        </Arg>
        <Set name="retainDays">90</Set>
        <Set name="append">true</Set>
        <Set name="extended">true</Set>
        <Set name="LogTimeZone">GMT</Set>
      </New>
    </Set>
    ...
  </Configure>
</attribute>
```

You can change the name and location of the request log by changing the arguments that are passed to the NCSARequestLog class as highlighted in the following code:

```
<attribute name="ConfigurationElement">
  <Configure class="org.mortbay.jetty.Server">
    ...
    <Set name="RequestLog">
      <New class="org.mortbay.http.NCSARequestLog">
        <Arg>
          <SystemProperty name="jboss.server.home.dir"/>
          <SystemProperty name="jetty.log" default="/log"/>
          /yyyy_mm_dd.request.log
        </Arg>
        ...
      </New>
    </Set>
    ...
  </Configure>
</attribute>
```

You can also set the following properties:

Property	Description
retainDays	The number of days the log file should be retained. The default value is 31.
append	If set to true, the log messages are appended to the existing file. Otherwise, new log files are created. The default value is true.

continues

149

Property	Description
extended	Stores the log messages in extended format. The default value is true. In the extended mode, the logger also writes the HTTP header information.
LogTimeZone	Defines the time zone to use. If not specified, this will use the default time zone on the server.

11.2.3.3 Enabling SSL on Jetty

You can configure Jetty to use HTTPS instead of HTTP to enable secure transport.

To enable HTTPS, first you need to uncomment the following configuration element in the jboss-service.xml Jetty SAR deployment descriptor:

```
<Call name="addListener">
  <Arg>
    <New class="org.mortbay.http.SunJsseListener">
      <Set name="Port">443</Set>
      <Set name="MinThreads">5</Set>
      <Set name="MaxThreads">255</Set>
      <Set name="MaxIdleTimeMs">30000</Set>
      <Set name="MaxReadTimeMs">10000</Set>
      <Set name="MaxStopTimeMs">5000</Set>
      <Set name="LowResourcePersistTimeMs">2000</Set>
      <Set name="Keystore">
        <SystemProperty name="jetty.home" default="."/>
        /ssl/ssl.keystore
      </Set>
      <Set name="Password">password</Set>
      <Set name="KeyPassword">password</Set>
    </New>
  </Arg>
</Call>
```

In addition to the attributes supported by the standard HTTP listener, the SSL listener requires the following extra attributes:

Attribute	Function
Keystore	Defines the location of the keystore that contains the key pair to use. In the previous example, it defaults to the ssl.keystore file in the \ssl directory under the current directory. The keystore location can also be set relative to the directory specified by the system property jetty.home.
Password	Defines the keystore password.

Attribute	Function
KeyPassword	Defines the key password. The keystore is protected by a password, and each private key within the keystore is protected further by passwords.
Port	Defines the port on which the SSL listener listens. The default SSL port is 443. If you specify any other value, the clients will have to explicitly specify the port number in the browser.
	Again, on Unix systems, you need root privileges to listen to a port number less than 1024.

In keystores, key pairs are keyed against unique alias names. Each keystore has a default key. Jetty uses the default key of the specified keystore. The next thing you need to do is install **Java Secure Socket Extension (JSSE)**. If you're using Java Development Kit (JDK) 1.4, you don't need to do this because JSSE bundles with JDK. If you're using an earlier version, refer to section 7.5, "Enabling SSL," for instructions.

Now you need to generate the key pair. Again refer to section 7.5, "Enabling SSL," for instructions.

Start JBoss and access the JMX console using the URL https://localhost/jmx-console. You'll get the following warning window saying the certificate isn't trusted. This is because your certificate is self-signed and not signed by a root Certificate Authority (CA):

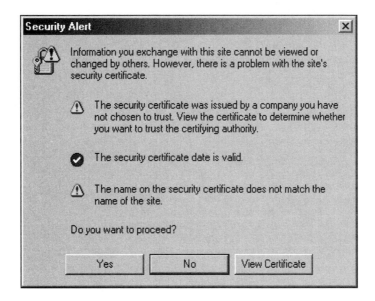

If you click Yes, the browser will display the JMX console. Please note that the protocol used is HTTPS and not HTTP.

11.2.4 Running Jetty with Other Web Servers

In this section, you'll look at how to configure Jetty with other web servers. The section covers Apache and IIS. Jetty provides a listener that implements the Jakarta **Apache JServ Protocol (AJP)** for integrating with both Apache and IIS.

Using the AJP protocol to connect to external web servers normally involves the following steps:

1. Register the web server plug-in. This plug-in will handle the communication from the web server to the web container. You can download the plug-ins required for IIS and Apache from http://jakarta.apache.org/builds/jakarta-tomcat-connectors/:

    ❑   For IIS, you can download the ISAPI filter called `isapi_redirector2.dll`.

    ❑   For Apache, you need to download the platform-specific `mod_jk` module that's available on the Jakarta connector web site. There are two versions: `mod_jk` and `mod_jk2`.

2. Configure the web server with information required for connecting to the web container. This information is normally specified in a configuration file available to the web server.

3. Configure the web server to provide information regarding the Uniform Resource Identifier (URI) patterns that should be handled by the web container. This information is also normally specified in a configuration file available to the web server.

To enable the AJP listener on Jetty, you need to add the following configuration element in your SAR deployment descriptor, `%JBOSS_HOME%\server\<config set>\deploy\jbossweb-jetty.sar\META-INF\jboss-service.xml`, as follows:

```
<attribute name="ConfigurationElement">
  <Configure class="org.mortbay.jetty.Server">
    <Call name="addListener">
      <Arg>
        <New class="org.mortbay.http.ajp.AJP13Listener">
          <Set name="port">8009</Set>
        </New>
      </Arg>
    </Call>
    ...
  </Configure>
</attribute>
```

The AJP listener supports the following attributes:

Attribute	Function
bufferSize	Size of the AJP data buffers (the default is 8192).
ConfidentialPort	The port to redirect to in case a servlet security constraint of CONFIDENTIAL isn't met. The default value of 0 means forbidden response.
ConfidentialScheme	The scheme to use for confidential redirections. The default is https.
host	The host or IP interface on which to listen. The default value of 0.0.0.0 means no interfaces.
identifyListener	Set the listener name as a request attribute. The default is false.
lingerTimeSecs	The socket linger time for closing sockets in seconds. The default is 30 seconds.
maxIdleTimeMs	Milliseconds that a thread can be idle before the thread pool shrinks. The default value is 10000.
maxReadTimeMs	Milliseconds that a read will block on a connection. The default value of 0 means connections don't timeout.
maxStopTimeMs	Milliseconds to wait before gently shutting down listener. The default value of −1 means the thread pool stops the thread without giving any time to the thread.
MaxThreads	Maximum threads in thread pool for listener. The default value is 256.
MinThreads	Minimum threads in thread pool for listener. The default value is 2.
name	Name of the listener.
port	Port to listen on. The default is 8009.
threadClass	The class to be used for threads in the thread pool.

11.2.4.1 Configuring Apache

To configure Apache to use the AJP protocol to connect to the AJP listener, you need to perform the following steps.

1. Download the latest version of the Apache web server from http://www.apache.org for your platform. (This example uses 2.0.43.)

2. Download the Apache AJP module from the Jakarta web site and copy it to the \modules directory of your Apache installation. Please note that even though these pages are available under Tomcat on the Jakarta web site, you can use the AJP module for integrating any web container with Apache using AJP.

3. Create the configuration files required for Apache for connecting to Jetty. Store the following contents toward the end of the httpd.conf file in Apache \conf directory:

```
LoadModule jk_module modules/mod_jk.dll
JKWorkersFile "%JBOSS_HOME%/server/default/conf/workers.properties"
JKLogFile "%JBOSS_HOME%/server/default/log/jk.log"
JKLogLevel warn
JKMount /jmx-console/* ajp13
```

This file defines the location of the workers file that contains the host and port of the AJP worker thread, and it asks Apache to delegate all requests with the URI pattern /jmx-console/* to the AJP worker thread. It also specifies the log file and log level for log messages produced by mod_jk. %JBOSS_HOME% should expand to the directory where you've installed the JBoss/Jetty bundle.

4. Next, you need to store the following contents to a file called workers.properties in the \conf directory of your JBoss default configuration set. This file specifies the details about the AJP worker process, such as the host, port number, and so on. You can also specify a variety of other properties to enable load balancing, use multiple versions of AJP, and so on:

```
ps=\
worker.list=ajp13
worker.ajp13.port=8009
worker.ajp13.host=localhost
worker.ajp13.type=ajp13
```

5. Make sure that Apache, and not a JBoss process, is listening on port 80. Start JBoss and then start Apache. You should now be able to access the JMX console from the browser without explicitly specifying the port number.

11.2.4.2 Configuring IIS

Configuring Jetty to run with IIS is the same as that for Apache on the Jetty side. The only thing you need to do is set up the AJP listener. Even though the configuration you need on the IIS side serves the same purpose as that for Apache, the actual task of configuration is significantly different. Please make sure you have IIS installed and running before you proceed with the configuration. The steps involved in configuring IIS (this example uses version 5) are as follows:

1. Create the configuration file used by the IIS web server plug-in to communicate with the AJP listener. This can be the same `workers.properties` file used for Apache.

2. Create a configuration file called `uriworkermap.properties` that defines the URI patterns that will be handled by the AJP listener. The contents of this file are as follows:

```
/jmx-console/*=ajp13
```

3. Store both the aforementioned files under the `\conf` directory of your default configuration set within JBoss.

4. Create the following registry entries so that the IIS web server plug-in can locate the worker properties and URI mapping files. The best way to do it is to store the following contents in a file with a `.reg` extension and double-click it from Windows Explorer:

```
REGEDIT4
[HKEY_LOCAL_MACHINE\SOFTWARE\Apache Software Foundation\Jakarta Isapi
Redirector\1.0]
"extension_uri"="/jakarta/isapi_redirect.dll"
"log_file"="%JBOSS_HOME%\\server\\default\\log\\iis_redirect.log"
"log_level"="info"
"worker_file"="%JBOSS_HOME%\\server\\default\\conf\\
                workers.properties"
"worker_mount_file"="%JBOSS_HOME%\\server\\default\\conf\\
                uriworkermap.properties"
```

Replace `%JBOSS_HOME%` in the previous snippet with the JBoss installation directory. The registry entries will also point to the log file to which the messages are to be written along with the log level.

5. Install the ISAPI filter that handles communication between IIS and the AJP listener. For Apache, you can use the Apache `mod_jk` module. You can use the ISAPI filter `isapi_redirect.dll` available from the Jakarta web site for IIS. Copy this file to the `\bin` directory of your JBoss installation. Run Control Panel | Administrative Tools | Internet Services Manager on your computer:

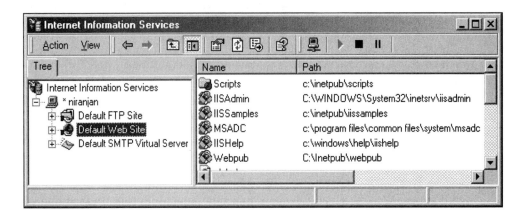

6. Right-click the Default Web Site and click Properties from the pop-up menu. In the Properties window, switch to the ISAPI Filters tab and click the Add button. In the pop-up window, enter the filter name as `jakarta`, and for the filter path, select the ISAPI redirector Dynamic Link Library (DLL) stored in the JBoss `\bin` directory:

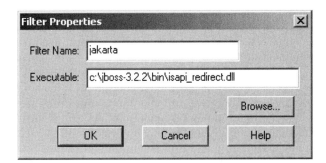

7. Restart IIS by right-clicking the Default Web Site and selecting Stop and then Start. Now, if you go back to the Properties window and the ISAP Filters tab, you should see that the newly added filter has been loaded. The green arrow seen against it, as depicted in the following figure, indicates this:

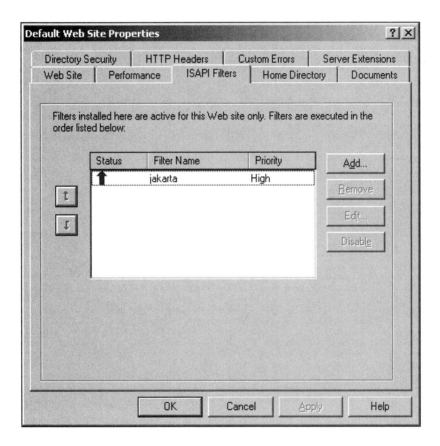

Now you need to create a virtual directory in the default web site by the name jakarta. For this, right-click Default Web Site and select New | Virtual Directory from the pop-up menu. In the wizard for creating the virtual directory, enter the name as jakarta. In the next window, select the path as the path to the JBoss \bin directory that contains the ISAPI redirector DLL. In the next window, assign all permissions apart from Write:

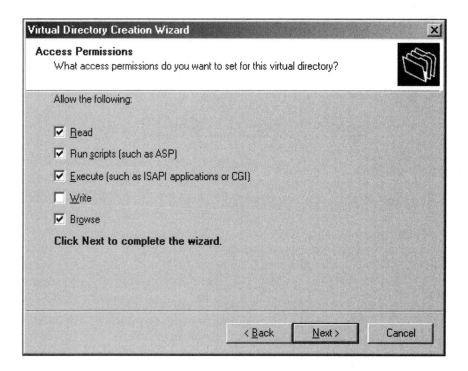

8. Complete the wizard and stop IIS. Start JBoss, making sure that none of the JBoss threads are listening on port 80 and then start IIS. You should now be able to access the JMX console from your browser without specifying the port number.

12

Configuring Tomcat

In the previous chapter, you looked at configuring the embedded Jetty web container with JBoss to deploy and run Java 2 Enterprise Edition (J2EE) web applications. JBoss also comes with an embedded Tomcat web container. In this chapter, you'll learn how to configure Tomcat with JBoss. You'll also look at how to run the JBoss/Tomcat combination with Internet Information Services (IIS) and Apache front-end web servers.

12.1 Configuring Tomcat

To run JBoss with Tomcat, you need to download the JBoss-3.*x* Tomcat-4.* variant from the JBoss or SourceForge web site.

> *As of version 3.2.2, Tomcat is the default web container, but for 3.2.1 there's a separate Tomcat download.*

The Tomcat bundle provides the org.jboss.web.catalina.EmbeddedCatalinaService41 implementation of the AbstractWebContainer class. Refer to section 11.1, "AbstractWebContainer," for more details on the AbstractWebContainer class. The installation will contain a jbossweb-tomcat41.sar exploded directory, which will contain all the required Tomcat libraries. The Tomcat embedded web container is made available as an MBean service. The MBean service descriptor is a `jboss-service.xml` file and is available in the `\META-INF` directory of the exploded `sar` directory in the `default` server configuration set. The MBean used for enabling embedded Catalina service is as follows:

```
<mbean
    code="org.jboss.web.tomcat.tc4.EmbeddedTomcatService41"
    name="jboss.web:service=WebServer">
    ...
</mbean>
```

Section 13.3.6.1, "Configuring Tomcat for HTTP Session Clustering," covers the embedded Catalina configuration to enable distributed sessions in detail.

Now, you'll look at the main attributes you can configure for the embedded Catalina service.

12.1.1 Deleting Work Directories

Tomcat normally doesn't delete work directories when the web applications are undeployed. This can cause JavaServer Pages (JSP) compilation problems in some cases during redeployment. You can use the `DeleteWorkDirs` attribute of the embedded Catalina service MBean to get Tomcat to delete the work directories during undeployment:

```
<mbean code="org.jboss.web.catalina.EmbeddedCatalinaService41"
       name="jboss.web:service=WebServer">
       <attribute name="DeleteWorkDirs">false</attribute>
    ...
</mbean>
```

12.1.2 Setting the Tomcat Home

The MBean supports two attributes to specify the Tomcat home directory, `CatalinaHome` and `CatalinaBase`. The value of the attribute `CatalinaHome` sets the `catalina.home` system property. If not specified, this will be determined based on the location of the

Java Archive (JAR) containing the `org.apache.catalina.startup.Embedded` class assuming a standard Catalina distribution structure. The `CatalinaBase` attribute sets the `catalina.base` system property. If not specified, the `catalina.home` value will be used.

12.1.3 Java 2 Classloading Behavior

Tomcat normally uses the parent classloader to load classes before resorting to the Web Archive (WAR) classloader. This is the standard Java 2 classloading behavior. However, the Servlet 2.3 specification requires WAR classloader to first try loading the classes by looking into the `\WEB-INF\classes` and `\WEB-INF\lib` directories. To enable Servlet 2.3 classloading, you need to set the `Java2ClassLoadingCompliance` attribute to `true` for the embedded Catalina service MBean:

```
<mbean
   code="org.jboss.web.catalina.EmbeddedCatalinaService41"
   name="jboss.web:service=EmbeddedCatalinaSX">
   <attribute name="Java2ClassLoadingCompliance">true</attribute>
   ...
</mbean>
```

12.1.4 Unpacking WAR Files

Tomcat normally unpacks WAR files for deploying. This is mostly necessary for compiling JSP files. You can turn off this default behavior by setting the `UnpackWars` attribute in the `jboss-service.xml` file for the Catalina service MBean:

```
<mbean
   code="org.jboss.web.tomcat.tc4.EmbeddedTomcatService"
   name="jboss.web:service=WebServer">
   <attribute name="UnpackWars">true</attribute>
</mbean>
```

12.1.5 Thread Count

You can get the active and maximum thread counts by accessing the attributes
`ActiveThreadCount` and `MaxActiveThreadCount` through the JMX console, as
shown in the following figure:

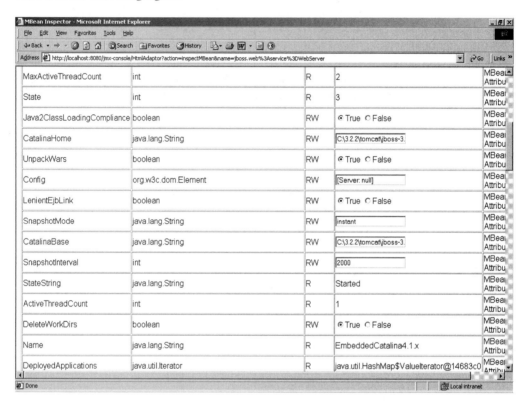

The information shown in this figure is available on the MBean page for the MBean
`jboss.web:service=WebServer`. The active thread count is the number of concurrent
requests across all contexts, and the maximum active thread count is the maximum
number of active requests across all contexts.

12.1.6 Invocation Statistics

The MBean also provides a read-only attribute for tracking statistics. The attribute is called `Stats` and provides information about the number of concurrent threads, the number of maximum concurrent threads, the minimum time processing requests, the maximum time processing request, and so on for each context that's deployed in the web container, as shown in the following figure. This information is also available on the MBean page for the MBean `jboss.web:service=WebServer`:

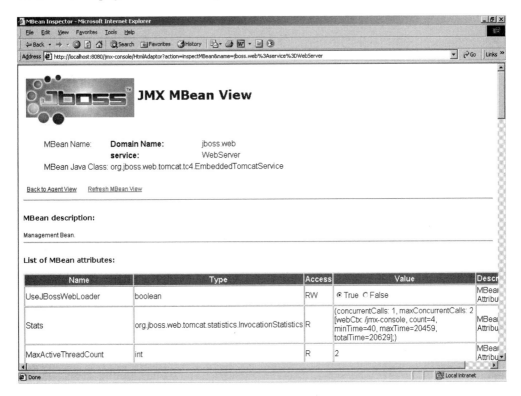

12.1.7 Custom Configuration

You can use the MBean attribute Config to define a custom Catalina configuration. The content of the element defines an XML fragment:

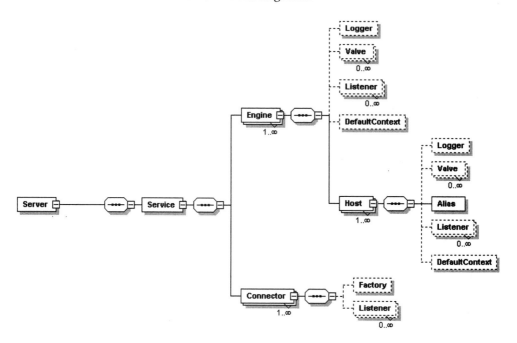

The following snippet shows the custom configuration that comes out of the box with the JBoss/Tomcat bundle:

```
<Server>
   <Service name="JBoss-Tomcat">
   <Engine name="MainEngine" defaultHost="localhost">
      <Logger className="org.jboss.web.tomcat.Log4jLogger"
             verbosityLevel="debug"
             category="org.jboss.web.localhost.Engine"/>
      <Host name="localhost">
```

```
        <!-- Access logger -->
        <Valve className="org.apache.catalina.valves.AccessLogValve"
               prefix="localhost_access" suffix=".log"
               pattern="common"
               directory="${jboss.server.home.dir}/log"/>

        <!-- This valve clears any caller identity set by the realm
             and provides access to the realm about the existence of an
             authenticated caller to allow a web app to run with a
             realm that support unauthenticated identities. It also
             establishes any run-as principal for the servlet
             being accessed. -->
        <Valve className=
            "org.jboss.web.tomcat.security.SecurityAssociationValve" />
        <!-- Default context parameters -->
        <DefaultContext cookies="true" crossContext="true"
                        override="true"/>
      </Host>
    </Engine>

    <!-- A HTTP/1.1 Connector on port 8080 -->
    <Connector className="org.apache.coyote.tomcat4.CoyoteConnector"
               port="8080" minProcessors="5" maxProcessors="100"
               enableLookups="true" acceptCount="10" debug="0"
               connectionTimeout="20000" useURIValidationHack="false"/>

    <!-- A AJP 1.3 Connector on port 8009 -->
    <Connector className="org.apache.coyote.tomcat4.CoyoteConnector"
               port="8009" minProcessors="5" maxProcessors="75"
               enableLookups="true" redirectPort="8443"
               acceptCount="10" debug="0" connectionTimeout="20000"
               useURIValidationHack="false"
               protocolHandlerClassName=
               "org.apache.jk.server.JkCoyoteHandler"/>

  </Service>
</Server>
```

The Server element represents the Tomcat embedded web container. This element contains one or more Service elements. The Service element contains one or more Connector elements and a single Engine element. The Engine element represents the main infrastructure for processing the requests that come through the various connectors represented by the Connector elements. The Service element has a name attribute to uniquely identify the service.

The `Engine` element is the main request processing machinery for the service. The `Engine` element receives a request from the connectors and returns responses to the connectors. The `Engine` element supports the following attributes:

Attribute	Description
`className`	This is the fully qualified name of the class that implements the interface `org.apache.catalina.Engine`. The default implementation is `org.apache.catalina.core.StandardEngine`.
`defaultHost`	The default host name, which identifies the host that will process requests directed to host names on this server but that aren't configured in this configuration file. This name must match the `name` attributes of one of the `Host` elements nested immediately inside.
`jvmRoute`	Identifier that must be used in load balancing scenarios to enable session affinity. The identifier, which must be unique across all Tomcat 4 servers that participate in the cluster, will be appended to the generated session identifier, therefore allowing the front-end proxy to always forward a particular session to the same Tomcat 4 instance.
`name`	Logical name of this engine, used in log and error messages.
`debug`	The level of debugging detail logged by this engine to the associated logger. Higher numbers generate more detailed output. If not specified, the default debugging detail level is zero (0).

The `Engine` element has the following child elements:

Child Element	Description
`<Host>`	You can nest one or more `Host` elements inside this `Engine` element, each representing a different virtual host associated with this server. At least one host is required, and one of the nested hosts *must* have a name that matches the name specified for the `defaultHost` attribute of the `Engine` element.
`<Logger>`	Configures a logger that will receive and process all log messages for this engine, plus messages from connectors associated with this engine in the surrounding service. In addition, this logger will log messages from subordinate hosts and contexts, unless overridden by a logger configuration at a lower level.

Child Element	Description
`<Valve>`	You can ask Catalina to check the Internet Protocol (IP) address, or host name, on every incoming request directed to the surrounding engine, host, or context element. The remote address or name will be checked against a configured list of accept and/or deny filters, which are defined using the regular expression syntax supported by the Jakarta `Regexp` regular expression library. Requests that come from locations that aren't accepted will be rejected with a Hypertext Transfer Protocol (HTTP) "Forbidden" error.
`<DefaultContext>`	You can optional nest a `DefaultContext` element inside this `Engine` element to define the default characteristics of web applications that are automatically deployed.
`<Listener>`	If you've implemented a Java object that needs to know when this engine is started or stopped, you can declare it by nesting a listener element inside this element. The class name you specify must implement the `org.apache.catalina.LifecycleListener` interface, and it will be notified about the occurrence of the corresponding lifecycle events.

Tomcat supports two types of connectors:

❑ Connectors that accept request directly from the browsers

❑ Connectors that accept connections through web servers

The connectors that accept connections from browsers are written in Java and are packages with the JBoss/Tomcat installation. The connectors that interact with web servers are composed of Java as well as C components. The Java components are bundled with the JBoss/Tomcat installation. The binary builds for the C components need to be separately downloaded from the Tomcat web site. The connector that's used by default by the JBoss/Tomcat bundle is the Coyote connector. The Coyote connector supports both HTTP 1.1 (for browser requests) and Apache JServe Protocol (AJP) 1.3 (for web server requests). The following snippet shows the two connectors in the custom configuration for the MBean descriptor:

```
<!-- A HTTP/1.1 Connector on port 8080 -->
<Connector className="org.apache.coyote.tomcat4.CoyoteConnector"
        port="8080" minProcessors="5" maxProcessors="100"
        enableLookups="true" acceptCount="10" debug="0"
        connectionTimeout="20000" useURIValidationHack="false"/>
```

```
<!-- A AJP 1.3 Connector on port 8009 -->
<Connector className="org.apache.coyote.tomcat4.CoyoteConnector"
          port="8009" minProcessors="5" maxProcessors="75"
          enableLookups="true" redirectPort="8443"
          acceptCount="10" debug="0" connectionTimeout="20000"
          useURIValidationHack="false"
          protocolHandlerClassName=
           "org.apache.jk.server.JkCoyoteHandler"/>
```

The HTTP 1.1 connector listens on port 8080, and the AJP connector listens on 8009. The Connector element supports the following attributes:

Attribute	Description
className	This is the Java class name of the implementation to use. This class must implement the org.apache.catalina.Connector interface. You must specify the standard value defined later.
enableLookups	Set this to true if you want calls to request.getRemoteHost() to perform Domain Name System (DNS) lookups in order to return the actual host name of the remote client. Set to false to skip the DNS lookup and return the IP address in string form instead (thereby improving performance). By default, DNS lookups are disabled.
redirectPort	If this Connector is supporting non–Secure Sockets Layer (SSL) requests and a request is received for which a matching <security-constraint> requires SSL transport, Catalina will automatically redirect the request to the port number specified here.
scheme	Set this attribute to the name of the protocol you want to have returned by calls to request.getScheme(). For example, you'd set this attribute to https for an SSL connector. The default value is http.
secure	Set this attribute to true if you want to have calls to request.isSecure() return true for requests received by this Connector (you'd want this on an SSL connector). The default value is false.

In addition, the Coyote connector supports the following attributes:

Attributes	Description
acceptCount	The maximum queue length for incoming connection requests when all possible request processing threads are in use. Any requests received when the queue is full will be refused. The default value is 10.
address	For servers with more than one IP address, this attribute specifies which address will be used for listening on the specified port. By default, this port will be used on all IP addresses associated with the server.
bufferSize	The size (in bytes) of the buffer to be provided for input streams created by this connector. By default, buffers of 2048 bytes will be provided.
compression	The connector may use HTTP/1.1 GZIP compression in an attempt to save server bandwidth. The acceptable values for the parameter are off (disables compression), on (allows compression, which causes text data to be compressed), force (forces compression in all cases), and a numerical integer value (which is equivalent to on but specifies the minimum amount of data before the output is compressed). If the content length isn't known and compression is set to on or more aggressive, the output will also be compressed. If not specified, this attribute is set to false.
connectionLinger	The number of milliseconds during which the sockets used by this connector will linger when they're closed. The default value is -1 (socket linger is disabled).
connectionTimeout	The number of milliseconds this connector will wait, after accepting a connection, for the request URI line to be presented. The default value is 60000 (for example, 60 seconds).
debug	The debugging detail level of log messages generated by this component, with higher numbers creating more detailed output. If not specified, this attribute is set to zero (0).

Attributes	Description
disableUploadTimeout	This flag allows the servlet container to use a different, longer connection timeout while a servlet is being executed, which in the end allows either the servlet a longer amount of time to complete its execution or a longer timeout during data upload. If not specified, this attribute is set to `false`.
maxProcessors	The maximum number of request processing threads to be created by this connector, which therefore determines the maximum number of simultaneous requests that can be handled. If not specified, this attribute is set to `20`.
minProcessors	The number of request processing threads that will be created when this connector is first started. This attribute should be set to a value smaller than that set for `maxProcessors`. The default value is `5`.
port	The Transmission Control Protocol (TCP) port number on which this connector will create a server socket and await incoming connections. Your operating system will allow only one server application to listen to a particular port number on a particular IP address.
proxyName	If this connector is being used in a proxy configuration, configure this attribute to specify the server name to be returned for calls to `request.getServerName()`.
proxyPort	If this connector is being used in a proxy configuration, configure this attribute to specify the server port to be returned for calls to `request.getServerPort()`.
tcpNoDelay	If set to `true`, the `TCP_NO_DELAY` option will be set on the server socket, which improves performance under most circumstances. This is set to `true` by default.

If you're using the Coyote connector to accept requests from a web server, you need to set the `protocolHandlerClassName` attribute to `org.apache.jk.server.JkCoyoteHandler`.

12.1.8 Enabling SSL on Tomcat

You can configure the embedded Tomcat service to use HTTPS instead of HTTP. To do this you need to perform the three main steps:

1. Install JSSE if not using JDK 1.4.

2. Create the keystore that contains the key pair.

3. Configure the JAAS security domain. As you saw in Section 7.3.6, "JAAS Security Domain," JAAS security domain extends JAAS security manager to provide cryptographic functionalities.

4. Set the SSL connection factory for embedded Catalina service connector to use the keystore.

Section 7.5, "Enabling SSL," covers the first two steps.

12.1.8.1 Configure the JAAS Security Domain

Next you need to configure the JAAS security domain MBean. You can either do this in jboss-service.xml file in the \conf directory of your configuration set, or in the jboss-service.xml file in the \deploy\jbossweb-tomcat41.sar\META-INF directory of the default configuration set, that contains the embedded Catalina service MBean. Use the following snippet to define the JAAS security domain MBean:

```
<mbean
    code="org.jboss.security.plugins.JaasSecurityDomain"
    name="jboss.security:service=JaasSecurityDomain,domain=RMI+SSL">
    <constructor>
        <arg type="java.lang.String" value="RMI+SSL"/>
    </constructor>
    <attribute name="KeyStoreURL">ssl/ssl.keystore</attribute>
    <attribute name="KeyStorePass">password</attribute>
</mbean>
```

The MBean listed previously uses the keystore ssl.keystore in the ssl directory under the bin directory of JBoss and defines the keystore password as password.

12.1.8.2 Set the SSL Connection Factory

Next, you need to configure the SSL connection factory for the Tomcat HTTP connector. The embedded Catalina service MBean uses the custom XML configuration `Connector` element for setting up protocol-specific listeners. This element can take an embedded `Factory` element to specify the factory class for creating the sockets. To use SSL, you can specify the SSL connection factory provided by JBoss. This factory expects the JNDI name of the JAAS security domain that it uses to obtain the keystore information. An example is as follows:

```
<Connector
   className="org.apache.catalina.connector.http.HttpConnector"
   port="443"
   scheme="https"
   secure="true">
   <Factory
      className="org.jboss.web.catalina.security.SSLServerSocketFactory"
      securityDomainName="java:/jaas/RMI+SSL"
      clientAuth="false"
      protocol="TLS"/>
</Connector>
```

Start JBoss and access the JMX console using the URL https://localhost/jmx-console. You'll get the following warning window saying the certificate isn't trusted. This is because your certificate is self-signed and not signed by a root CA:

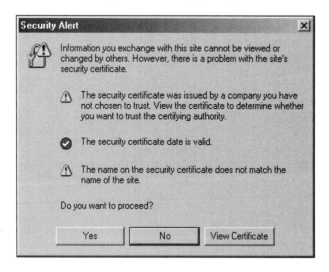

If you click Yes, the browser will display the JMX console. Please note that the protocol used is HTTPS and not HTTP.

12.1.8.3 Running Tomcat with Other Web Servers

In this section, you'll learn how to configure Tomcat with other web servers. This section covers Apache and IIS. Tomcat provides a listener that implements the Jakarta AJP for integrating with both Apache and IIS.

Using the AJP protocol to connect to external web servers normally involves the following steps:

1. Register a web server plug-in. This plug-in will handle the communication from the web server to the web container. You can download the plug-ins required for IIS and Apache from http://jakarta.apache.org/builds/jakarta-tomcat-connectors/.

   ❑ For IIS, you can download the Internet Server Application Programming Interface (ISAPI) filter called `isapi_redirector2.dll`.

   ❑ For Apache, you need to download the platform-specific `mod_jk` module available on the Jakarta connector web site. There are two versions: `mod_jk` and `mod_jk2`.

2. Configure the web server with the information required for connecting to the web container. This information is normally specified in a configuration file available to the web server.

3. Configure the web server to provide information regarding the Uniform Resource Identifier (URI) patterns that should be handled by the web container. This information is also normally specified in a configuration file available to the web server.

The out-of-the-box JBoss/Tomcat bundle comes with a Coyote connector configuration that listens on port 8009 for AJP connections from web servers, as shown in section 12.1.7, "Custom Configuration."

12.1.8.3.1 Configuring Apache

To configure Apache to use the AJP protocol to connect to the AJP listener, you need to perform the following steps. This example uses Apache 2:

1. Download the latest version of the Apache web server from http://www.apache.org for your platform. The version in this example is 2.0.43.

2. Download the Apache AJP module from the Jakarta web site and copy it to the `modules` directory of your Apache installation. Please note that even though these pages are available under Tomcat on the Jakarta web site, you can use the AJP module for integrating any web container with Apache using AJP.

3. Create the configuration files required for Apache for connecting to Tomcat by storing the following contents toward the end of the `httpd.conf` file in Apache `\conf` directory:

```
LoadModule jk_module modules/mod_jk.dll
JKWorkersFile "%JBOSS_HOME%/server/default/conf/workers.properties"
JKLogFile "%JBOSS_HOME%/server/default/log/jk.log"
JKLogLevel warn
JKMount /jmx-console/* ajp13
```

The previous file defines the location of the workers file that contains the host and port of the AJP worker thread and asks Apache to delegate all requests with the URI pattern /jmx-console/* to the AJP worker thread. It also specifies the log file and log level for log messages produced by mod_jk. %JBOSS_HOME% should expand to the directory where you've installed the JBoss/Tomcat bundle.

4. Now you need to store the following contents to a file called `workers.properties` in the `\conf` directory of your configuration set. This file specifies the details about the AJP worker process, such as host, port number, and so on. You can also specify a variety of other properties to enable load balancing, use multiple versions of AJP, and so on:

```
ps=\
worker.list=ajp13
worker.ajp13.port=8009
worker.ajp13.host=localhost
worker.ajp13.type=ajp13
```

5. Make sure that Apache, and not a JBoss process, is listening on port 80. Start JBoss and then start Apache. You should now be able to access the Java Management Extensions (JMX) console from the browser without explicitly specifying the port number.

12.1.8.3.2 Configuring IIS

Configuring Tomcat to run with IIS is similar to that for Apache. The only thing you need to do is set up the AJP listener. Even though the configuration you need on the IIS side serves the same purpose as that for Apache, the actual task of configuration is significantly different. Please make sure you have IIS installed and running before you proceed with the configuration. The steps involved in configuring IIS (this example uses version 5) are as follows:

1. Create the configuration file used by the IIS web server plug-in to communicate with the AJP listener. This can be the same `workers.properties` file used for Apache.

2. Create a configuration file called `uriworkermap.properties` that defines the URI patterns that will be handled by the AJP listener. The contents of this file are as follows:

```
/jmx-console/*=ajp13
```

3. Store both the aforementioned files under the `\conf` directory of your default configuration set within JBoss.

4. Create the following registry entries so that the IIS web server plug-in can locate the worker properties and URI mapping files. The best way to do it is to store the following contents in a file with `.reg` extension and then double-click it from Windows Explorer:

```
REGEDIT4
[HKEY_LOCAL_MACHINE\SOFTWARE\Apache Software Foundation\Jakarta Isapi
Redirector\1.0]
"extension_uri"="/jakarta/isapi_redirect.dll"
"log_file"="%JBOSS_HOME%\\server\\default\\log\\iis_redirect.log"
"log_level"="info"
"worker_file"="%JBOSS_HOME%\\server\\default\\conf\\
                workers.properties"
"worker_mount_file"="%JBOSS_HOME%\\server\\default\\conf\\
                uriworkermap.properties"
```

Replace `%JBOSS_HOME%` in the previous snippet with the JBoss installation directory. The registry entries will also point to the log file to which the messages are to be written along with the log level.

5. Install the ISAPI filter that handles communication between IIS and the AJP listener. For Apache, the example used the Apache `mod_jk` module. This example uses the ISAPI filter `isapi_redirect.dll` available from the Jakarta web site for IIS. Copy this file to the `\bin` directory of your JBoss installation. Run Control Panel | Administrative Tools | Internet Services Manager on your computer:

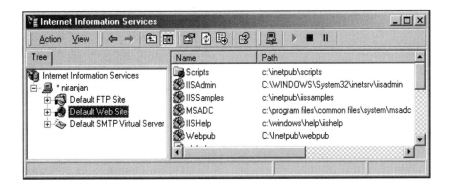

6. Right-click the Default Web Site node and click Properties from the pop-up menu. In the Properties window, switch to the ISAPI Filters tab and click the Add button. In the pop-up window, enter the filter name as jakarta, and for the filter path, select the ISAPI redirector DLL stored in the JBoss \bin directory:

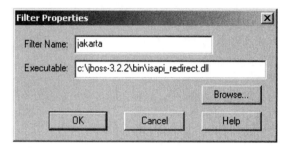

7. Restart IIS by right-clicking the Default Web Site and selecting Stop and then Start. Now, if you go back to the Properties window and the ISAP Filters tab, you should see that the newly added filter has been loaded. The green arrow shown next to it, as depicted here, indicates this:

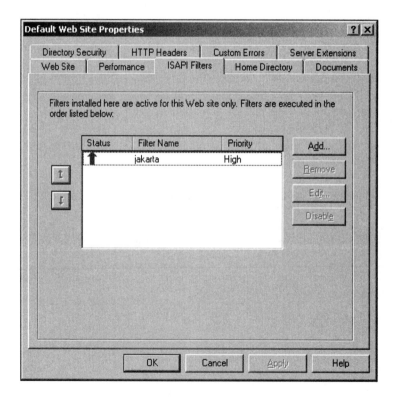

8. Now you need to create a virtual directory in the default web site by the name jakarta. For this, right-click the **Default Web Site** node and select **New | Virtual Directory** from the pop-up menu. In the wizard for creating the virtual directory, enter the name as jakarta. In the next window, select the path as the path to the JBoss \bin directory that contains the ISAPI redirector DLL. In the next window, assign all permissions apart from Write:

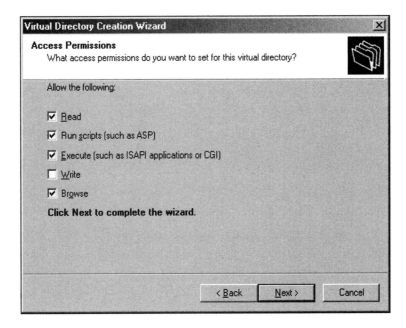

Complete the wizard and stop IIS. Start JBoss, making sure that none of the JBoss threads are listening on port 80, and then start IIS. You should now be able to access the JMX console from your browser without specifying the port number.

13

Configuring Clusters

JBoss 3.*x* provides clustering functionality to enhance the availability and scalability of your Java 2 Enterprise Edition (J2EE) applications. In this chapter, you'll learn how to configure JBoss clusters in detail.

13.1 An Overview of Clustering

A cluster is a group of server instances that work as a single entity to achieve some common goals for the applications they host:

❑   High availability

❑   Fault tolerance

❑   Performance and scalability

❑   Load balancing

The server instances may run on separate physical machines or on the same machine. The following diagram depicts a typical cluster topology:

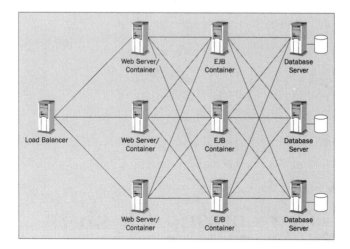

All the requests from the client normally come to a single point often called a load balancer or dispatcher. Normally, this load balancer will send the request to a web server/container node, based on some configured algorithm. The web container will use the clustering functionality provided by the Enterprise JavaBean (EJB) container to connect to an appropriate EJB container. The EJB containers may connect to cluster of replicated database servers.

13.1.1 Load Balancers

You can implement load balancers using a wide variety of techniques:

- ❑ Domain Name System (DNS) round robin
- ❑ Hardware load balancers
- ❑ Web server proxies

13.1.1.1 DNS Round Robin

In load balancing using a DNS round robin, the DNS server that resolves the domain names to Internet Protocol (IP) addresses will have multiple IP addresses mapped to the same domain. As clients ask the DNS server for the IP address for a domain name, it'll serve the first IP address in the queue. This IP address is then pushed to the back of the queue. This solution is very cost-effective.

However, even if one of the servers mapped in the domain lookup table goes down, the DNS server will forward the request to that server. This is because the DNS server doesn't know the status of the servers to which the domain name is mapped. This means that even though the DNS round robin method provides load balancing, it doesn't guarantee availability; however, some advanced DNS servers can keep track of the status of the servers stored in the DNS lookup table.

Another significant handicap with DNS round robin is that it doesn't guarantee server affinity. In J2EE distributed web applications, it's required that once the load balancer pins down a server in the cluster for a user request, all the subsequent requests in that session should be sent to the same server. However, DNS round robin doesn't have any way of tracking cookies or Uniform Resource Locator (URL) rewriting to keep track of sessions.

13.1.1.2 Hardware Load Balancers

Hardware load balancers provide a more sophisticated approach for balancing the load. Hardware load balancers normally use virtual IP addresses that show a single IP address (which maps to multiple addresses in a cluster) to the outside world. An example of a hardware load balancer is Cisco CSS 11150 Content Services Switch.

When a request comes to a hardware load balancer, it amends the request header to point to one of the machines in the cluster. Hardware load balancers address many of the disadvantages associated with DNS round robin by providing high availability, transparent failover, server affinity, and so on. Most of the hardware load balancers provide a variety of matrix information including the number of requests per second, active sessions, active sessions per server instance, and so on.

However, hardware load balancers are quite expensive and relatively complex to set up. Another disadvantage is that the load balancer itself is a single point of failure.

13.1.1.3 Web Server Proxies

Web server proxies use a front-end web server to accept all the requests. This web server will perform tasks such as accepting Hypertext Transfer Protocol (HTTP) requests, decrypting Secure Sockets Layer (SSL) requests, and so on. Then, based on the nature of the request, the web server will pass it onto the appropriate web container for processing. A web server may be configured with multiple instances of web containers.

An example of this is an Apache or Internet Information Services (IIS) instance connecting to multiple instances of Tomcat or Jetty using the Apache JServ Protocol (AJP). Here, the mod_jk module or the AJP ISAPI filter will perform the task of balancing load. Section 13.3.5, "EJBs in a Cluster," explains this in detail.

13.2 Clustering Requirements

In this section, you'll at the application behaviors that should be addressed by clustering from a J2EE perspective:

- **Transparent HTTP Session Failover**
  Even if the web server/container to which the user is connected goes down, the next request from the client should be forwarded to another server in the cluster.

- **Replication of HTTP Session Data**
  If the web server/container to which a client is connected goes down, it isn't just required to forward the request to a new server in the cluster. It should also replicate the session data held by the old server to the new server.

- **Transparent Failover for EJB Home and Remote Objects**
  If an EJB server that hosts the home or remote object owned by a client goes down, the cluster mechanism should forward the next invocation to another EJB container in the cluster.

- **State Replication for Stateful Session Beans**
  If an EJB container that hosts a stateful session bean goes down, the state should be transferred to the new EJB container that will be servicing the invocations on the stateful session bean.

- **Cluster-Side JMS Destinations**
  JMS destinations should be available cluster-wide as the failure of one server in the cluster wouldn't affect the Java Message Service (JMS) clients that send and receive messages.

- **Cluster-Wide JNDI Namespace**
  Java Naming and Directory Interface (JNDI) is the heart of most of the J2EE applications. Clients will bind and/or look up objects such as EJB home objects, JMS connection factories, and destinations, mail sessions, datasources, and so on from the JNDI namespace. One important thing about JNDI in a clustered environment is that the location of the namespace to which an object is bound should be transparent to the client.

- **Cluster-Wide Hot Deployment**
  Application servers that support clustering should provide a way of deploying applications cluster-wide. One solution is to share the code between all the nodes in the cluster. This means that the physical device that hosts the code is a single point of failure. Another alternative is to deploy the applications on all the nodes in the cluster.

13.3 JBoss Clustering

JBoss 3.*x* clustering functionality provides the following features:

- ❏ The ability of nodes in a cluster to discover each other automatically
- ❏ High availability and load balancing for JNDI, entity beans, and session beans
- ❏ State replication for stateful session beans
- ❏ HTTP session state replication with both Jetty and Tomcat
- ❏ Shared JNDI tree in the cluster
- ❏ Ability for clients to automatically discover JNDI servers
- ❏ Ability for cluster-wide hot deployment by deploying on one node in the cluster
- ❏ Customizable load balancing policies
- ❏ Ability to cluster custom objects using clustered RMI

13.3.1 Clustering Architecture

In JBoss, a **partition** identifies a group of server instances that work together as a cluster. Each server instance expresses its desire to participate in a partition by configuring an `org.jboss.ha.framework.server.ClusterPartition` MBean, which lets you specify a name for the partition in which the server should participate.

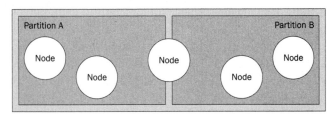

A server instance can be part of multiple partitions. Server instances in a partition can run on a single physical machine, on multiple machines, or across subnets. However, when they run on the same machine, you need to make sure they don't try to listen on conflicting port numbers for the various services such as HTTP, Remote Method Invocation (RMI), JNDI, or Internet Inter-Orb Protocol (IIOP).

JBoss provides an abstract communication layer that can be used by the servers in a partition to discover each other. The structure of a cluster at any given time is termed as its **view**. The view of the cluster is updated each time a node enters or leaves the partition. You can plug in any communication framework to the JBoss abstract communication layer to allow the nodes in a partition to communicate with each other. JBoss currently uses the highly configurable **Javagroups Framework** (http://www.javagroups.com) for enabling communication between the nodes in a partition.

13.3.2 JBoss Proxies

JBoss uses a set of server instances as a partition to provide a clustered environment. However, there should be some scheme by which the client invocations are routed to an appropriate server instance in the partition to provide transparent load balancing and failover. JBoss provides a solution that utilizes the most appropriate location to host this dispatcher logic. The dispatcher logic is implemented in the RMI stub proxies that are downloaded into the client process space during runtime.

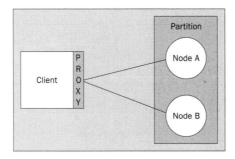

These proxies have enough information about all the nodes that participate in the partition. Hence, if an invocation to a particular node in the partition fails, the proxy can fall back to another node in the partition. In addition, each time that the client makes an invocation, JBoss updates the client proxies with the latest partition view.

> **In JBoss, the String HA- prefixes the services that are cluster-enabled. HA is an abbreviation for High Availability. For example, cluster-based JNDI is called HA-JNDI, and cluster-based RMI is called HA-RMI.**

13.3.3 Configuring Clusters

The all configuration set that comes with JBoss comes preconfigured to enable clustering. In addition to the required Java Archive (JAR) files, one important file is cluster-service.xml, present in the \deploy directory. This file contains the core MBean definitions for enabling the cluster service. The most important among these is the ClusterPartition MBean. This MBean is used by a server instance to be part of a named partition or start one if it doesn't already exist. The MBean definition is as follows:

```
<mbean
    code="org.jboss.ha.framework.server.ClusterPartition"
    name="jboss:service=MyPartition">
```

The MBean supports the following attributes:

Attribute	Function
PartitionName	An optional attribute used for specifying the name of the partition in which the node wants to participate. As mentioned earlier, the node can be part of more than one partition. The default value of this attribute is DefaultPartition.
DeadlockDetection	An optional attribute used for setting a flag to run message deadlock detection. The default value is false.
PartitionProperties	An optional attribute used for specifying the properties required by the underlying communication framework. Currently, JBoss uses the Javagroups communication framework, which by default uses a User Datagram Protocol (UDP)–based multicast protocol. However, Javagroups is highly configurable, and you can use other protocols if you want.

The following snippet shows the default partition property that's used when the PartitionProperties attribute isn't specified:

```
<Config>
  <UDP mcast_addr="228.1.2.3" mcast_port="45566"
      ip_ttl="64" ip_mcast="true"
      mcast_send_buf_size="150000" mcast_recv_buf_size="80000"
      ucast_send_buf_size="150000" ucast_recv_buf_size="80000"
      loopback="false" />
  <PING timeout="2000" num_initial_members="3"
      up_thread="true" down_thread="true" />
  <MERGE2 min_interval="5000" max_interval="10000" />
  <FD shun="true" up_thread="true" down_thread="true"
      timeout="2500" max_tries="5" />
  <VERIFY_SUSPECT timeout="3000" num_msgs="3"
                  up_thread="true" down_thread="true" />
  <pbcast.STABLE desired_avg_gossip="20000"
                  up_thread="true" down_thread="true" />
  <pbcast.NAKACK gc_lag="50"
                  retransmit_timeout="300,600,1200,2400,4800"
                  up_thread="true" down_thread="true" />
```

```
<UNICAST timeout="5000" window_size="100" min_threshold="10"
        down_thread="true" />
<FRAG frag_size="8192"
      down_thread="true" up_thread="true" />
<pbcast.GMS join_timeout="5000" join_retry_timeout="2000"
            shun="true" print_local_addr="true" />
<pbcast.STATE_TRANSFER up_thread="true" down_thread="true" />
</Config>
```

Please refer to documentation from http://www.javagroups.com for more information on partition properties.

An example of the MBean configuration is as follows:

```
<mbean
   code="org.jboss.ha.framework.server.ClusterPartition"
   name="jboss:service=MyPartition">
   <attribute name="PartitionName">MyPartition</attribute>
</mbean>
```

The previous MBean starts a new partition called MyPartition if it isn't already started and makes the server in which the MBean is deployed a member of that partition.

13.3.4 Configuring HA-JNDI

In a clustered configuration, JBoss supports a cluster-wide JNDI namespace (HA-JNDI) as well as a local JNDI namespace for each server in the cluster. Clients can use either the local JNDI service or the HA-JNDI service to look up objects. If they use the local JNDI service, the object is looked for only in the local JNDI namespace. However, if the HA-JNDI service is used, JBoss first looks in the HA-JNDI namespace. If the object isn't found, the HA-JNDI service delegates the lookup to the local JNDI service of the server to which the client is connected. If it still can't find the object, it'll ask the local JNDI of all the nodes in the partition until it finds the looked-up object:

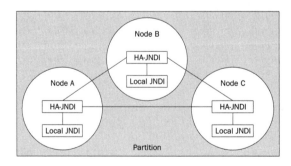

> **Please note that EJB home objects are always bound to the local JNDI context of the server on which the particular EJB is deployed.**

HA-JNDI is also normally configured in the `cluster-service.xml` file in the `\deploy` directory of every server participating in the partition using the HA-JNDI MBean explained next. The MBean definition is as follows:

```
<mbean
  code="org.jboss.ha.jndi.HANamingService"
  name="jboss:service=HAJNDI">
```

The MBean supports the following attributes:

Attribute	Function
PartitionName	The name of the partition to which the HA-JNDI context is available. The default value is `DefaultPartition`.
BindAddress	The address to which the HA-JNDI server will bind, if you're using a machine that supports multiple IPs.
Port	The port on which the HA-JNDI server listens. The default value is `1100`.
BackLog	Serves the same purpose as that for the local JNDI service MBean. Please refer to section 6.1, "The JBoss Naming Service," for further details.
RmiPort	Serves the same purpose as that for the local JNDI service MBean. Please refer to section 6.1, "The JBoss Naming Service," for further details.
AutoDiscoveryAddress	The multicast address to listen for automatic discovery.
AutoDiscoveryGroup	The multicast group to listen for automatic discovery.

The following example shows an example HA-JNDI MBean configuration:

```
<mbean
  code="org.jboss.ha.jndi.HANamingService"
  name="jboss:service=HAJNDI">
  <depends>jboss:service=MyPartition</depends>
  <attribute name="PartitionName">MyPartition</attribute>
  <attribute name="Port">2000</attribute>
</mbean>
```

The previous example defines the HA JNDI service listening on port 2000 for the partition `MyPartition`.

> **Please note that it's always better to deploy your EJBs on all the nodes in the cluster because it'll speed up the lookup process through HA-JNDI.**

13.3.4.1 Configuring Clients for Automatic Discovery

In a nonclustered environment, clients normally use the `Context.PROVIDER_URL` property to specify the JNDI server to which they want to connect. In JBoss, the default port is 1099, and the protocol is Java Network Programming (JNP). In a clustered environment, however, there are multiple servers, and each server will be listening on two different ports: one for local JNDI and the other for HA-JNDI. In this scenario, how will the client specify the provider URL?

One solution is for the client to specify the HA-JNDI port of one of the servers in the partition as follows:

```
prop.put(Context.PROVIDER_URL, "jnp://poseidon:1100");

Context ctx = new InitialContext(prop);
```

Once the client gets the remote stub, the stub will have information regarding the partition view. Thus, even if the original server goes down, the client can connect to another server in the partition. However, if the server that the client is initially trying to connect to is down, the client won't be able to connect at all. To circumvent this problem, JBoss allows the clients to specify a comma-separated list of JNDI servers as follows:

```
prop.put(Context.PROVIDER_URL,
    "jnp://poseidon:1100,jnp://pegasus:1100,jnp://hercules:1100");

Context ctx = new InitialContext(prop);
```

In the aforementioned scenario, the client will try establishing a connection with the servers in the list starting from the first one until it's successful or it fails connecting to any of the servers in the list. However, this can at times be cumbersome if there are a lot of servers in the partition. Hence, JBoss provides a third method where you don't specify any provider URL, and if any of the servers in the list are reachable, the clients will try to connect to a HA-JNDI server through a multicast call on the address 230.0.0.4:1102.

13.3.5 EJBs in a Cluster

JBoss allows you to cluster both session (stateful and stateless) as well as entity EJBs. The behavior of EJBs in a cluster is configured using the <cluster-config> element of the JBoss-specific EJB deployment descriptor (jboss.xml). Section 17.3, "Container Configuration Details," covers this in detail.

However, to get clustered stateful session EJBs working, you need to configure one key MBean service. This is the HASessionState service, which is used for in-memory state replication of stateful session EJBs. This MBean is available in the cluster-service.xml file, and its definition is as follows:

```
<mbean
    code="org.jboss.ha.hasessionstate.server.HASessionStateService"
    name="jboss:service=HASessionState">
```

The MBean supports the following attributes:

Attribute	Function
JndiName	An optional attribute to specify the JNDI name under which the service is bound. The default value is /HAPartition/Default.
PartitionName	To specify the name of the partition in which the session state service is used. The default value is DefaultPartition.
BeanCleaningDelay	To specify an optional time interval in which the session state service can clean up the state of a session bean that hasn't been modified. The default value is 30 minutes.

The following snippet shows an example of the session state MBean configuration:

```
<mbean
    code="org.jboss.ha.hasessionstate.server.HASessionStateService"
    name="jboss:service=HASessionState">
    <depends>jboss:service=MyPartition</depends>
    <JndiName>/HAPartition/MyService</JndiName>
    <PartitionName>MyPartition</PartitionName>
</mbean>
```

The previous example defines the MBean definition for replicating stateful session beans deployed on servers participating in the cluster partition MyPartition.

13.3.5.1 Load Balancing Policy

JBoss provides two load balancing policies that you can configure your EJBs with:

- **Round robin**
  Always favors the next available target when an invocation is made.

- **First available**
  Always favors the first available target. This does not mean that failover will not occur if the first member in the list dies. In this case, failover will occur, a new target will become the first member, and invocation will continuously be invoked on the same new target until its death.

You specify your load balancing policy in the JBoss-specific EJB deployment descriptor, jboss.xml. Section 17.3, "Container Configuration Details," covers EJB clustering in detail. You can write your own load balancing policy by implementing the JBoss org.jboss.ha.framework.interfaces.LoadBalancePolicy interface.

13.3.6 HTTP Session Clustering

JBoss allows HTTP session replication for both the Tomcat and Jetty flavors. However, transparent session failover should be implemented at the load balancer level, which pins the JBoss server instance to a user session. You can do this using hardware load balancers or web server proxies. When using AJP, you can configure IIS or Apache in the workers properties file to work with multiple instances of JBoss/Tomcat and JBoss/Jetty instances, and AJP will take care of load balancing. One thing you need to make sure is that whatever load balancing strategy you use, it should accommodate server affinity for user sessions.

At the JBoss level, you need to have the clustering MBean, explained in section 13.3.3, "Configuring Clusters," and the jbossha-httpsession.sar Service Archive (SAR) component deployed. This MBean provides support for clustered HTTP sessions.

13.3.6.1 Configuring Tomcat for HTTP Session Clustering

The embedded Catalina service MBean, discussed in section 12.1, "Configuring Tomcat," for configuring embedded Tomcat service defined in `jboss-service.xml`, provides two attributes for configuring clustered HTTP sessions:

Attribute	Function
SnapshotMode	To specify the mode for replicating session state across nodes in a partition. If set to `instant`, the state is replicated whenever it's changed. If the state is set to `interval`, it's replicated at regular intervals specified by the `SnapShotInterval` attribute.
SnapShotInterval	To specify the interval at which the state should be replicated when the snapshot mode is set to `interval`. The default value is 2,000 milliseconds.

13.3.6.2 Configuring Jetty for HTTP Session Clustering

Unlike Tomcat, Jetty provides two options for HTTP session state replication:

❑ Custom session replication provided by Jetty

❑ JBoss replication as used by Tomcat

To enable Jetty session replication, you need to have the following element in the custom configuration element of the Jetty service MBean in the `deploy\jbossweb-jetty.sar\META-INF\jboss-service.xml` file.

```
<Configure class="org.mortbay.jetty.Server">
  ...
  <Set name="DistributableSessionManagerPrototype">
    <New class="org.mortbay.j2ee.session.Manager">
      <Set name="scavengerPeriod">600</Set>
      <Set name="interceptorStack">
      <Array type="org.mortbay.j2ee.session.StateInterceptor">
        <Item>
          <New class="org.mortbay.j2ee.session.DebugInterceptor"/>
        </Item>
        <Item>
          <New class="org.mortbay.j2ee.session.ValidatingInterceptor"/>
        </Item>
        <Item>
          <New class=
            "org.mortbay.j2ee.session.TypeCheckingInterceptor"/>
        </Item>
```

191

```xml
        <Item>
         <New class="org.mortbay.j2ee.session.BindingInterceptor"/>
        </Item>
        <Item>
         <New class="org.mortbay.j2ee.session.PublishingInterceptor"/>
        </Item>
        <Item>
         <New class="org.mortbay.j2ee.session.SubscribingInterceptor"/>
        </Item>
        <Item>
         <New class=
             "org.mortbay.j2ee.session.SynchronizingInterceptor"/>
        </Item>
       </Array>
      </Set>
      <!-- Session store to use -->
      <Set name="store">
         <New class="org.mortbay.j2ee.session.JGStore">
           <Set name="actualMaxInactiveInterval">604800</Set>
           <Set name="scavengerPeriod">3600</Set>
           <Set name="scavengerExtraTime">900</Set>
           <Set name="protocolStack">
               UDP(mcast_addr=228.8.8.8;mcast_port=45566;
               ip_ttl=32;ucast_recv_buf_size=16000;
               ucast_send_buf_size=16000;mcast_send_buf_size=32000;
               mcast_recv_buf_size=64000;
               loopback=true):PING(timeout=2000;
               num_initial_members=3):MERGE2(min_interval=5000;
               max_interval=10000):FD_SOCK:
                 VERIFY_SUSPECT(timeout=1500):
                 pbcast.STABLE(desired_avg_gossip=20000):
                 pbcast.NAKACK(gc_lag=50;
               retransmit_timeout=300,600,1200,2400,4800;
               max_xmit_size=8192):UNICAST(timeout=2000):
                 FRAG(frag_size=8192;
               down_thread=false;
               up_thread=false):pbcast.GMS(join_timeout=5000;
               join_retry_timeout=2000;
               shun=false;print_local_addr=true):pbcast.STATE_TRANSFER
           </Set>
           <Set name="subClusterName">DefaultSubCluster</Set>
           <Set name="retrievalTimeOut">20000</Set>
           <Set name="distributionTimeOut">5000</Set>
           <Set name="distributionMode">GET_ALL</Set>
         </New>
       </Set>
     </New>
   </Set>
 </Configure>
```

192

The class `org.mortbay.j2ee.session.Manager` uses the `store` attribute of type `org.mortbay.j2ee.session.Store` for session management. To enable distributed sessions you can use an implementation of this interface called `org.mortbay.j2ee.session.JGStore`. This class uses the Javagroups communication framework for distributing the session state. Ths `JGStore` class supports the following attributes:

Attribute	Description
actualMaxIntervalTime	This is the interval before the session is garbage collected. The default value is `604800` (the number of seconds in a week).
scavengerPeriod	Interval between which distributable sessions without local versions are garbage collected. The default value is `3600` (the number of seconds in an hour).
protocolStack	Javagroups protocol stack to use.
subClusterName	Name of the subcluster.
retrievalTimeOut	Time interval for a starting Jetty instance to get the session replicas from the participating nodes in the cluster.
distributionTimeOut	Time interval before which the session replication across the cluster is considered as a failure.
distributionMode	This is an enumerated value to indicate at what point session replication is considered successful. Available values are `GET_ALL` to indicate the session should be replicated across all nodes, `GET_MAJORITY` to indicate the session should be replicated across majority of all working nodes, `GET_ABS_MAJORITY` to indicate the session should be replicated across majority of all nodes regardless of whether they're working, `GET_FIRST` to indicate the session should be replicated to the first node in the cluster, and `GET_NONE` to indicate when the ID doesn't.

To use JBoss clustering, you can use the store as `org.jboss.jetty.session.ClusterStore` instead of the JGStore as shown below:

```
<Set name="store">
    <New class="org.jboss.jetty.session.ClusterStore">
        <Set name="actualMaxInactiveInterval">604800</Set>
        <Set name="scavengerPeriod">3600</Set>
        <Set name="scavengerExtraTime">900</Set>
    </New>
</Set>
```

13.3.6.3 Configuring AJP for HTTP Session Clustering

To achieve load balancing using AJP, you need multiple instances of JBoss/Tomcat or JBoss/Jetty running. The AJP module on the Apache/IIS web server should be made aware of the multiple instances of the JBoss instances using the workers properties file (discussed in section 11.2.4, "Running Jetty with Other Web Servers," and section 12.1.8.3, "Running Tomcat with Other Web Servers") as follows:

```
ps=\
```

Define the worker list:

```
worker.list=JBoss1, JBoss2, loadbalancer
```

Define the second JBoss worker:

```
worker.JBoss1.port=1009
worker.JBoss1.host=poseidon
worker.JBoss1.type=ajp13
worker.JBoss1.lbfactor=100
```

Define the second JBoss worker:

```
worker.JBoss2.port=1009
worker.JBoss2.host=pegasus
worker.JBoss2.type=ajp13
worker.JBoss2.lbfactor=100
```

The load balancer (type lb) worker performs weighted round-robin load balancing with sticky sessions. If a worker dies, the load balancer will check its state once in a while. Until then all work is redirected to a peer worker:

```
worker.loadbalancer.type=lb
worker.loadbalancer.balanced_workers=JBoss1, JBoss2
```

13.3.7 Clustered Deployment

JBoss also supports farming, which enables the components that are deployed on one server to be made available on all the other servers in the partition. This isn't enabled by default. You can enable it by configuring the FarmMemberService MBean. The MBean definition is as follows:

```
<mbean
    code="org.jboss.ha.framework,server.FarmMemberService"
    name="jboss:service=FarmMember,partition=MyPartition">
```

It supports the following attributes:

Attribute	Function
PartitionName	The partition for which farming is enabled. The default value is `DefaultPartition`.
FarmDeployDirectory	The directory that the JBoss deployment scanner component watches for deployment archives.
ScannerName	The object name of the deployment scanner MBean that's used. Section 15.1, "Deployers," covers the deployment scanner MBean.

The following snippet shows an example of this MBean service:

```
<mbean
   code="org.jboss.ha.framework,server.FarmMemberService"
   name="jboss:service=FarmMember,partition=MyPartition">
   <depends>jboss:service=MyPartition</depends>
   <attribute name="PartitionName">MyPartition</attribute>
   <attribute name="FarmDeployDirectory">./deploy</attribute>
   <attribute name="ScannerName">
      jboss.deployment:type=DeploymentScanner,flavor=URL
   </attribute>
</mbean>
```

The previous snippet defines the MBean service responsible for distributed deployment. This MBean will deploy a J2EE component across all the servers in the `MyPartition` partition. Please note that this MBean itself should be deployed on all the servers in the partition.

Configuring Logging

Logging is one of the key aspects of enterprise application development, used extensively for diagnostic and bug tracking purposes. In this chapter, you'll look at how to configure logging within JBoss. JBoss uses **Log4J** as its sole logging Application Programming Interface (API), and version 3.*x* comes with Java Archive (JAR) files required for Log4J 1.2.*x*.

> **Please note that an in-depth coverage of Log4J is beyond the scope of this book. You can find more information about Log4J at http://jakarta.apache.org/log4j/.**

14.1 The Logging MBean

JBoss provides an MBean that can be used for configuring logging options. This MBean is normally defined in the root configuration file `jboss-service.xml` available in the `\conf` directory of the server configuration set you're running. The MBean definition is as follows:

```
<mbean
   code="org.jboss.logging.Log4jService"
   name="jboss.system:type=Log4jService,service=Logging">
```

This MBean supports the following attributes:

Attribute	Function
ConfigurationURL	Specifies the location of the Log4J configuration file used for defining appenders, patterns, categories, and priorities. JBoss supports both properties' file formats as well as an Extensible Markup Language (XML) format for configuring Log4J.
RefreshPeriod	Specifies the refresh period in seconds for reloading the configuration information. The default value is 60.
Log4jQuietMode	The org.apache.log4j.helpers.LogLog.setQuietMode flag setting. This class used to output log statements from within the log4j package. Log4J components can't make Log4J logging calls. However, it's sometimes useful for the user to learn about what Log4J is doing. You can enable Log4J internal logging by defining the log4j.configDebug variable. All Log4J internal debug calls go to System.out where internal error messages are sent to System.err. All internal messages are prepended with the string "log4j:". In quiet mode Log4J generates strictly no output, not even for errors.

The following listing shows an example for the Log4J MBean definition:

```
<mbean
    code="org.jboss.logging.Log4jService"
    name="jboss.system:type=Log4jService,service=Logging">
    <attribute name="ConfigurationURL">resource:log4j.xml</attribute>
    <attribute name="Log4jQuietMode">true</attribute>
</mbean>
```

This will load the logging configuration from the file log4j.xml, present in the \conf directory of the server home.

14.2 Log4J Overview

In this section, you'll get a brief overview of the Log4J API.

The three main components of Log4J are **loggers**, **appenders**, and **layouts**. Loggers decide what is logged, appenders decide where it's logged, and layouts decide in what format it's logged.

14.2.1 Category/Logger

Log4J allows you to disable certain log statements while allowing others to print unhindered. To do this, Log4J uses a logging space, where all logging statements are categorized according to some developer-chosen criteria. Prior to version 1.2, the class Category was used to represent an entity for which logging statements were enabled or disabled based on a severity level. However, since version 1.2, the Logger class has replaced the Category class. The Logger class extends the Category class.

Loggers are named entities that follow a hierarchical naming rule. A logger is said to be an ancestor of another logger if its name, followed by a dot, is a prefix of the descendant logger name. A logger is said to be a parent of a child logger if there are no ancestors between it and the descendant logger. For example, the logger named com.foo is a parent of the logger named com.foo.Bar. Similarly, java is a parent of java.util and an ancestor of java.util.Vector.

The root logger resides at the top of the logger hierarchy. It always exists, and it can't be retrieved by name. Invoking the class static Logger.getRootLogger() method retrieves it. All other loggers are instantiated and retrieved with the class static Logger.getLogger() method. This method takes the name of the desired logger as a parameter. Some of the basic methods in the Logger class are as follows.

Methods for creating and retrieving loggers are as follows:

```
public static Logger getRootLogger();
public static Logger getLogger(String name);
```

Methods for logging messages with varying levels of priority are as follows:

```
public void debug(Object message);
public void info(Object message);
public void warn(Object message);
public void error(Object message);
public void fatal(Object message);
```

A generic logging method where you can specify a severity level is as follows:

```
public void log(Level 1, Object message);
```

Loggers may be assigned levels. The set of possible levels—that is, DEBUG, INFO, WARN, ERROR, and FATAL—is defined in the org.apache.log4j.Level class. If a given logger isn't assigned a level, then it inherits one from its closest ancestor with an assigned level. The inherited level for a given logger is equal to the first non-null level in the logger hierarchy, starting at that logger and proceeding upward in the hierarchy toward the root logger.

Logging requests are made by invoking one of the printing methods of a logger instance. These printing methods are debug(), info(), warn(), error(), fatal(), and log(). By definition, the printing method determines the level of a logging request. For example, if logger is a logger instance, then the statement logger.info("..") is a logging request of level INFO. A logging request is said to be enabled if its level is higher than or equal to the level of its logger. Otherwise, the request is said to be disabled. A logger without an assigned level will inherit one from the hierarchy. For the standard levels, the order is DEBUG < INFO < WARN < ERROR < FATAL.

Calling the getLogger() method with the same name will always return a reference to the same Logger object. For example, in the following:

```
Logger x = Logger.getLogger("wombat");
Logger y = Logger.getLogger("wombat");
```

x and y refer to the same Logger object.

Thus, it's possible to configure a logger and then to retrieve the same instance somewhere else in the code without passing around references.

Configuring the Log4J environment is typically done at application initialization. The preferred way is by reading a configuration file.

Log4J makes it easy to name loggers by software component. You can accomplish this by statically instantiating a logger in each class, with the logger name equal to the fully qualified name of the class. This is a useful and straightforward method of defining loggers. Because the log output bears the name of the generating logger, this naming strategy makes it easy to identify the origin of a log message.

14.2.2 Appenders

The ability to selectively enable or disable logging requests based on their loggers is only part of the picture. Log4J allows logging requests to print to multiple destinations. In Log4J an output destination is called an **appender**. Currently, appenders exist for the console, files, Graphical User Interface (GUI) components, remote socket servers, Java Message Service (JMS), NT event loggers, and remote Unix Syslog daemons. It's also possible to log asynchronously. See section 14.3.1.1, "Prebuilt Appenders," for more details on these existing appenders and how to use them.

You can attach more than one appender to a logger. The addAppender() method adds an appender to a given logger. Each enabled logging request for a given logger will be forwarded to all the appenders in that logger as well as the appenders higher in the hierarchy. In other words, appenders are inherited additively from the logger hierarchy. For example, if a console appender is added to the root logger, then all enabled logging requests will at least print on the console. If in addition a file appender is added to a logger, say `logger`, then enabled logging requests for `logger` and `logger`'s children will print on a file and on the console. It's possible to override this default behavior so that appender accumulation is no longer additive by setting the additivity flag to `false`.

14.2.3 Layout

More often than not, users want to customize not only the output destination but also the output format. You accomplish this by associating a layout with an appender. The layout is responsible for formatting the logging request according to the user's wishes, whereas an appender takes care of sending the formatted output to its destination. The `PatternLayout`, part of the standard Log4J distribution, lets the user specify the output format according to conversion.

For example, the `PatternLayout` with the conversion pattern `%r [%t] %-5p %c - %m%n` will output something akin to the following:

```
176 [main] INFO  org.foo.Bar - Located nearest gas station.
```

The first field is the number of milliseconds elapsed since the start of the program. The second field is the thread making the log request. The third field is the level of the log statement. The fourth field is the name of the logger associated with the log request. The text after the - is the message of the statement.

14.2.4 Renderers

Log4J allows you to specify custom renderers for objects that are logged frequently. Please note that the print functions on the logger accept any type of Java objects and not just strings. Object rendering follows the class hierarchy. For example, assuming oranges are fruits, if you register a `FruitRenderer`, all fruits including oranges will be rendered by the `FruitRenderer`, unless of course you registered an orange-specific `OrangeRenderer`.

Object renderers have to implement the `ObjectRenderer` interface.

14.3 Configuring Logging

The Log4J configuration MBean discussed in the previous section uses Extensible Markup Language (XML)–based configuration. The configuration file as specified by the default JBoss installation is `log4j.xml` located in the `\conf` directory of the default configuration set. It has the following structure:

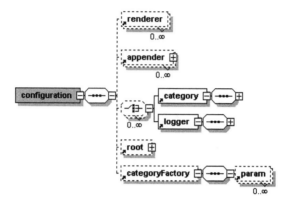

The root element for XML-based configuration is called `configuration`. The `configuration` element takes two attributes, `threshold` and `debug`:

❑   The `threshold` attribute takes a level value such that all logging statements with a level equal or below this value are disabled. The available levels are `DEBUG`, `INFO`, `WARN`, `ERROR`, and `FATAL` in increasing order of severity. However, the threshold defined here can be overridden at appender and filter/category levels.

❑   Setting the `debug` attribute to `true` enables the printing of internal Log4J logging statements. By default, the `debug` attribute is set to `false`, meaning that you don't touch internal Log4J logging settings.

In the next few sections you'll take a closer look at the `appender`, `root`, `category`, and `logger` elements in detail.

> **For a more thorough coverage of configuring Log4J refer to its documentation at http://jakarta.apache.org/log4j/docs/ documentation.html.**

14.3.1 Appender

The `configuration` element can contain zero or more appender elements to configure Log4J appenders. Appenders in Log4J decide where the messages are logged. The appender element has the following structure:

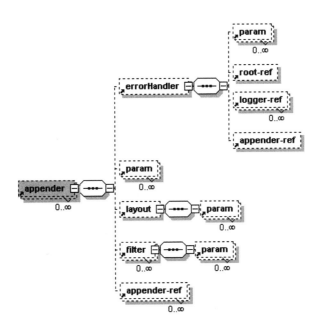

The appender element has two mandatory attributes, name and class. The name attribute assigns a unique name to the appender, and the class attribute defines the class name of the appender that implements the Log4J Appender interface. The appender element can have the following child elements:

Element	Description
errorHandler	An optional errorHandler element sets an error handler for the appender. This element has a class attribute to specify the fully qualified name of the class that implements the Log4J ErrorHandler interface. This element can also have zero or more param elements to set options specific to the error handler being used. Log4J defines a set of predefined filters. If an error handler isn't specified, there won't be any error handling done. JBoss provides an ErrorHandler implementation called org.jboss.logging.util.OnlyOnceErrorHandler.
param	Zero or more param elements set options specific to the appender. The param element supports the attributes name and value used to specify the name and value of the option. All the appenders that extend the Log4J AppendorSkeleton class support the option Threshold to specify the level of the log messages that can be logged.

continues

Element	Description
layout	An optional `layout` element specifies the class that will be responsible for formatting the log messages. This element has a `class` attribute to specify the fully qualified name of the class that extends the Log4J `Layout` class. This element can also have zero or more `param` elements to set options specific to the layout being used. If a `layout` isn't specified, the appender will use a layout specific to the appender. Different appenders have different default layouts.
filter	Zero or more `filter` elements define custom filtering of log messages. This element has a `class` attribute to specify the fully qualified name of the class that extends the Log4J `Filter` class. This element can also have zero or more `param` elements to set options specific to the filter being used. Log4J defines a set of predefined filters. If a filter isn't specified, then all messages sent to the appender will be logged.
appender-ref	Zero or more `appender-ref` elements are used for chaining appenders. When you chain appenders, the messages sent to the referring appender are sent to the referred appenders. This element takes a `ref` attribute that will refer to the name attribute of the referred appender.

14.3.1.1 Prebuilt Appenders

Log4J provides quite a few prebuilt appenders, which you can find in the JBoss `log4j.xml` configuration file.

14.3.1.1.1 ConsoleAppender

This appender sends the messages to the console and supports the following parameter:

- ❑ Target
  Specifies whether the messages should be sent to `System.out` or `System.err`

The following snippet shows an example `ConsoleAppender` configuration:

```
<appender name="CONSOLE" class="org.apache.log4j.ConsoleAppender">
  <errorHandler class="org.jboss.logging.util.OnlyOnceErrorHandler"/>
  <param name="Threshold" value="INFO"/>
  <param name="Target" value="System.out"/>

  <layout class="org.apache.log4j.PatternLayout">
    <param name="ConversionPattern"
      value="%d{ABSOLUTE} %-5p [%c{1}] %m%n"/>
  </layout>

</appender>
```

This snippet defines an appender called CONSOLE that uses the Log4J console appender and uses the Log4J pattern layout. The threshold is set to INFO, and the log messages are sent to System.out.

14.3.1.1.2 FileAppender

This appender sends the messages to a file and supports the following parameters:

❑ Append
Specifies whether the messages should be appended to an existing file or if a new file should be created

❑ BufferedIO
A Boolean flag to specify whether buffering should be enabled

❑ BufferSize
The buffer size if buffering is enabled

❑ File
The file to which the messages are written

This appender has subclasses called DailyRollingFileAppender, which rolls the log file every day, and RollingFileAppender, which can roll the log file based on date and/or size. The RollingFileAppender supports two additional parameters:

❑ MaxFileSize
The maximum size the logging file can grow to before being rolled over into a new file

❑ MaxBackupIndex
The number of backup log files that should be held at any time

The following snippet shows an example FileAppender configuration:

```
<appender
  name="FILE"
  class="org.jboss.logging.appender.RollingFileAppender">
  <errorHandler class="org.jboss.logging.util.OnlyOnceErrorHandler"/>
  <param name="Threshold" value="DEBUG"/>
  <param name="File" value="${jboss.server.home.dir}/log/server.log"/>
  <param name="Append" value="false"/>
  <param name="MaxFileSize" value="500KB"/>
  <param name="MaxBackupIndex" value="1"/>

  <layout class="org.apache.log4j.PatternLayout">
    <param name="ConversionPattern" value="%d %-5p [%c] %m%n"/>
  </layout>
</appender>
```

This snippet defines an appender called FILE that uses the Log4J rolling file appender and the Log4J pattern layout. The threshold is set to DEBUG, and the log messages are sent to the server.log file under the \log directory of the configuration set you use. The file is rolled every 500 kilobytes (KB), and the last file that was rolled is archived.

14.3.1.1.3 JMSAppender

This is a simple appender that publishes events to a JMS topic. The events are serialized and transmitted as a JMS object message. JMS appenders are useful for logging from Enterprise JavaBeans (EJBs) where file Input/Output (I/O) isn't allowed according to the specification. This appender supports the following parameters:

- InitialContextFactoryName
  Specifies the initial context factory to use when creating a Java Naming and Directory Interface (JNDI) initial context to look up the JMS connection factory and topic

- ProviderURL
  Specifies the provider Uniform Resource Locator (URL) to use when creating a JNDI initial context to look up the JMS connection factory and topic

- URLPkgPrefixes
  Specifies the URL package prefixes to use when creating a JNDI initial context to look up the JMS connection factory and topic

- SecurityCredentials
  Specifies the security credentials to use when creating a JNDI initial context to look up the JMS connection factory and topic

- SecurityPrincipalName
  Specifies the security principal to use when creating a JNDI initial context to look up the JMS connection factory and topic

- TopicName
  Specifies the JNDI name of the topic connection that's used

- TopicConnectionFactoryName
  Specifies the JNDI name of the JMS topic connection factory

- UserName
  Specifies the user name used for creating topic sessions

- Password
  Specifies the password used for creating topic sessions

The following snippet shows an example JMSAppender configuration:

```
<appender name="JMS" class="org.apache.log4j.net.JMSAppender">
  <errorHandler class="org.jboss.logging.util.OnlyOnceErrorHandler"/>
  <param name="Threshold" value="DEBUG"/>
  <param name="TopicConnectionFactoryBindingName"
    value="java:/ConnectionFactory"/>
  <param name="TopicBindingName" value="topic/MyErrorsTopic"/>
</appender>
```

If the initial context properties aren't specified (as in the previous code), the appender will create the initial context without specifying any properties.

The previous snippet defines an appender called JMS that logs messages to the topic MyErrorsTopic with a threshold set to DEBUG.

14.3.1.1.4 SMTPAppender

This appender sends an e-mail when a specific logging event occurs, typically on errors or fatal errors. This appender supports the following parameters:

❏ From
A string value that should be the e-mail address of the sender.

❏ SMTPHost
A string value that should be the host name of the Simple Mail Transfer Protocol (SMTP) server that will send the e-mail message.

❏ To
A string value that should be a comma-separated list of the e-mail addresses of the recipients.

❏ Subject
Specifies the security credentials to use when creating a JNDI initial context to look up the JMS connection factory and topic.

❏ BufferSize
A positive integer representing the maximum number of logging events to collect in a cyclic buffer. When the buffer size is reached, the oldest events are deleted as new events are added to the buffer. By default the size of the cyclic buffer is 512 events.

❏ LocationInfo
A Boolean value. By default, it's set to false, which means there will be no effort to extract the location information related to the event. As a result, the layout that formats the events as they're sent out in an e-mail is likely to place the wrong location information (if present in the format). Location information extraction is comparatively very slow and should be avoided unless performance isn't a concern.

The following snippet shows an example `SMTPAppender` configuration:

```
<appender name="SMTP" class="org.apache.log4j.net.SMTPAppender">
  <errorHandler class="org.jboss.logging.util.OnlyOnceErrorHandler"/>
  <param name="Threshold" value="ERROR"/>
  <param name="From" value="fred@flintstone.com"/>
  <param name="To" value="barney@rubble.com"/>
  <param name="Subject" value="Error"/>
  <param name="SMTPHost" value="mail.exchb01.com"/>
</appender>
```

This snippet defines an appender called `SMTP` that sends an e-mail message for messages with severity as `ERROR`.

14.3.1.1.5 AsyncAppender

`AsyncAppender` lets users log events asynchronously. It uses a bounded buffer to store logging events. `AsyncAppender` will collect the events sent to it and then dispatch them to all the appenders that are attached to it. You can attach multiple appenders to an `AsyncAppender`. The `AsyncAppender` uses a separate thread to serve the events in its bounded buffer. It supports the following single option:

- ❑ `BufferSize`
  Specifies the buffer size for the asynchronous appender. By default this appender can buffer 128 logging events.

The following snippet shows an example `AsyncAppender` configuration:

```
<appender name="ASYNC" class="org.apache.log4j.AsyncAppender">
  <errorHandler class="org.jboss.logging.util.OnlyOnceErrorHandler"/>
  <appender-ref ref="FILE"/>
  <appender-ref ref="CONSOLE"/>
  <appender-ref ref="SMTP"/>
</appender>
```

This snippet defines an appender called `ASYNC` that uses the Log4J asynchronous appender. The appender buffers messages sent to it and later sends it to the named appenders defined using the `appender-ref` elements. You can use asynchronous appenders for improving performance.

14.3.1.1.6 Other Appenders

Other appenders provided by Log4J include the following (please refer to the Log4J API documentation for the configurable attributes of the appenders listed):

- ❏ JDBCAppender
  For logging to a database.

- ❏ LF5Appender
  Logs events to a Swing-based logging console. The Swing console supports turning categories on and off and multiple detail level views, as well as full-text searching and many other capabilities.

- ❏ NTEventLogAppender
  Logs to the NT event log system. This appender can only be installed and used on a Windows system.

- ❏ SocketAppender
  Sends the log messages to a remote log server.

- ❏ SyslogAppender
  Sends log messages to the Unix Syslog daemon.

14.3.2 Renderer

The renderer element defines classes that will provide custom conversion of message objects to string patterns as explained in section 14.2.4, "Renderers." This element takes two attributes, renderingClass and renderedClass. The rendered class is the class for which the renderer is defined, and the rendering class is a class that implements the Log4J object renderer interface:

```
<renderer
  renderingClass="com.MyRenderer"
  renderedClass="com.MyClass"/>
```

In the previous scenario, whenever a print method on a logger is called with an object of type com.MyClass, Log4J will ask an instance of com.MyRenderer to render the object. com.MyRenderer needs to implement the Log4J ObjectRenderer interface.

14.3.3 Root

The root element defines the logging properties for the root category/logger. Category is a class provided by Log4J for logging messages. The Log4J Logger class that extends `Category` and `Category` has now been deprecated. Previously, to log messages from a class, you had to call this:

```
Category cat = Category.getInstance(getClass());
cat.info("My message");
```

or the following:

```
Category cat = Category.getInstance(getClass().getName());
cat.info("My message");
```

The argument that's passed to these methods defines a named category. It's a common practice to use the fully qualified class name of the class from where the messages are logged as the category name. You can associate appenders and priorities/levels with categories. The Log4J class `Level` extends the `Priority` class, and the `Priority` class has been deprecated now. These classes set a threshold for the severity of the messages that are logged.

However, the recommended approach now is to use the `Logger` class as follows:

```
Logger log = Logger.getLogger(getClass());
log.info("My message");
```

or as follows:

```
Logger log = Logger.getLogger(getClass().getName());
log.info("My message");
```

The `root` element defines appenders and threshold for the root category/logger. The threshold defined here can be overridden at individual category/logger level. Log4J also allows you to have a hierarchy of loggers/categories similar to the Java package structure. For example, a named logger `com.foo` is considered as the parent of `com.foo.bar`. If you don't specify an explicit threshold for `com.foo.bar`, it'll inherit the priority of `com.foo`. If there's no threshold defined anywhere in the hierarchy, Log4J will use the threshold defined for the root category. If the `root` category hasn't got a threshold, Log4J will set the threshold at `DEBUG`. Similarly categories/loggers also inherit the appenders set for parent categories/loggers.

The structure of the `root` element is as follows:

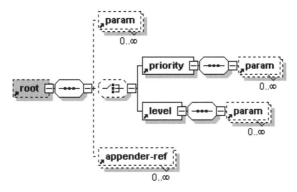

- ❏ The `param` element sets options specific to the root.

- ❏ The `priority` or `level` element sets a threshold for the root category or logger. Prior to version 1.2, the `Priority` class represented message severity. The `Level` class in version 1.2 has replaced this.

- ❏ The `appender-ref` elements set one or more appenders to the root category/logger. See section 14.3.1.1, "Prebuilt Appenders," for a list of appenders.

The following snippet shows an example of the `root` category/logger configuration:

```
<root>
  <level value="INFO"/>
  <appender-ref ref="CONSOLE"/>
  <appender-ref ref="FILE"/>
</root>
```

The previous example sets the threshold for the root category/logger at `INFO` and sets the two named appenders `CONSOLE` and `FILE`. This means for any named category/logger for which the threshold isn't explicitly defined, it'll use the `INFO` level, and all the categories/loggers within the system will send messages to the `CONSOLE` and `FILE` appenders.

14.3.4 Category/Logger

The `configuration` element can have zero or more `category` or `logger` elements to define thresholds and appenders for named categories or loggers. The structure of these elements is as follows:

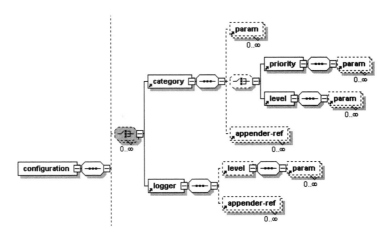

Both `category` and `logger` elements have a name attribute to define the name of the category/logger. Both of them can define their own list of appenders in addition to the appenders defined for their parent categories/loggers using the `appender-ref` elements. The `category` element can use the `priority` or `level` element to override the threshold set for its parent category whereas the `logger` element can use the `level` element to do the same.

In the following snippet, the category `foo.bar` overrides the threshold set by its parent category to define that `foo.bar` and its subcategories will log all messages with a priority greater than `DEBUG` and will use a named appender `SOCKET` *in addition to* the appenders defined for its parent category:

```
<category name="foo.bar">
  <priority value="DEBUG"/>
  <appender-ref ref="SOCKET"/>
</category>
```

Log4J also allows you to define custom priorities and levels. Section 14.5, "TRACE Priority," explains this in detail.

14.3.5 JBoss Default Logging Configuration

The default configuration that comes out of the box with JBoss is as follows:

```xml
<?xml version="1.0" encoding="UTF-8"?>
<!DOCTYPE log4j:configuration SYSTEM "log4j.dtd">

<log4j:configuration xmlns:log4j="http://jakarta.apache.org/log4j/"
                     debug="false">

  <!-- A time/date based rolling appender -->
  <appender name="FILE"
    class="org.jboss.logging.appender.DailyRollingFileAppender">
    <errorHandler class=
       "org.jboss.logging.util.OnlyOnceErrorHandler"/>
    <param name="File"
      value="${jboss.server.home.dir}/log/server.log"/>
    <param name="Append" value="false"/>

    <!-- Rollover at midnight each day -->
    <param name="DatePattern" value="'.'yyyy-MM-dd"/>

    <layout class="org.apache.log4j.PatternLayout">
      <!-- The default pattern: Date Priority [Category] Message\n -->
      <param name="ConversionPattern" value="%d %-5p [%c] %m%n"/>
    </layout>
  </appender>

  <!-- Console appender -->
  <appender name="CONSOLE" class="org.apache.log4j.ConsoleAppender">
    <param name="Threshold" value="INFO"/>
    <param name="Target" value="System.out"/>

    <layout class="org.apache.log4j.PatternLayout">
      <!-- The default pattern: Date Priority [Category] Message\n -->
      <param name="ConversionPattern"
        value="%d{ABSOLUTE} %-5p [%c{1}] %m%n"/>
    </layout>
  </appender>

  <appender name="JSR77" class="org.apache.log4j.FileAppender">
    <errorHandler class=
       "org.jboss.logging.util.OnlyOnceErrorHandler"/>
    <param name="Append" value="false"/>
    <param name="File"
          value="${jboss.server.home.dir}/log/jsr77.log"/>
    <layout class="org.apache.log4j.PatternLayout">
      <param name="ConversionPattern"
            value="%d{ABSOLUTE} %-5p [%c{1}] %m%n"/>
    </layout>
  </appender>

  <!-- Limit the org.apache.commons category to INFO as its DEBUG
       is verbose -->
  <category name="org.apache.commons">
```

```
        <priority value="INFO"/>
   </category>

 <!-- Setup the Root category -->
   <root>
     <appender-ref ref="CONSOLE"/>
     <appender-ref ref="FILE"/>
   </root>

 </log4j:configuration>
```

This configuration defines two appenders: one a date/time-based rolling file appender that's rolled every day, the other a console appender. The file appender writes to the file server.log under the \logs directory of your configuration set. The console appender has a threshold of INFO, and the file appender has a threshold of DEBUG. The root category is configured to use both the appenders. The configuration also specified the threshold for the category org.apache.commons as INFO.

14.4 Administering Logging

As with any other MBean, you can administer the Log4J MBean using the JMX console:

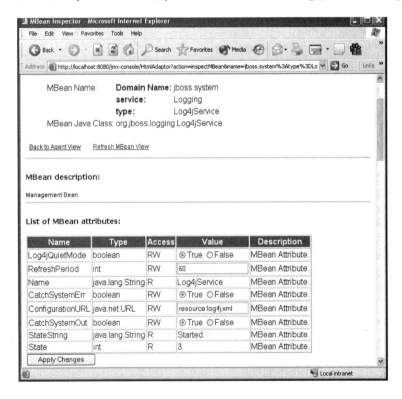

Using the JMX console you can modify the values for the configuration URL and refresh period MBean attributes. In addition to this, you can invoke the following operations to control the behavior of the logging service:

```
public void setLoggerPriority(String logger, String priority)
public String getLoggerPriority(String loggerName)
```

You use the previous methods get and set priorities for a named logger in the Log4J configuration file:

```
public void reconfigure(String configurationURL)
public String reconfigure ()
```

You use the previous methods to reconfigure the logging behavior. The first method accepts a URL pointing to the Log4J configuration file, and the second method uses the configuration URL already in use.

14.5 TRACE Priority

JBoss also introduces a custom priority level called TRACE. This is below the level of the standard Log4J DEBUG priority. This lower priority is useful for logging events that should only be displayed when deep debugging is required. The class org.jboss.logging.Logger that acts as a wrapper around the Log4J Category class provides the utility method isTraceEnabled(). You can use this method before sending a log message with TRACE priority.

The following snippet shows how to use this priority for a named category in the Log4J configuration file, log4j.xml, which is available in the \conf directory of your configuration set:

```xml
<category
  name="org.jboss.ejb.plugins">
  <priority
    value="TRACE"
    class="org.jboss.logging.XLevel"/>
</category>
```

215

15

The JBoss Deployment Architecture

One of the important issues addressed during deployment is the resolution of class dependencies across your components. Hence, it's important that you're well versed with the deployment architecture of the application server you use. In this chapter, you'll look at the deployment architecture that JBoss uses. You should also refer to section 5.1, "JBoss Classloading," for a discussion on the JBoss classloading architecture.

15.1 Deployers

In this section, you'll look at the various deployers available with JBoss and how they're organized. JBoss uses a main deployer to orchestrate all deployment processes. This main deployer delegates the actual deployment process of specific components to subdeployers. Hence, JBoss comes with six different subdeployers to handle the deployment of Web Archive (WAR), Enterprise Archive (EAR), Java Archive (JAR), Enterprise JavaBean (EJB), Resource Archive (RAR), and Service Archive (SAR) components as shown in the figure on the following page.

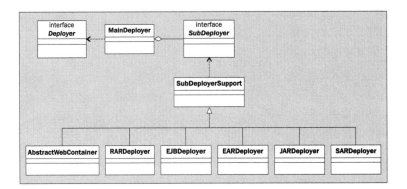

The main deployer is represented by the org.jboss.deployment.Deployer interface, and JBoss provides the org.jboss.deployment.MainDeployer implementation class. An instance of this class is registered as an MBean during server startup. All the subdeployers implement the org.jboss.deployment.SubDeployer interface by extending the org.jboss.deployment.SubDeployerSupport adapter class.

The deployers are as follows:

❑ MainDeployer
The main deployer is registered statically as an MBean during JBoss startup and is responsible for initiating the deployment of the services specified in the root configuration file.

❑ AbstractWebContainer
This deployer MBean is responsible for deploying WAR components. It deploys files with a war extension and directories with web.xml available in a \META-INF subdirectory.

❑ JARDeployer
This deployer is again registered statically during startup and is responsible for deploying all JAR files that don't contain a \WEB-INF directory. Please note that JAR deployers are different from EJB deployers. The responsibility of the JAR deployer is to load the classes present in the JAR files and make them available in the unified classloader repository.

❑ SARDeployer
This deployer is also registered statically during server startup and is responsible for SAR deployment. It deploys files with a sar extension and directories with jboss-service.xml available in a \META-INF sub-directory. It also deploys stand-alone Extensible Markup Language (XML) files whose name ends with service.xml, as in jboss-service.xml.

❑ RARDeployer
This deployer is responsible for deploying Java Connector Architecture
(JCA) resource adapter components and is normally dynamically loaded
from the SAR deployment descriptor `jca-service.xml` file located in the
`\deploy` directory of the configuration set. This deploys files with the `rar`
extension and directories with `ra.xml` available in a `\META-INF`
subdirectory.

❑ EARDeployer
This deployer is responsible for deploying EAR components and is
normally dynamically loaded from the root deployment descriptor
`jboss-service.xml` file located in the `\conf` directory of the configuration set. It deploys archives with an `ear` extension and directories with
`application.xml` available in a `\META-INF` subdirectory.

❑ EJBDeployer
This deployer is responsible for deploying EJB components and is
normally dynamically loaded from the root deployment descriptor
`jboss-service.xml` file located in the `\conf` directory of the configuration set. It deploys archives with a `jar` extension and directories with
`ejb-jar.xml` available in a `\META-INF` subdirectory.

Each deployer is capable of recursive deployment. For example, during the process of
deployment, an EAR deployer will delegate the deployment of component EJB, WAR,
RAR components, and so on to the relevant subdeployers through the main deployer.
The subdeployers are also capable of reading the classpath manifest attribute to deploy
the JAR files specified in the manifest through the JAR deployer. During the deployment
of the components, the subdeployers create a unified classloader pointing to the
Uniform Resource Locator (URL) of the component archive being deployed and register
it with loader repository. See section 5.1.3, "UnifiedClassLoader," for a discussion on
how classloading works for Java 2 Enterprise Edition (J2EE) components.

15.2 Hot Deployment

Hot deployment is the process of adding new components—such as enterprise beans,
servlets, and JavaServer Pages (JSP)—to a running server without having to stop the
application server process and restart it. In JBoss, deployment scanners perform hot
deployment. JBoss provides two deployment scanners, as MBean services, which are
capable of performing hot deployment.

15.2.1 The URLDeploymentScanner MBean

This MBean is the scanner that's enabled out of the box in JBoss in the `jboss-service.xml` of the `/conf` directory, and its definition is as follows:

```
<mbean
    code="org.jboss.deployment.scanner.URLDeploymentScanner"
    name="jboss.deployment:type=DeploymentScanner,flavor=URL">
```

The URL deployment scanner accepts the following attributes:

Attribute	Function
URLComparator	Used to check whether files have changed. JBoss provides the following comparators: ❑ `org.jboss.deployment.DeploymentSorter` Enabled by default, this sorts by file extension, as follows: `sar`, `service.xml`, `rar`, `jar`, `war`, `wsr`, `ear`, `zip`, and `*`. ❑ `org.jboss.deployment.scanner.Prefix-DeploymentSorter` If the name portion of the URL begins with one or more digits, those digits are converted to an `int` (ignoring leading zeroes), and files are deployed in that order. Files that don't start with any digits will be deployed last, and they'll be sorted by extension as previously mentioned with the `DeploymentSorter`. You can use this comparator if you want more control on the order in which the various components are deployed.
Filter	A filter for files that don't require deployment. The filter `org.jboss.deployment.scanner.DeploymentFilter`, which comes with JBoss, provides a file filter that filters a variety of extensions, such as `*.old`, `*.orig`, `*.rej`, `*.bak`, and so on.
URLs	URLs are comma separated and are resolved relative to the server home (specific to the configuration set you use) unless the given path is absolute. Any referenced directories can't be unpackaged archives; use the parent directory of the unpacked archive instead. A `file:` protocol will be assumed if not specified otherwise (for example, `http:`).

Attribute	Function
ScanPeriod	The scanning interval period specified in milliseconds. This can be useful when deploying across a network because the JBoss deployer can sometimes throw exceptions when trying to deploy components that are still being transmitted across the network. This happens because the write to the \deploy directory hasn't finished yet.
RecursiveSearch	If set to true, the deployer will recursively search all directories that do not contain a period (.) in their name. This allows you to group similar configuration properties in a relevant directory, such as the jms subdirectory in the deploy directory.

The following listing shows an example URL deployment scanner MBean service for handling hot deployment:

```
<mbean
  code="org.jboss.deployment.scanner.URLDeploymentScanner"
  name="jboss.deployment:type=DeploymentScanner,flavor=URL">
  <depends optional-attribute-name="Deployer">
    jboss.system:service=MainDeployer
  </depends>
  <attribute name="URLComparator">
    org.jboss.deployment.DeploymentSorter
  </attribute>
  <attribute name="Filter">
    org.jboss.deployment.scanner.DeploymentFilter
  </attribute>
  <attribute name="ScanPeriod">5000</attribute>
  <attribute name="URLs">./deploy</attribute>
  <attribute name="RecursiveSearch">True</attribute>
</mbean>
```

15.2.2 The URLDirectoryScanner MBean

This MBean allows you to specify which URLs are directories to scan and which are URLs to be deployed directly. URLDeploymentScanner assumes that all directories are to be scanned, which can cause problems if the directory referred to in the deploy attribute is an exploded archive. The MBean definition is as follows:

```
<mbean
  code="org.jboss.deployment.scanner.URLDirectoryScanner"
  name="jboss.deployment:type=DeploymentScanner,flavor=URL">
```

The URL directory scanner MBean supports the following attributes:

Attribute	Function
URLComparator	Has the same meaning as that for the URLDeploymentScanner. See section 15.2.1, "The URLDeploymentScanner MBean."
Filter	Has the same meaning as that for the URLDeploymentScanner. See section 15.2.1, "The URLDeploymentScanner MBean."
URLs	Each entry specifies either a dir (directory to be scanned) or url (URL to be deployed). Like the URLs for the URLDeploymentScanner previously mentioned, a file: protocol will be assumed if not specified otherwise.
ScanPeriod	Has the same meaning as that for the URLDeploymentScanner. See section 15.2.1, "The URLDeploymentScanner MBean."

The following listing shows an example URL directory scanner MBean service for handling hot deployment:

```
<mbean
  code="org.jboss.deployment.scanner.URLDirectoryScanner"
  name="jboss.deployment:type=DeploymentScanner,flavor=URL">

  <depends optional-attribute-name="Deployer">
    jboss.system:service=MainDeployer
  </depends>
  <attribute name="URLComparator">
    org.jboss.deployment.DeploymentSorter
  </attribute>
  <attribute name="Filter">
    org.jboss.deployment.scanner.DeploymentFilter
  </attribute>
  <attribute name="ScanPeriod">5000</attribute>
  <attribute name="URLs">
    <urls>
      <dir name="./deploy" />
      <url name="./deploy/examples/myapp.ear" />
      <dir name="./deploy/examples" />
      <url name="http://www.test.com/samples/myapp.ear" />
    </urls>
  </attribute>
</mbean>
```

15.3 The Deployment Process

In JBoss you can initiate a deployment process by simply copying the deployment unit to one of the locations scanned by the deployment scanner. The deployment scanner will then delegate the deployment process to the main deployer. The main deployer depending on the type of the deployment unit will delegate the deployment to one of the relevant subdeployers. Once the deployment is successful, you'll be able to see a deployment completed message on the console as well as the log file:

```
C:\WINNT\System32\cmd.exe - run
mp/deploy/server/default/deploy/petstore.ear/61.petstore.ear-contents/signon-ejb
-client.jar is already deployed
16:14:26,743 INFO  [MainDeployer] Package: file:/C:/jboss-3.0.4/server/default/t
mp/deploy/server/default/deploy/petstore.ear/61.petstore.ear-contents/customer-e
jb-client.jar is already deployed
16:14:26,743 INFO  [MainDeployer] Package: file:/C:/jboss-3.0.4/server/default/t
mp/deploy/server/default/deploy/petstore.ear/61.petstore.ear-contents/po-ejb-cli
ent.jar is already deployed
16:14:26,743 INFO  [MainDeployer] Package: file:/C:/jboss-3.0.4/server/default/t
mp/deploy/server/default/deploy/petstore.ear/61.petstore.ear-contents/cart-ejb-c
lient.jar is already deployed
16:14:26,743 INFO  [MainDeployer] Package: file:/C:/jboss-3.0.4/server/default/t
mp/deploy/server/default/deploy/petstore.ear/61.petstore.ear-contents/uidgen-ejb
-client.jar is already deployed
16:14:26,743 INFO  [MainDeployer] Package: file:/C:/jboss-3.0.4/server/default/t
mp/deploy/server/default/deploy/petstore.ear/61.petstore.ear-contents/asyncsende
r-ejb-client.jar is already deployed
16:14:27,494 INFO  [EjbModule] Creating
16:14:27,534 INFO  [EjbModule] Deploying ShoppingCartEJB
16:14:27,725 INFO  [EjbModule] Created
16:14:27,865 INFO  [EjbModule] Creating
16:14:27,885 INFO  [EjbModule] Deploying CounterEJB
16:14:28,045 INFO  [EjbModule] Deploying UniqueIdGeneratorEJB
16:14:28,095 INFO  [EjbModule] Created
16:14:28,365 INFO  [EjbModule] Creating
```

If the deployment fails, JBoss writes appropriate error messages to the console and the log file:

```
C:\WINNT\System32\cmd.exe - run
16:14:29,497 INFO  [EjbModule] Starting
16:14:29,808 WARN  [ServiceController] Problem starting service jboss.j2ee:jndiN
ame=ejb/local/petstore/uidgen/Counter,service=EJB
org.jboss.deployment.DeploymentException: Error: can't find data source: java:/j
dbc/petstore/PetStoreDB; - nested throwable: (javax.naming.NameNotFoundException
: jdbc not bound)
        at org.jboss.ejb.plugins.cmp.jdbc.bridge.JDBCEntityBridge.<init>(JDBCEnt
ityBridge.java:99)
        at org.jboss.ejb.plugins.cmp.jdbc.JDBCStoreManager.initStoreManager(JDBC
StoreManager.java:397)
        at org.jboss.ejb.plugins.cmp.jdbc.JDBCStoreManager.start(JDBCStoreManage
r.java:339)
        at org.jboss.ejb.plugins.CMPPersistenceManager.start(CMPPersistenceManag
er.java:198)
        at org.jboss.ejb.EntityContainer.start(EntityContainer.java:376)
        at org.jboss.ejb.Container.invoke(Container.java:756)
        at org.jboss.ejb.EntityContainer.invoke(EntityContainer.java:1058)
        at org.jboss.mx.server.MBeanServerImpl.invoke(MBeanServerImpl.java:517)
        at org.jboss.system.ServiceController$ServiceProxy.invoke(ServiceControl
ler.java:978)
        at $Proxy5.start(Unknown Source)
        at org.jboss.system.ServiceController.start(ServiceController.java:398)
        at sun.reflect.GeneratedMethodAccessor6.invoke(Unknown Source)
        at sun.reflect.DelegatingMethodAccessorImpl.invoke(DelegatingMethodAcces
sorImpl.java:25)
```

The previous error message was caused because the datasources weren't configured on the server before deploying the Container-Managed Persistence (CMP) beans that referred to the datasource. You can also access the main deployer MBean through the

JMX console to check the deployment status. The object name for this MBean is
`jboss.system:service=MainDeployer`. You can find this MBean on the JMX
console home page under the **jboss.system** domain, as shown here:

You can view the MBean page by clicking its object name. The MBean provides a
variety of operations to check the deployment status. These methods returns a
collection or String of currently deployed packages:

```
public Collection listDeployed()
public String listDeployedAsString()
```

This method returns a list of packages that haven't deployed completely:

```
public Collection listIncompletelyDeployed()
```

While this method returns a collection of packages waiting to be deployed:

```
public Collection listWaitingForDeployer()
```

These methods deploy the package identified by the URL:

```
public void deploy(String urlspec)
public void deploy(URL url)
```

These methods redeploy the package identified by the URL:

```
public void redeploy(String urlspec)
public void redeploy(URL url)
```

Finally, these methods undeploy the package identified by the URL:

```
public void undeploy(String urlspec)
public void undeploy(URL url)
```

16

Configuring WAR Deployment

In this chapter, you'll look at deploying Web Archive (WAR) components within JBoss/Jetty and JBoss/Tomcat. JBoss supports WAR deployment in both stand-alone WAR format and part of an Enterprise Archive (EAR) file. You can also deploy WAR files in exploded format by copying the directory containing the web application root, and its contents, to any location monitored by your deployment scanner. See section 15.3, "The Deployment Process," for more information on how WARs are deployed.

16.1 The JBoss Web Deployment Descriptor

You can use a JBoss-specific web deployment descriptor for accomplishing the following tasks:

- ❑ Mapping resource references

- ❑ Mapping resource environment references

- ❑ Mapping Enterprise JavaBean (EJB) remote references

- ❑ Setting up security domains

- ❑ Setting virtual hosts

- ❑ Setting context paths

This file should be called jboss-web.xml and should be made available in the \WEB-INF directory of your web application. The descriptor uses the jboss-web_3_0.dtd, which describes the following XML structure:

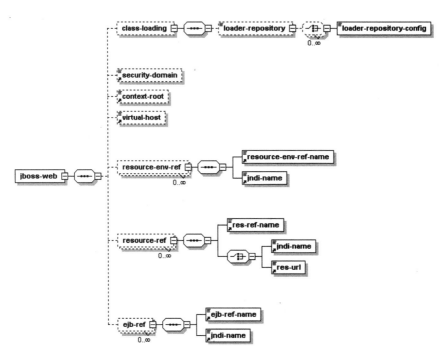

16.1.1 Classloading

The class-loading element allows you to override the default class loading behavior of the web container. The element has the attribute java2ClassLoadingCompliance, when set to true will disable standard Java delegation-based classloading and first try to load the classes from the /WEB-INF/lib and /WEB-INF/classes directories. The loader-repository specifies the name of the UnifiedLoaderRepository MBean to use for the WAR to provide WAR-level scoping of classes deployed in the WAR. It's a unique Java Management Extensions (JMX) ObjectName string. It may also specify an arbitrary configuration by including a loader-repository-config element. The loader-repository-config element specifies any arbitrary configuration fragment for use in configuring the loader-repository instance. The actual content of this element is specific to the loaderRepositoryClass and the code parsing the element. The configParserClass attribute gives the class name of the org.jboss.mx.loading.LoaderRepositoryFactory.LoaderRepositoryConfigParser implementation to use to parse the loader-repository-config content.

The following is an example:

```
<class-loading
  java2ClassLoadingCompliance="false">
  <loader-repository
    loaderRepositoryClass="com.apress.jboss.LoaderRepository">
    com.apress:loader=custom-repository
    <loader-repository-config
      configParserClass="com.apress.LoaderParser">
        java2ParentDelegaton=true
    </loader-repository-config>
  </loader-repository>
</class-loading>
```

16.1.2 Security Domain

You can restrict access to your web application Uniform Resource Identifier (URI) methods by using the security-role and security-constraint elements in the standard web deployment descriptor. However, enforcement of this declarative security in an operational environment is performed in a web container-specific manner. In section 7.3.3, "Login Configuration," you looked at how to use Java Authentication and Authorization Service (JAAS) within JBoss to define login modules in the login-config.xml file.

When a request comes in for a secure URI, JBoss tries to evaluate the credentials of the thread using the security-domain element in the JBoss web deployment descriptor. This element should refer to a login module configured within the system. The JBoss JAAS security manager will use the login module to resolve the caller's credentials and access rights. The following snippet shows how to define a security domain for performing authentication/authorization:

```
<jboss-web>
  <security-domain>java:jaas/MyLoginModule</security-domain>
  ...
</jboss-web>
```

Here, MyLoginModule is a login module configured within JBoss. For a detailed discussion on how to configure login modules, please refer to section 7.3.3.3, "Login Configuration Data."

16.1.3 JNDI References

It's good practice to refer to Java Naming and Directory Interface (JNDI) objects using a coded name within your web applications, instead of referring to the actual JNDI name. Coded names are defined in the java:comp/env/ namespace of the web application using `web-ref`, `resource-env-ref`, `ejb-ref`, and `ejb-local-ref` in the standard web deployment descriptor. These elements are used for defining coded names for the following:

❑ Resource factories such as datasources, mail sessions, Java Message Service (JMS) connection factories, Uniform Resource Locators (URLs), and so on

❑ JMS destinations (queues and topics)

❑ EJB remote references

❑ EJB local references

The mapping of coded JNDI names to actual JNDI names is performed in a web container-specific way. In JBoss, this is performed in `jboss-web.xml` using the following elements:

❑ `resource-ref` for resource references such as data sources, mail sessions, URL connection factories, JMS connection factories, and so on

❑ `resource-env-ref` for resource environment references such as JMS queues and topics

❑ `ejb-ref` for remote EJB references

16.1.3.1 Mapping EJB References

Because local EJBs need to co-exist in the same Virtual Machine (VM) as the web application, you don't need to use the JBoss web deployment descriptor for mapping the coded name to the actual EJB. You can do this using the `ejb-local-ref/ejb-link` element in the standard web deployment descriptor as follows:

```
<web-app>

  <display-name>AdminWAR</display-name>
  <description>
    WebTier for the Admin Client for the PetStore
  </description>

  ...

  <ejb-local-ref>
    <ejb-ref-name>ejb/local/AsyncSender</ejb-ref-name>
    <ejb-ref-type>Session</ejb-ref-type>
    <local-home>
      com.sun.j2ee.blueprints.asyncsender.ejb.AsyncSenderLocalHome
    </local-home>
    <local>com.sun.j2ee.blueprints.asyncsender.ejb.AsyncSender</local>
    <ejb-link>AsyncSenderAdminEJB</ejb-link>
  </ejb-local-ref>
```

```
</web-app>

</ejb-jar>
```

Here, the `ejb-local-ref/ejb-link` element refers to the EJB name of the referred bean. However, you can't do this if the referred bean is remote. In such scenarios, you have to use the JBoss EJB deployment descriptor, as follows, for mapping the coded name of the EJB to the remote JNDI name:

```
<jboss-web>

  <ejb-ref>
    <ejb-ref-name>ejb/remote/OPCAdminFacade</ejb-ref-name>
    <jndi-name>ejb/remote/opc/opc/OPCAdminFacadeEJB</jndi-name>
  </ejb-ref>

</jboss-web>
```

Here, `ejb-ref/ejb-ref-name` refers to the coded name, and `ejb-ref/jndi-name` refers to the remote JNDI name.

16.1.3.2 Resource Environment References

Coded names for resource environment references are mapped to the actual JNDI names using the `resource-env-ref` element as follows:

```
<jboss-web>

  ...

  <resource-env-ref>
    <resource-env-ref-name>
      jms/topic/opc/InvoiceTopic
    </resource-env-ref-name>
    <jndi-name>topic/opc/InvoiceTopic</jndi-name>
  </resource-env-ref>

</jboss-web>
```

Here, the `resource-env-ref-name` is the coded name, and `jndi-name` is the actual name.

16.1.3.3 Resource References

In JBoss, you can use the `resource-ref` element for mapping coded names of resource factories to actual JNDI names or URLs. Non-URL resources are mapped as follows:

```
<jboss-web>

  <resource-ref>
    <res-ref-name>jms/topic/TopicConnectionFactory</res-ref-name>
    <jndi-name>ConnectionFactory</jndi-name>
  </resource-ref>

</jboss-web>
```

Here, the `res-ref-name` refers to the coded name of the resource, and `jndi-name` refers to the actual JNDI name. URL resources are mapped as follows:

```
<jboss-web>

  <resource-ref>
    <res-ref-name>url/CatalogDAOSQLURL</res-ref-name>
    <res-url>
      http://localhost:8080/petstore/CatalogDAOSQL.xml
    </res-url>
  </resource-ref>

</jboss-web>
```

Here, the `res-ref-name` refers to the coded name of the resource, and `res-url` refers to the URL of the resource.

16.1.4 Context Path

If you deploy a WAR component by copying the unexploded WAR file to the `\deploy` directory, JBoss will use the name of the WAR file as the context path. Thus, if the file is called `petstore.war`, the context path will be **/petstore**. If you're deploying the WAR as an exploded directory, JBoss will use the name of the root folder as the context path.

> **If you're deploying the WAR as part of an EAR, the context URI is specified in `application.xml`.**

However, sometimes you may want to specify a context path other than the WAR file name in stand-alone EAR files. In JBoss, you can specify this using the `context-root` element in the JBoss web deployment descriptor as follows:

```
<jboss-web>
  ...
  <context-root>
    /
  </context-root>
  ...
<jboss-web>
```

In the previous example, you'll be able to access the web application without specifying a context path.

> **With Tomcat, accessing the web application without specifying a context path is also possible by calling the `ROOT.war` WAR component. Please note that the name is case sensitive.**

16.1.5 Virtual Host

You can use virtual hosts within JBoss to group your web applications into different Domain Name System (DNS) names. Although Java 2 Enterprise Edition (J2EE) specifications don't mention anything about virtual hosts, you can specify them in JBoss using the `virtual-host` element in the JBoss web deployment descriptor:

```
<jboss-web>
  ...
  <virtual-host>
    www.flintstone.com
  </virtual-host>
  ...
</jboss-web>
```

The virtual host you define should be available in the web container's operation environment.

17

Developing EJBs with JBoss

In this chapter you'll look at how to configure Enterprise JavaBeans (EJBs) within JBoss. JBoss 3.*x* provides an EJB 2.0–compliant EJB container. Unlike some of the mainstream EJB containers that require an additional step of compiling the EJBs between packaging and deployment to generate stubs and skeletons, JBoss relies on dynamic proxies and an interceptor-based architecture to integrate the client-side and server-side artifacts of the EJB container. This means you can package and deploy your EJBs to the JBoss container without any additional EJB compilation process.

The behavior of the client-side and server-side EJB containers is configured through a JBoss-specific deployment descriptor called `jboss.xml`, which is present in the `META-INF` directory of the EJB Java Archive (JAR) file. An EJB's client view comprises mainly its home and component interfaces. When an EJB is deployed, the deployer creates proxy objects for the home and component interfaces. The proxy for the home interface is bound to the Java Naming and Directory Interface (JNDI) namespace. The proxy instances mainly contain the client-side interceptors and a dynamic proxy invocation handler that implements the home interface of the EJB and binds it to the JNDI namespace.

When clients perform a strongly typed invocation on the home and component objects, the client-side EJB container "detypes" the invocation and sends it through a chain of client-side interceptors. The types and number of the client-side interceptors can be configured through the JBoss-specific EJB deployment descriptor. The client-side interceptors can be used to enable logging, security, transactions, and so on. The last component in the interceptor chain is a transport-specific invoker that connects to the server-side skeleton and sends the invocation through the server. The component that handles the invocation on the server is called a **detached invoker**. This architecture allows JBoss to accept EJB invocation through a variety of protocols including Java Remote Method Protocol (JRMP), Internet Inter-Orb Protocol (IIOP), Hypertext Transfer Protocol (HTTP), Simple Object Access Protocol (SOAP), and so on.

Once the invocation reaches the server side, it travels through a chain of server-side interceptors before it reaches the target EJB. The server-side interceptors implement a variety of functionalities including security, persistence, locking, caching, pooling, and so on. You can configure the types and numbers of server-side interceptors through the JBoss-specific EJB deployment descriptor.

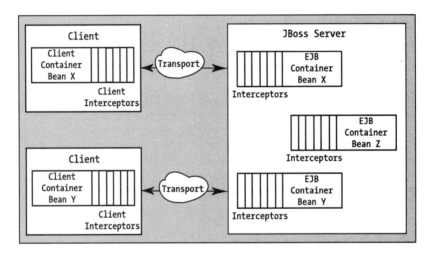

17.1 Container Configuration

You configure the behavior of the client-side and server-side containers through the JBoss-specific deployment file `jboss.xml`, which is present in the META-INF directory of the EJB JAR file. However, JBoss comes with a set of standard container configurations in the file `standardjboss.xml`, which is available in the conf directory of the configuration set you use. If you don't specify a container configuration to use, JBoss will choose an appropriate container configuration from the standard set depending on the type of the EJB. JBoss also allows you to do the following:

- ❑ Define a new container configuration in `jboss.xml` and associate it with your EJB

- ❑ Extend an existing standard configuration set, override some of the configurations, and associate with your EJB

The following list shows the standard configuration sets that come out of the box with JBoss:

- ❏ Standard Container-Managed Persistence (CMP) 2.*x* entity bean
- ❏ Clustered CMP 2.*x* entity bean
- ❏ Standard CMP 2.*x* entity bean with cache invalidation
- ❏ Instance per transaction CMP 2.*x* entity bean
- ❏ Standard CMP entity bean
- ❏ Clustered CMP entity bean
- ❏ Instance per transaction CMP entity bean
- ❏ Standard stateless session bean
- ❏ Clustered stateless session bean
- ❏ Standard stateful session bean
- ❏ Clustered stateful session bean
- ❏ Standard Bean-Managed Persistence (BMP) entity bean
- ❏ Clustered BMP entity bean
- ❏ Instance per transaction BMP entity bean
- ❏ Standard Message-Driven Bean (MDB)

Both the `jboss.xml` and `standardjboss.xml` files share the same content model as follows. However, some of the elements are more often used in the global deployment descriptor, `standardjboss.xml`, and some are used more often in the deployment unit-level deployment descriptor, `jboss.xml`.

237

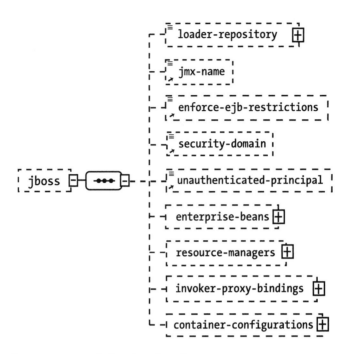

Container configurations are defined within the container-configurations element contains zero or more container-configuration elements, each for a given container configuration. The container-configuration element defines a variety of component behavior including the following:

- Caching
- Pooling
- Commit option
- Security
- Client-side interceptors
- Server-side interceptors
- Cluster configuration
- Call logging

The following diagram shows the structure of the container-configuration element:

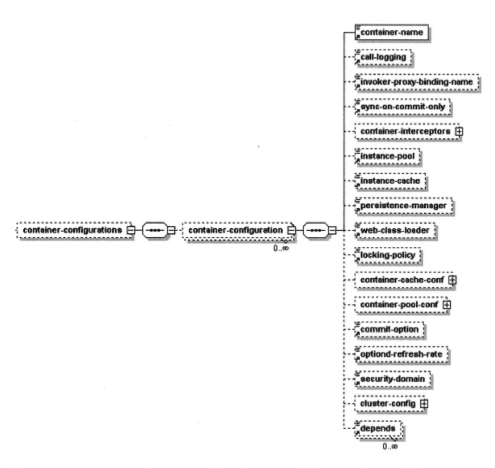

The `container-name` element specifies the name of the container as follows. If you're extending an existing container configuration instead of defining one from scratch, you can use the `extends` attribute to specify the extended container configuration:

```
<jboss>
  ...
  <container-configurations>
    <container-configuration
      extends="Instance Per Transaction CMP 2.x EntityBean">
      ...
      <container-name>Optimistic Locking Container</container-name>
      ...
    <container-configuration>
  </container-configurations>
  ...
</jboss>
```

239

You can associate a container configuration with an EJB using the `configuration-name` element available in the `session`, `entity`, or `message-driven` elements available under the `enterprise-beans` element as follows. If you don't specify a container configuration, JBoss will choose a container configuration from the standard set based on the type of the EJB:

```
<jboss>
  ...
  <enterprise-beans>
    <entity>
      ...
      <configuration-name>
        Optimistic Locking Container
      </configuration-name>
      ...
    </entity>
  </enterprise-beans>
  ...
</jboss>
```

17.2 Invoker Proxy Binding

The `invoker-proxy-bindings` element defines the invokers available for use with the EJB container configurations. This element contains one or more `invoker-proxy` elements, each for a given invoker configuration. The structure of this element is as follows:

The `standardjboss.xml` file contains the following invoker configurations:

❑   `entity-rmi-invoker`

❑   `clustered-entity-rmi-invoker`

❑   `stateless-rmi-invoker`

❏ `clustered-stateless-rmi-invoker`

❏ `stateful-rmi-invoker`

❏ `clustered-stateful-rmi-invoker`

❏ `message-driven-bean`

❏ `iiop`

A given invoker proxy binding is associated with the container configuration using the `invoker-proxy-binding-name` element under the `container-configuration` element. The invoker proxy binding uses the following child elements:

Element	Description
name	The name gives a unique name for the `invoker-proxy-binding`.
invoker-mbean	Gives the Java Management Extensions (JMX) `Object-Name` of the invoker MBean service. JBoss provides a variety of invokers that support EJB invocation over Remote Method Invocation (RMI), HTTP, and so on.
proxy-factory	The `org.jboss.ejb.EJBProxyFactory` implementation class. This class creates the proxy instances for the home and component objects.
proxy-factory-config	Defines the client interceptors stack and other configuration options to use for the various EJB proxies.

The following snippet shows the invoker proxy binding for entity bean invocation over RMI:

```
<invoker-proxy-binding>
  <name>entity-rmi-invoker</name>
  <invoker-mbean>jboss:service=invoker,type=jrmp</invoker-mbean>
  <proxy-factory>org.jboss.proxy.ejb.ProxyFactory</proxy-factory>
  <proxy-factory-config>
    <client-interceptors>
      <home>
        <interceptor>
          org.jboss.proxy.ejb.HomeInterceptor
        </interceptor>
```

```
            <interceptor>
               org.jboss.proxy.SecurityInterceptor
            </interceptor>
            <interceptor>
               org.jboss.proxy.TransactionInterceptor
            </interceptor>
            <interceptor>
               org.jboss.invocation.InvokerInterceptor
            </interceptor>
         </home>
         <bean>
            <interceptor>
               org.jboss.proxy.ejb.EntityInterceptor
            </interceptor>
            <interceptor>
               org.jboss.proxy.SecurityInterceptor
            </interceptor>
            <interceptor>
               org.jboss.proxy.TransactionInterceptor
            </interceptor>
            <interceptor>
               org.jboss.invocation.InvokerInterceptor
            </interceptor>
         </bean>
         <list-entity>
            <interceptor>
               org.jboss.proxy.ejb.ListEntityInterceptor
            </interceptor>
            <interceptor>
               org.jboss.proxy.SecurityInterceptor
            </interceptor>
            <interceptor>
               org.jboss.proxy.TransactionInterceptor
            </interceptor>
            <interceptor>
               org.jboss.invocation.InvokerInterceptor
            </interceptor>
         </list-entity>
      </client-interceptors>
   </proxy-factory-config>
</invoker-proxy-binding>
```

The following diagram shows the content model of the `proxy-factory-config` element:

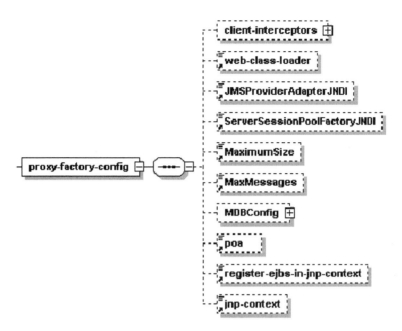

The `client-interceptors` element defines the stack of client-side interceptors for home and component invocations:

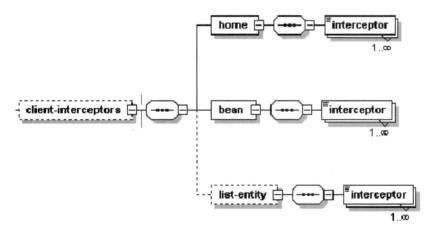

The home element contains the interceptors for home invocation, the bean element contains the interceptors for component invocation, and the list-entity element contains the interceptors for invocations involving entity lists. The declared order of the interceptor elements corresponds to the order of the interceptor chain.

The web-class-loader element gives the class name of the web classloader JBoss must use in this configuration. This class must be a subclass of org.jboss.web.WebClassLoader. The default is org.jboss.web.WebClassLoader. Web classloaders allow dynamic loading of resources and classes from deployed Enterprise Archives (EARs), EJB JARs, and Web Archives (WARs).

The JMSProviderAdaptorJNDI element specifies the JNDI name of the JMS provider adapter in the java:/ namespace. This is mandatory for an MDB and must implement org.jboss.jms.jndi.JMSProviderAdapter. The value used by the default JMS invoker is DefaultJMSProvider.

The ServerSessionPoolFactoryJNDI specifies the JNDI name of the session pool in the java:/ namespace. This is mandatory for an MDB and must implement org.jboss.jms.asf.ServerSessionPoolFactory. The value used by the default JMS invoker is StdJMSPool.

MaxMessages specify the maximum number of messages parameter for the MDB's connection consumer.

The MDBConfig element specifies additional configuration for MDBs:

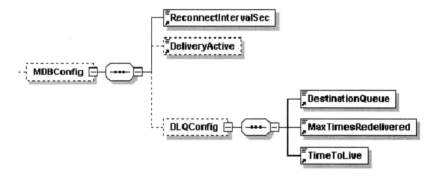

The ReconnectIntervalSec specifies the time to wait before trying to recover the connection to the Java Message Service (JMS) server. The value used by the default MDB invoker binding is 10. The DeliveryActive element specifies whether delivery of messages is active during startup. The DLQConfig element configures the MDB's dead letter queue, when there are too many failed deliveries. The Destination-Queue specifies the JNDI name of the queue in which these messages are stored, MaxTimesRedelivered specifies the maximum number of times messages are redelivered, and TimeToLive specifies the time the message lives in the dead letter queue. The following snippet shows the default MDB invoker biding used by JBoss:

```
<invoker-proxy-binding>
  <name>message-driven-bean</name>
  <invoker-mbean>default</invoker-mbean>
  <proxy-factory>
    org.jboss.ejb.plugins.jms.JMSContainerInvoker
  </proxy-factory>
  <proxy-factory-config>
    <JMSProviderAdapterJNDI>
      DefaultJMSProvider
    </JMSProviderAdapterJNDI>
    <ServerSessionPoolFactoryJNDI>
      StdJMSPool
    </ServerSessionPoolFactoryJNDI>
    <MaximumSize>15</MaximumSize>
    <MaxMessages>1</MaxMessages>
    <MDBConfig>
      <ReconnectIntervalSec>10</ReconnectIntervalSec>
      <DLQConfig>
        <DestinationQueue>queue/DLQ</DestinationQueue>
        <MaxTimesRedelivered>10</MaxTimesRedelivered>
        <TimeToLive>0</TimeToLive>
      </DLQConfig>
    </MDBConfig>
  </proxy-factory-config>
</invoker-proxy-binding>
```

The poa element is used by the IIOP invoker binding and should be either `perservant` or `shared`. The element `register-ejbs-in-jnp-context` is used as a flag to specify whether to register the EJBs in the JNDI namespace. The `jnp-context` specifies the JNDI context to which the home object is bound. The only standard invoker binding that uses this element is the IIOP binding, and it sets the value of the `jnp-context` element to `iiop`.

17.3 Container Configuration Details

Now you'll look at the configuration information that can be specified per container configuration. The following snippet shows the container configuration that comes with JBoss for standard CMP 2.*x* entity beans:

```
<container-configuration>
  <container-name>Standard CMP 2.x EntityBean</container-name>
  <call-logging>false</call-logging>
  <invoker-proxy-binding-name>
    entity-rmi-invoker
  </invoker-proxy-binding-name>
  <sync-on-commit-only>false</sync-on-commit-only>
```

```
<insert-after-ejb-post-create>false</insert-after-ejb-post-create>
<container-interceptors>
    <interceptor>
      org.jboss.ejb.plugins.ProxyFactoryFinderInterceptor
    </interceptor>
    <interceptor>
      org.jboss.ejb.plugins.LogInterceptor
    </interceptor>
    <interceptor>
      org.jboss.ejb.plugins.SecurityInterceptor
    </interceptor>
    <interceptor>
      org.jboss.ejb.plugins.TxInterceptorCMT
    </interceptor>
    <interceptor metricsEnabled="true">
      org.jboss.ejb.plugins.MetricsInterceptor
    </interceptor>
    <interceptor>
      org.jboss.ejb.plugins.EntityCreationInterceptor
    </interceptor>
    <interceptor>
      org.jboss.ejb.plugins.EntityLockInterceptor
    </interceptor>
    <interceptor>
      org.jboss.ejb.plugins.EntityInstanceInterceptor
    </interceptor>
    <interceptor>
      org.jboss.ejb.plugins.EntityReentranceInterceptor
    </interceptor>
    <interceptor>
      org.jboss.resource.connectionmanager.
      CachedConnectionInterceptor
    </interceptor>
    <interceptor>
      org.jboss.ejb.plugins.EntitySynchronizationInterceptor
    </interceptor>
    <interceptor>
      org.jboss.ejb.plugins.cmp.jdbc.JDBCRelationInterceptor
    </interceptor>
</container-interceptors>
<instance-pool>
  org.jboss.ejb.plugins.EntityInstancePool
</instance-pool>
<instance-cache>
  org.jboss.ejb.plugins.InvalidableEntityInstanceCache
</instance-cache>
<persistence-manager>
  org.jboss.ejb.plugins.cmp.jdbc.JDBCStoreManager
</persistence-manager>
```

```
    <locking-policy>
      org.jboss.ejb.plugins.lock.QueuedPessimisticEJBLock
    </locking-policy>
    <container-cache-conf>
      <cache-policy>
         org.jboss.ejb.plugins.LRUEnterpriseContextCachePolicy
      </cache-policy>
        <cache-policy-conf>
          <min-capacity>50</min-capacity>
          <max-capacity>1000000</max-capacity>
          <overager-period>300</overager-period>
          <max-bean-age>600</max-bean-age>
          <resizer-period>400</resizer-period>
          <max-cache-miss-period>60</max-cache-miss-period>
          <min-cache-miss-period>1</min-cache-miss-period>
          <cache-load-factor>0.75</cache-load-factor>
        </cache-policy-conf>
    </container-cache-conf>
    <container-pool-conf>
        <MaximumSize>100</MaximumSize>
    </container-pool-conf>
    <commit-option>B</commit-option>
  </container-configuration>
```

The `container-name` element specifies a unique name for the container configuration. The `call-logging` element specifies whether the container should log every method invocation on the bean. The `invoker-proxy-binding-name` specifies the preconfigured invoker proxy config you should use with this container.

The `sync-on-commit-only` element determines the behavior of `ejbStore()` calls on finds, selects, and removes. If set to `true`, `ejbStore()` will only be called on transaction commit. The `insert-after-post-create` element is a flag used to indicate that the insert SQL should be sent to the Database Management System (DBMS) for entity beans only after `ejbPostCreate()` returns. This is useful if you have non-nullable foreign keys and you set your Container-Managed Relationship (CMR) fields in `ejbPostCreate()`. The EJB 2.0 specification forbids setting CMR fields in the `ejbCreate()` method; hence, if the insert SQL is sent to the DBMS after `ejbCreate()`, the foreign key columns will be null and can cause constraint violation errors in the database.

The `container-interceptors` elements contain zero or more `interceptor` elements to define the server-side interceptor chains. Server-side interceptors are used for implementing locking, persistence, security, transactions, and so on.

247

JBoss allows you to configure instance pools for stateless session beans, entity beans, and MDBs using the `instance-pool` and `container-pool-conf` elements. The `instance-pool` element should contain the fully qualified name of the class that implements the `org.jboss.ejb.InstancePool` interface. The standard container configurations use the following instance pool implementations:

❑ `org.jboss.ejb.plugins.MessageDrivenInstancePool` for MDBs

❑ `org.jboss.ejb.plugins.EntityInstancePool` for entity beans

❑ `org.jboss.ejb.plugins.StatelessSessionInstancePool` for stateless session beans

The instance pool configurations may use the contents of the `container-pool-conf` element whose content model is as follows for configuring the pool. The `container-pool-conf` element holds configuration data for the instance pool. JBoss doesn't read the subtree directly for this element; instead, it's passed to the instance pool instance (if it implements `org.jboss.metadata.XmlLoadable`) for it to load its parameters. The default instance pools, `EntityInstancePool` and `StatelessSessionInstancePool`, both accept the following configuration:

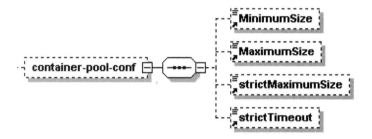

`MaximumSize` specifies the capacity of the pool. For pools where reclaim is possible, the pool will also be repopulated when the instance is free to be reused. This isn't a hard limit; if instances are needed when the pool is at its `MaximumSize`, new instances will be created following the demand unless a `strictMaximumSize` of `true` is specified. `MinimumSize` isn't currently used by the JBoss pools. The `strictMaximumSize` is a Boolean flag indicating whether attempts to access the pool will block when `MaximumSize` instances are active. The default is `false`. The `strictTimeout` specifies the time in milliseconds to wait for the `strictMaximumSize` semaphore. The default is `Long.MAX_VALUE`.

JBoss also allows you to configure caching behavior for stateful session and entity beans. You do this using the `instance-cache` and `container-cache-conf` elements. The `instance-cache` element should contain the fully qualified name of the class that implements `org.jboss.ejb.InstanceCache` interface. JBoss uses the following instance cache implementations:

❑ `org.jboss.ejb.plugins.InvalidableEntityInstanceCache` for CMP 2.x entity beans

❑ `org.jboss.ejb.plugins.EntityInstanceCache` for clustered CMP 2.x entity beans

❑ `org.jboss.ejb.plugins.StatefulSessionInstanceCache` for stateful session beans

The `container-cache-conf` element holds dynamic configuration data for the instance cache. JBoss doesn't read the subtree directly for this element; instead, it's passed to the instance cache instance (if it implements `org.jboss.metadata.XmlLoadable`) for it to load its parameters:

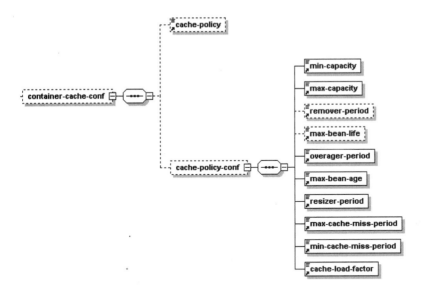

The `cache-policy` element specifies the implementation class for the cache policy, which controls when instances will be passivated and so on. The `cache-policy-conf` element specifies the configuration settings for the selected cache policy. This is currently only valid for the Least Recently Used (LRU) cache. When the cache is the LRU one for the stateful container, the elements `remover-period` and `max-bean-life` specify the period of the remover task that removes stateful beans (that normally have been passivated) that have age greater than the specified `max-bean-life` element. The configuration elements are as follows:

Element	Description
`min-capacity`	The minimum capacity of this cache.
`max-capacity`	The maximum capacity of this cache.
`remover-period`	The period of the remover's runs.
`max-bean-life`	The period of the remover task that removes stateful beans (that normally have been passivated) that have an age greater than the specified `max-bean-life` element.
`overager-period`	The period of the overager's runs.
`max-bean-age`	The age after which a bean is automatically passivated.
`resizer-period`	The period of the resizer's runs.
`max-cache-miss-period`	Shrink cache capacity if there's a cache miss every or more than this member's value.
`min-cache-miss-period`	Enlarge cache capacity if there's a cache miss every or less than this member's value.
`cache-load-factor`	The resizer will always try to keep the cache capacity so that the cache is this member's value loaded of cached objects.

The `security-domain` element specifies the JNDI name of the Java Authentication and Authorization Service (JAAS) security manager that will be used to authenticate and authorize invocations to this bean. You can also specify this at the deployment unit level or the individual bean level.

> **The** `locking-policy`, `commit-option`, **and** `optiond-refresh-rate` **elements are explained in section 18.14, "Locking and Concurrency".**

The `cluster-config` element allows to specify cluster specific settings:

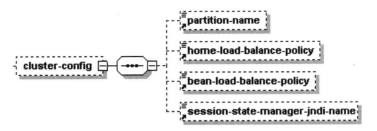

The `partition-name` element indicates the name of the HA partition to be used by the container to exchange clustering information. This is a name and not a JNDI name. The given name will be prefixed by `/HASessionState/` by the container to get the actual JNDI name of the HA partition. If not provided, JBoss will assume `partition-name` to be `DefaultPartition`.

The `home-load-balance-policy` element indicates the Java class name to be used to load balance calls in the home proxy. If not provided, JBoss will assume `home-load-balance-policy` to be `org.jboss.ha.framework.interfaces.RoundRobin`.

The `bean-load-balance-policy` element indicates the Java class name to be used to load balance calls in the bean proxy. If not specified, JBoss will assume it to be `org.jboss.ha.framework.interfaces.RoundRobin`.

The `session-state-manager-jndi-name` element indicates the name of the HA session state to be used by the container as a back end for state session management in the cluster and is applicable for stateful session beans. This is a JNDI name. If not specified, JBoss will assume it to be `/HASessionState/Default`.

The `depends` element indicates dependency on other MBeans by specifying their object names.

17.4 Bean-Level Configuration

Container configurations define global defaults for the EJB containers. If you don't explicitly specify a container configuration, JBoss will choose a container configuration, depending on the bean types, from the default container configurations available in the `standardjboss.xml` file. You've also seen that you can extend the standard configuration and override the behaviors you need. In addition to this, you can specify certain behavior at individual bean level. You do this using the `session`, `entity`, and `message-driven` elements under the `enterprise-beans` elements in the `jboss.xml` file in the `META-INF` directory of the EJB JAR file. In the following sections, you'll at the parameters that are configurable at the bean level.

17.4.1 Session Bean Configuration

You configure session beans using the `session` element. For each session bean in the standard deployment descriptor `ejb-jar.xml`, you can have a corresponding `session` element in the `jboss.xml` file. The content model of this element is as follows:

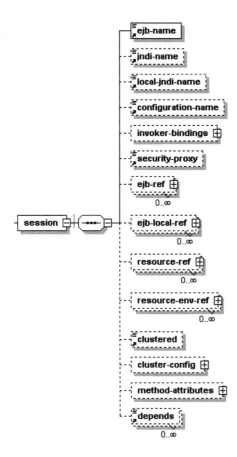

The `ejb-name` element should correspond to the name of the EJB in `ejb-jar.xml`. The `jndi-name` should specify the JNDI name by which the bean's remote home object is bound, and the `local-jndi-name` is the JNDI name to which the bean's local home object is bound. The `configuration-name` element specifies the container configuration to use. If you don't specify one, JBoss will choose one of the standard container configurations.

The `invoker-bindings` element contains the invocation configurations for the bean. JBoss 3.*x* allows the same bean to be invoked through multiple invocation protocols:

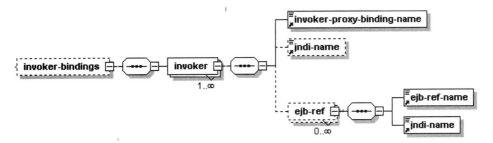

The `invoker-bindings` element contains one or more `invoker` elements. The `invoker` element contains a mandatory `invoker-proxy-binding-name` element that should refer to an existing invoker proxy binding. If the `jndi-name` isn't specified, the invoker will be available for lookup on the default JNDI name. The `jndi-name` element is useful when you specify multiple invocation bindings for a given EJB. As explained earlier, your invocation binding mainly comprises the client-side interceptors and transport specific invocation MBean. Hence, if you want your EJB to be accessed over multiple transport protocols, you need specify unique JNDI name for each protocol.

You use the `security-proxy` element for externalizing security logic from the bean classes. Security proxies are covered in detail in section 7.4, "Security Proxies."

The `ejb-ref`, `ejb-local-ref`, `resource-ref`, and `resource-env-ref` elements map the EJB references, EJB local references, resource references, and resource environment references, respectively, defined in the `java:comp/env` namespace of the bean in the standard deployment descriptor to real JNDI names in the operational environment:

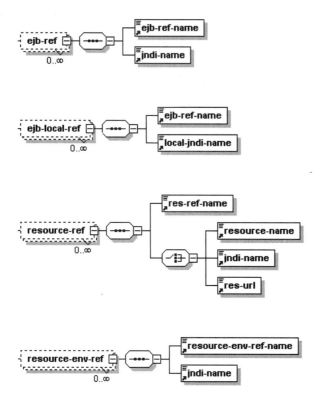

For EJB references, the ejb-ref-name should match the ejb-ref-name defined in ejb-jar.xml, and jndi-name should match the JNDI name to which the referred bean's remote home is bound. You can also resolve EJB references using the ejb-link element in ejb-jar.xml without relying on jboss.xml. The following snippet shows how map EJB references:

```
<ejb-ref>
  <ejb-ref-name>ejb/myBean</ejb-ref-name>
  <jndi-name>MyBeanHome</ejb-ref-name>
</ejb-ref>
```

For resource environment references such as JMS destinations, you can use the resource-env-ref to perform the mapping as follows:

```
<resource-env-ref>
  <resource-env-ref-name>jms/topic/myTopic</resource-env-ref-name>
  <jndi-name>MyTopic</ejb-ref-name>
</resource-env-ref>
```

Here, `resource-env-ref-name` should match the reference defined in `ejb-jar.xml`, and `jndi-name` should have the JNDI name to which the JMS destination is bound.

For resource references, the `res-ref-name` should match the resource reference name defined in `ejb-jar.xml`. You can do the mapping using `jndi-name`, `resource-name`, or `res-url`. If the resource reference is a Uniform Resource Locator (URL) connection factory, you should use the `res-url` to specify the actual JNDI name. For other resource references such as datasources, JMS connection factories, and so on, you can use the `jndi-name` element to specify the actual JNDI name to which the resource reference is bound. The following snippet shows how map resource references:

```
<resource-ref>
  <ejb-ref-name>url/Catalog</ejb-ref-name>
  <res-url>http://localhost:8080/Catalog.xml</res-url>
</ejb-ref>
```

Alternatively, you can use the `resource-name` element; it should match one of the preconfigured resource managers using the top-level `resource-managers` element in `jboss.xml`, whose content model is as follows:

Here, `res-name` should match the `resource-name` element used in the `resource-ref` element. For URL connection factories, you can use `res-url` to specify the URL; for other connection factories, you can use `res-jndi-name` to specify the actual JNDI name. This mechanism is preferred if the same resource is used across multiple EJBs to specify the mapping only once.

The `clustered` element indicates whether the bean is clustered and whether the `cluster-config` element has the same semantics as the same element covered in section 17.3, "Container Configuration Details." However, the cluster configuration defined here will override the one defined at the container configuration level.

The `method-attributes` element can specify which methods are read-only or idempotent. This reduces the need for locks and replication. Idempotent methods are those methods that can be invoked more than once without causing any state changes on the server.

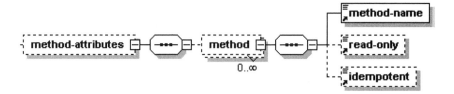

17.4.2 Entity Beans

Bean-level configuration for entity beans is done using the `entity` element under the `enterprise-bean` element. The content model for the `entity` element is similar to that of the `session` element. Hence, this section will cover only those elements unique to the `entity` element. The three elements that are uniquely available for the entity element are `read-only`, `cache-invalidation`, and `cache-invalidation-config` elements. The `read-only` element defines the entire entity bean as read-only.

The `cache-invalidation` element indicates if this bean cache should listen to cache invalidation events and clear its cache accordingly as well as send cache invalidation messages. It's provided by the deployer. If not, JBoss will assume `cache-invalidation` is `true`. The value will only be applied if the correct cache plug-in and interceptor(s) are defined in the container configuration. This is applicable only for commit options A and D. JBoss provides a standard container configuration, `Standard CMP 2.x EntityBean with cache invalidation`, which enables cache invalidation with the appropriate server-side interceptors and commit option.

The `cache-invalidation-config` element allows to specify cache invalidation specific settings:

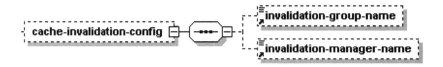

The `invalidation-group-name` element indicates the name of a group in which all invalidation messages are exchanged; in other words, all beans sharing a given `invalidation-group-name` should share the same Primary Key (PK) semantic. By default, `invalidation-group-name` is equal to the EJB name. Thus, when using cache invalidation across a cluster, it isn't necessary to specify a name because all beans will have the same name across the cluster. Nevertheless, if you deploy the same EJB on the same node, once with commit option C (read/write access) and once in commit option A (read only), and want the read/write EJB to invalidate entries of the read-only EJB, each will obviously have its own EJB name. Consequently, you can assign a common `invalidation-group-name` to both EJBs so that they share their cache invalidation messages. The `invalidation-manager-name` references the `InvalidationManager` MBean to be used. By default, the default `Invalidation-Manager` is used.

17.4.3 Message-Driven Beans

MDBs are configured using the `message-driven` elements, one each for each MDB that's configured. In addition to the standard child elements used by session and entity elements, the `message-driven` element uses additional child elements specific to MDBs:

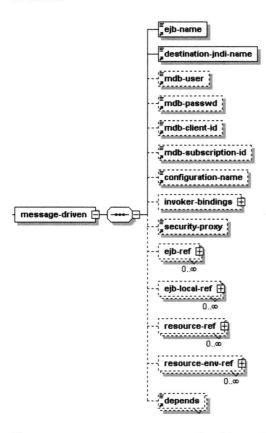

The `destination-jndi-name` should specify the JNDI name of the JMS destination on which the MDB listens. The `mdb-user` and `mdb-password` elements specify the user name and password to access secured destinations. The `mdb-client-id` specifies the client ID for JMS connections, and `mdb-subscription-id` specifies the ID to use for durable subscriptions.

257

17.5 EJB Security

In this section, you'll see how to configure the various aspects of security using the JBoss EJB deployment descriptor.

17.5.1 Method Permissions

You can restrict access to your EJB methods by using the `security-role` and `method-permission` elements in the standard EJB deployment descriptor. However, enforcing this declarative security in an operational environment is performed in an application server–specific manner. In section 7.3.3.3, "Login Configuration Data," you saw how to use JAAS within JBoss to define login modules in the `login-config.xml` file.

When a thread tries to access a secure method, JBoss tries to evaluate the credentials of the thread using the `security-domain` element in the JBoss EJB deployment descriptor. This element should refer to a login module configured within the system. The JBoss JAAS security manager will use the login module to resolve the caller's credentials and access rights. The following snippet shows how to define a security domain for performing authentication/authorization:

```
<jboss>
  <security-domain>java:jaas/MyLoginModule</security-domain>
  <enterprise-beans>
    ...
  <enterprise-beans>

</jboss>
```

Here, `MyLoginModule` is a login module configured within JBoss. For a detailed discussion on how to configure login modules, please refer to Section 7.3.3, "Login Configuration."

> **Method permissions are checked only for remote references. For local references, it's always assumed that the client has been authenticated and has been granted sufficient access rights.**

17.5.2 Unauthenticated Principal

You can use the element `unauthenticated-principal` to define a value that should be returned when `EJBContext.getCallerPrincipal()` is called in an unauthenticated thread:

```
<jboss>
  <unauthenticated-principal>
    Bob the Builder
  </unauthenticated-principal >
  <enterprise-beans>
    ...
  <enterprise-beans>

</jboss>
```

17.5.3 Security Proxy

J2EE provides a declarative way of handling security for EJB and web applications, where user identities are mapped to roles. Even though this is a powerful way of handling security, it falls short when your security policies are tightly coupled to your domain data. For example, if you want to make security decisions based on the argument values that are passed to bean methods, there's no way you can handle this using declarative security.

JBoss provides a nonintrusive way of handling this by decoupling the security logic from the bean code using the interceptor architecture. You can define security interceptors at the bean level in the JBoss-specific EJB deployment descriptor as follows:

```
<jboss>

  <enterprise-beans>
    <session>
      <ejb-name>ShoppingControllerEJB</ejb-name>
      ...
      <security-proxy>
        com.acme.security.MySecurityInterceptor
      <security-proxy>
      ...
    </session>
  <enterprise-beans>

</jboss>
```

The `security-proxy` element should define the fully qualified name of the class that implements the interface `org.jboss.security.SecurityProxy`. If a `security-proxy` element is present, JBoss dynamically adds an interceptor of type `org.jboss.ejb.plugins.SecurityProxyInterceptor` during deployment. This interceptor will delegate the running of custom security logic to the proxy implementation. The proxy class needs to implement the following methods:

```
public void init(Class beanHome,
                 Class beanRemote,
                 Object securityMgr) throws InstantiationException;
```

This method is called after the instance is initialized:

```
public void setEJBContext(EJBContext ctx);
```

This method is called prior to any method invocation to set the current EJB context:

```
public void invokeHome(Method m,
                        Object[] args) throws SecurityException;
```

This method is called to allow the security proxy to perform any custom security checks required for the EJB home interface method:

```
public void invoke(Method m,
                        Object[] args, Object bean)
    throws SecurityException;
```

This method is called to allow the security proxy to perform any custom security checks required for the EJB remote interface method.

18

Configuring CMP 2.0

Container-managed persistent Enterprise JavaBeans (EJBs) are one of the most widely used Java 2 Enterprise Edition (J2EE) components. The significance of Container-Managed Persistence (CMP) beans has become manifold in the J2EE world since the introduction of EJB 2.0 and the support for container-managed relations. JBoss 3.*x* comes with a pluggable CMP engine that supports almost all features of CMP 2.0. In this chapter, you'll look at the JBoss CMP 2.0 implementation.

Throughout this chapter, I'll use examples from the petstore implementation to illustrate the various CMP features that are available with JBoss 3.x. In particular, the chapter uses the purchase order component.

18.1 CMP Configuration Files

The CMP features provided by JBoss are as follows:

❑   Table creation during bean deployment, and removal during bean undeployment.

❑   Allowing different entities within a deployment unit to map to different datasources from different database vendors.

❑   Mapping of CMP fields: Mapping of container-managed relationship fields using both foreign keys and relationship tables.

❑   Extending EJB-QL.

❑   Mapping JavaBean-style persistent fields to multiple database columns.

❑   Tuning performance using eager/lazy loading.

❑   Customizing the CMP behavior by mapping database vendor-specific
     functionality to CMP operations.

To start with, you'll look at the main configuration files used within JBoss for configuring the CMP engine as well as CMP components:

❑   `standardjbosscmp-jdbc.xml`
     This file is used for defining the global configuration for CMP 2.0
     EJBs. This file is used for defining various default values when those
     values aren't defined in bean-level CMP configuration files, as well as
     providing mapping information for some of the mainstream database
     vendors. This mapping information mainly includes the SQL specific for
     the database vendors for creating primary keys/foreign keys, SQL
     functions to EJB-QL functions, SQL to attain row locking, and so on.

❑   `jbosscmp-jdbc.xml`
     This file is used for defining bean-level configuration for CMP EJBs. This file
     can be used for defining type mapping, relation mapping, finder mapping,
     and so on. This file should be present in the `\META-INF` directory of your
     EJB JAR file. This file will mainly contain the object-to-relational mapping
     information for all the entity EJBs as well as their relations specified in the
     `ejb-jar.xml` file.

Both the previous files follow the Document Type Definition (DTD) specified in the
`jbosscmp-jdbc_3_2.dtd` file. The basic structure of the XML is as follows:

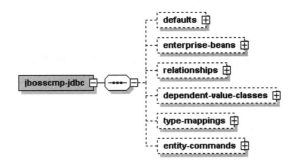

The previous structure contains the following children for the
jbosscmp-jdbc root element:

❑ defaults
This element defines container-wide or deployment-unit-wide defaults.
The container-wide defaults are set in the standardjbosscmp-jdbc.xml
file present in the \conf directory of the configuration set you use. The
default set at deployment unit level will be defined in the jbosscmp-
jdbc.xml file, which is present in the \META-INF directory for the
deployment unit. The following diagram shows the structure of this
element. The subsequent sections discuss various subelements of
this element:

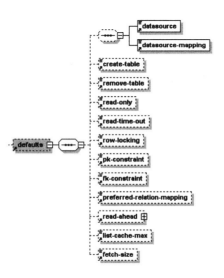

❑ enterprise-beans
This element is used mainly within the jbosscmp-jdbc.xml file of the
deployment unit for mapping the entity EJBs defined in the ejb-jar.xml
file to database tables. The element contains one or more entity elements.
The entities defined within this element can use its various child elements
to override the defaults set at container level or deployment unit level.
The following diagram depicts the structure of the entity element. The
subsequent sections discuss the various subelements of this element:

263

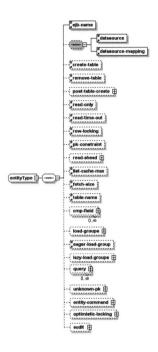

❑ relationships:
This element is used mainly within the jbosscmp-jdbc.xml file of the deployment unit for mapping the entity EJBs defined in the ejb-jar.xml file to database tables. The following diagram depicts the structure of this element. Section 18.9, "Mapping Relationships," discusses its various subelements:

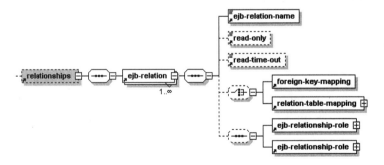

❑ dependent-value-classes
This element is used mainly within the jbosscmp-jdbc.xml file of the deployment unit for defining dependent value classes. The following diagram depicts the structure of this element. The section 18.8, "Mapping CMP Fields," discusses the various subelements of this element:

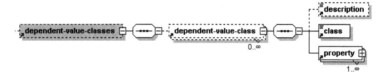

❏ type-mappings
This element is mainly used in `standardjbosscmp-jdbc.xml` file for mapping Java types to SQL types as well as some of the JBoss custom functions used in finders to database functions for some of the major database vendors. The database vendors that come preconfigured with JBoss include Sybase, Oracle, DB2, Hypersonic, MySQL, PostgreSQL, and so on. The following diagram depicts the structure of this element. The subsequent sections discuss the various subelements of this element:

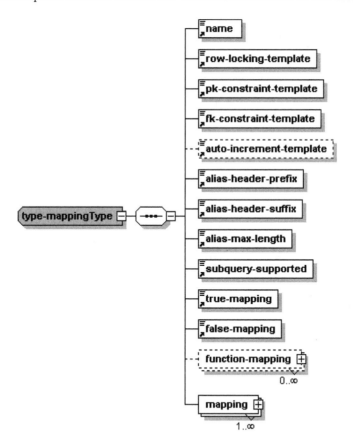

❏ entity-commands
Entity commands are used for using pluggable key generation strategies.

18.2 Mapping EJB Names

The content of the `ejb-name` elements defined in the `jbosscmp-jdbc.xml` file should match those defined in the standard `ejb-jar.xml` file for the deployment unit. The following snippet shows the excerpts from the `ejb-jar.xml` file for the purchase order component:

```
<?xml version="1.0" encoding="US-ASCII"?>

<!DOCTYPE ejb-jar
    PUBLIC "-//Sun Microsystems, Inc.//DTD Enterprise JavaBeans 2.0//EN"
    "http://java.sun.com/dtd/ejb-jar_2_0.dtd">

<ejb-jar>
    <description>PO</description>
    <display-name>PurchaseOrderJAR</display-name>
    <enterprise-beans>

        <entity>
            <description>PurchaseOrder CMP EJB</description>
            <display-name>PurchaseOrderEB</display-name>
            <ejb-name>PurchaseOrderEJB</ejb-name>
            ...
        </entity>
        ...
    </enterprise-beans>
    ...
</ejb-jar>
```

The following snippet shows excerpts from the corresponding `jbosscmp-jdbc.xml` file:

```
<?xml version="1.0" encoding="UTF-8"?>

<!DOCTYPE jbosscmp-jdbc PUBLIC
    "-//JBoss//DTD JBOSSCMP-JDBC 3.0//EN"
    "http://www.jboss.org/j2ee/dtd/jbosscmp-jdbc_3_2.dtd">

<jbosscmp-jdbc>
    ...
    <enterprise-beans>
        <entity>
            <ejb-name>PurchaseOrderEJB</ejb-name>
            ...
        </entity>
        ...
    </enterprise-beans>
    ...
</jbosscmp-jdbc>
```

> **Please note that JBoss currently requires the EJB names to be unique across multiple deployment units in a server instance.**

18.3 Datasource Mapping

JBoss uses datasource mapping to map the entity object model to a relational model specific to the target database system. When you deploy entity beans within JBoss, you need to specify the datasource mapping for the entity beans defined in the deployment unit. This specified mapping should be one of the predefined datasource mappings defined in the `standardjbosscmp-jdbc.xml` file or one you define within your deployment unit in the `jbosscmp-jdbc.xml` file.

You can define this at the entity bean level, deployment level, or globally. Defining the datasource mapping for the individual entity bean is useful if you have different entity beans persisted to different database systems within the same deployment unit. An example is as follows:

```
<jbosscmp-jdbc>
  ...
  <enterprise-beans>
    ...
    <entity>
      ...
      <datasource-mapping>Sybase<datasource-mapping>
      ...
    <entity>
    <entity>
      ...
      <datasource-mapping>Oracle9i<datasource-mapping>
      ...
    <entity>
    ...
  <enterprise-beans>
  ...
</jbosscmp-jdbc>
```

If all the entity beans defined in a deployment unit are persisted to the same type of database system, you can define a default datasource mapping for all the entity EJBs in the `jbosscmp-jdbc.xml` for that deployment unit, as follows:

```
<jbosscmp-jdbc>
  <defaults>
    ...
    <datasource-mapping>Sybase<datasource-mapping>
    ...
  <defaults>
  ...
</jbosscmp-jdbc>
```

If you don't specify EJB-level or deployment unit-wide default, JBoss will use the global default specified in `standardjbosscmp-jdbc.xml` file. The default global datasource mapping set for JBoss is Hypersonic SQL.

The global default is set in the same way as the deployment unit level default. The only difference is that for the deployment unit level default, the `datasource-mapping` is specified in the `jbosscmp-jdbc.xml` file available in the `\META-INF` directory of the deployment unit, and for global defaults it is specified in the `standardjbosscmp-jdbc.xml` file available in the `\conf` directory of the configuration set you use. If you want, you can modify `standardjbosscmp-jdbc.xml` to change the global default.

18.3.1 Type Mappings

JBoss defines the named datasource mappings for various database management systems using the `type-mappings` element in the `standardjbosscmp-jdbc.xml` file. This element can contain zero or more `type-mapping` elements to specify type mapping information for each database vendors.

18.3.1.1 Type Mapping Name

The `type-mapping` element uses the `name` element to define a unique name for the datasource mapping. This is used to define the datasource mapping for entity EJBs as explained in the last section. JBoss supports the following database management systems:

- ❏ InterBase
- ❏ DB2
- ❏ Oracle 9i, 6, and 7
- ❏ Oracle 8
- ❏ Oracle 7
- ❏ Sybase
- ❏ PostgreSQL 7.2
- ❏ Hypersonic SQL
- ❏ PointBase
- ❏ SOLID
- ❏ mySQL
- ❏ MS SQL Server 7.0 and 2000
- ❏ DB2/400
- ❏ SapDB
- ❏ Cloudscape
- ❏ Informix

You can add new datasource mappings to this file, if your preferred database is not in the previous list.

18.3.1.2 Row Locking Template

This is the template used to create a row lock on the selected rows. The arguments supplied are as follows:

- ❑ SELECT clause
- ❑ FROM clause
- ❑ WHERE clause

If row locking isn't supported in the SELECT statement, this element should be empty. The most common form of row locking is SELECT FOR UPDATE as in the following example:

```
<row-locking-template>
    SELECT ?1 FROM ?2 WHERE ?3 FOR UPDATE
</row-locking-template>
```

You can specify whether you require row locking at entity level in jbosscmp-jdbc.xml as follows:

```
<jbosscmp-jdbc>
    ...
    <enterprise-beans>
       ...
       <entity>
          ...
          <row-locking>true</row-locking>
          ...
       <entity>
       ...
    <enterprise-beans>
    ...
</jbosscmp-jdbc>
```

If all the entity beans defined in a deployment unit need row locking, you can define a default row locking for all the entity EJBs in the jbosscmp-jdbc.xml for that deployment unit as follows:

```
<jbosscmp-jdbc>
    <defaults>
       ...
       <row-locking>true</row-locking>
       ...
    <defaults>
    ...
</jbosscmp-jdbc>
```

If you don't specify an EJB-level or a deployment unit-wide default, JBoss will use the global default specified in the `standardjbosscmp-jdbc.xml` file. The default row locking policy set for JBoss is `false`.

The global default is set in the same way as the deployment unit level default. The only difference is, for the deployment unit level default, the `row-locking` option is specified in the `jbosscmp-jdbc.xml` file available in the `\META-INF` directory of the deployment unit, and for global defaults it's specified in the `standardjbosscmp-jdbc.xml` file available in the `\conf` directory of the configuration set you use. If you want, you can modify `standardjbosscmp-jdbc.xml` to change the global default.

18.3.1.3 Primary Keys

This is the template used to create a primary key constraint in the CREATE TABLE statement. The arguments supplied are as follows:

- ❑ Primary key constraint name, which is always pk_{table-name}
- ❑ Comma-separated list of primary key column names

If a primary key constraint clause isn't supported in a CREATE TABLE statement, this element should be empty. An example is as follows:

```
<type-mapping>
  ...
  <pk-constraint-template>
    CONSTRAINT ?1 PRIMARY KEY (?2)
  </pk-constraint-template>
  ...
</type-mapping>
```

18.3.1.4 Foreign Keys

This is the template used to create a foreign key constraint in a separate statement. The arguments supplied are as follows:

- ❑ Table name
- ❑ Foreign key constraint name, which is always fk_{table-name}_ {cmr-field-name}
- ❑ Comma-separated list of foreign key column names

- ❏ References table name
- ❏ Comma-separated list of the referenced primary key column names

If the datasource doesn't support foreign key constraints, this element should be empty. An example is as follows:

```
<type-mapping>
  ...
  <fk-constraint-template>
    ALTER TABLE ?1 ADD CONSTRAINT ?2 FOREIGN KEY (?3)
    REFERENCES ?4 (?5)
  </fk-constraint-template>
  ...
</type-mapping
```

18.3.1.5 Aliases

An alias header is prefixed to a generated table alias by the EJB-QL compiler to prevent name collisions. An alias header is composed of the contents of `alias-header-prefix`, `alias-header-suffix`, and an incrementing value. An alias header is constructed as `alias-header-prefix` + `int_counter` + `alias-header-suffix`. The maximum length of aliases is limited by `alias-max-length`:

```
<type-mapping>
  ...
  <alias-header-prefix>t</alias-header-prefix>
  <alias-header-suffix>_</alias-header-suffix>
  <alias-max-length>32</alias-max-length>
  ...
<type-mapping>
```

For example, if your EJB-QL contains three tables, with the previous example the aliases generated by JBoss in the generated SQL for the tables will be `t0_`, `t1_`, and `t2_`.

18.3.1.6 Subquery

This specifies whether the database system supports subqueries. If `true`, the JBoss EJB-QL compiler will use subqueries to generate the SQL for the target database, for certain EJB-QL queries. Otherwise, it'll use a `LEFT JOIN` and the `isNull` function:

```
<sub-query>true</sub-query>
```

18.3.1.7 True and False

The TRUE and FALSE literals defined in EJB-QL map to the values used in the target database system, as follows:

```
<true-mapping>1</true-mapping>
<false-mapping>0</false-mapping>
```

18.3.1.8 Data Type Mapping

JBoss uses the mapping element to map the Java types of the persistent fields to the SQL types on the target database system. A type-mapping element may contain zero or more mapping elements. The content model of this element is as follows:

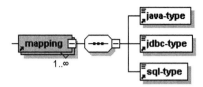

The java-type defines the Java type, the jdbc-type the type defined in the JDBC Types interface, and sql-type the type on the target database system. JBoss uses these types for getting and setting persistent data as well as generating Data Definition Languages (DDLs) when create tables on deployment are set to true. Section 18.5, "Create and Remove Table," covers how to create tables. The following snippet shows an example:

```
<mapping>
  <java-type>java.lang.Byte</java-type>
  <jdbc-type>SMALLINT</jdbc-type>
  <sql-type>NUMBER(3)</sql-type>
</mapping>
```

If JBoss is to find a type mapping for a type in a given datasource mapping information, it'll try to serialize and store that field.

18.3.1.9 Function Mapping

You can use the function-mapping element for mapping a function defined in EJB-QL or its extension JBoss-QL to an SQL function used in the target database system. A type-mapping element may contain zero or more function-mapping elements. The content model of this element is as follows:

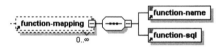

The `function-name` defines the name of the function in EJB-QL or JBoss-QL and `function-sql` is the SQL to which the function is mapped. The SQL can contain parameters specified with a question mark followed by the base parameter number. The following snippet shows an example:

```
<function-mapping>
    <function-name>concat</function-name>
    <function-sql>(?1 || ?2)</function-sql>
</function-mapping>
```

18.4 Datasource

When you deploy an entity EJB, you need to specify the data store to which the state of the entity will be persisted. Most of the EJB containers allow you to do this by specifying the Java Naming and Directory Interface (JNDI) name of a datasource that points to the database to which the entity will be persisted. In JBoss, you can specify this in three different ways.

The first is to define the datasource for the individual entity bean. This is useful if you have different entity beans persisted to different database systems within the same deployment unit. An example is as follows:

```
<jbosscmp-jdbc>
   ...
   <enterprise-beans>
     ...
     <entity>
       ...
       <datasource>java:/jdbc/opc/OPCDB</datasource>
       ...
     <entity>
     <entity>
       ...
       <datasource>java:/jdbc/opc/OPCDB</datasource>
       ...
     <entity>
       ...
   <enterprise-beans>
   ...
</jbosscmp-jdbc>
```

If all the entity beans defined in a deployment unit are persisted to the same data store, you can define a default datasource for all the entity EJBs in the `jbosscmp-jdbc.xml` for that deployment unit as follows:

```
<jbosscmp-jdbc>
  <defaults>
    ...
    <datasource>java:/jdbc/opc/OPCDB</datasource>
    ...
  <defaults>
  ...
</jbosscmp-jdbc>
```

If you don't specify EJB-level or deployment unit-wide default, JBoss will use the global default specified in the `standardjbosscmp-jdbc.xml` file. The default global datasource set for JBoss is `java:/DefaultDS`.

The global default is set in the same way as the deployment unit level default. The only difference is for deployment unit level default, the datasource is specified in `jbosscmp-jdbc.xml` file available in the `\META-INF` directory of the deployment unit, and for global defaults, it's specified in `standardjbosscmp-jdbc.xml` file available in the `\conf` directory of the configuration set you use. If you want, you can modify the `standardjbosscmp-jdbc.xml` file to change the global default.

18.5 Create and Remove Table

JBoss allows you to create tables (if they don't already exist) when you deploy the entity EJBs and remove tables when you undeploy them. You can set this option at entity bean level, deployment level, or globally for all entity beans installed within a server instance. Along with the table creation and removal options, you can also specify whether you want the CMP engine to create primary keys and foreign keys at database level to reflect the entity bean primary keys and relationships.

> **Please note that you can't set the option to create foreign keys at entity bean level because obviously foreign key creation involves two tables.**

The following example shows how to set these options on for individual entity beans:

```
<jbosscmp-jdbc>
  ...
  <enterprise-beans>
```

```
    ...
  <entity>
      ...
    <create-table>true</create-table>
    <remove-table>true</remove-table>
    <pk-constraint>true</pk-constraint>
      ...
  <entity>
    ...
<enterprise-beans>
  ...
</jbosscmp-jdbc>
```

You can set these options globally for entity beans included in the deployment unit in the jbosscmp-jdbc.xml:

```
<jbosscmp-jdbc>
  <defaults>
      ...
    <create-table>true</create-table>
    <remove-table>true</remove-table>
    <pk-constraint>true</pk-constraint>
    <fk-constraint>true</fk-constraint>
      ...
  <defaults>
    ...
</jbosscmp-jdbc>
```

If you don't specify EJB level or deployment unit-wide default, JBoss will use the global default specified in standardjbosscmp-jdbc.xml file. JBoss sets the create-table and pk-constraint options to true and the remove-table and fk-constraint options to false.

The global default is set in the same way as the deployment unit level default. The only difference is for the deployment unit level default, the table creation or removal defaults are specified in the jbosscmp-jdbc.xml file available in the \META-INF directory of the deployment unit, and for global defaults it's specified in the standardjbosscmp-jdbc.xml file available in the \conf directory of the configuration set you use. If you want, you can modify standardjbosscmp-jdbc.xml to change the global default.

You can also get the CMP engine to execute an SQL statement after the table is created by specifying the SQL using the post-table-create element. This element can contain one or more sql-statement element, each containing the SQL to be executed. This is useful if you want to prepopulate the table or create indices.

275

18.6 Table Name

You can specify the database table to which the entity bean is mapped using the table-name element within the entity element, as follows:

```
<jbosscmp-jdbc>
  ...
  <enterprise-beans>
    ...
    <entity>
      ...
      <table-name>CONTACT_INFO</table-name>
      ...
    <entity>
    ...
  <enterprise-beans>
  ...
</jbosscmp-jdbc>
```

If you don't specify the table name, the JBoss CMP engine will assume the contents of the ejb-name element as the table name.

18.7 Read-Only

You can set an entity bean as read-only with a read timeout value. The JBoss CMP engine wouldn't allow you to change the values of the fields of an entity bean declared as read-only. You can set the read-only option globally for all entity beans deployed within a server instance (normally you wouldn't be doing this), all entity beans included in a deployment unit, individual entity beans, or individual CMP fields.

The following example shows how to set the read-only option for individual entity beans in the jbosscmp-jdbc.xml file:

```
<jbosscmp-jdbc>
  ...
  <enterprise-beans>
    ...
    <entity>
      ...
      <read-only>true</read-only>
      <read-time-out>100</read-time-out>
      ...
    <entity>
    ...
  <enterprise-beans>
  ...
</jbosscmp-jdbc>
```

The `read-time-out` value specifies the time in milliseconds before the values are refreshed. The `0` value means the values are refreshed at the beginning of each transaction, and `-1` means they're never refreshed.

You can set these options globally for entity beans included in the deployment unit in `jbosscmp-jdbc.xml`:

```
<jbosscmp-jdbc>
  <defaults>
    ...
    <read-only>true</read-only>
    <read-time-out>100</read-time-out>
    ...
  <defaults>
    ...
</jbosscmp-jdbc>
```

If you don't specify an EJB level or deployment unit-wide default, JBoss will use the global default specified in the `standardjbosscmp-jdbc.xml` file. JBoss sets read-only to `false` and `read-time-out` to 300 milliseconds for all the EJBs deployed within the server instance.

The global default is set in the same way as the deployment unit level default. The only difference is for the deployment unit level default, the table `read-only` and `read-time-out` options are specified in the `jbosscmp-jdbc.xml` file available in the `\META-INF` directory of the deployment unit, and for global defaults, they're specified in the `standardjbosscmp-jdbc.xml` file available in the `\conf` directory of the configuration set you use. If you want, you can modify `standardjbosscmp-jdbc.xml` to change the global default.

18.8 Mapping CMP Fields

In this section, you'll look at how to map CMP fields to database columns. The CMP fields of an entity bean are mapped to database columns using zero or more `cmp-field` elements within the corresponding `entity` element in the `jbosscmp-jdbc.xml` file. The structure of the `cmp-field` element is as follows:

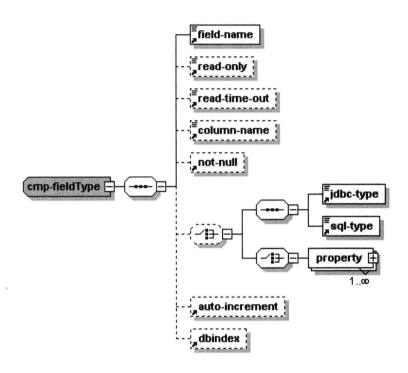

The following are the elements it supports:

Element Name	Description
field-name	Contains the name of the CMP field. This should match the corresponding cmp-field element in ejb-jar.xml file.
read-only	Sets the field as read-only; see section 18.7, "Read-Only."
read-time-out	Sets the timeout value, in milliseconds, before the field is refreshed; see section 18.7, "Read-Only."
column-name	Represents a database column to which the CMP field is mapped. If the column-name element isn't present, JBoss will use the CMP name as the column name. The CMP engine will also use these column names while creating the tables.
jdbc-type sql-type	Used for mapping the Java type of the CMP field to an SQL type on the target database system. If not specified, the CMP engine will resolve the mapping using the type mappings specified for the datasource mapping that's used.

Element Name	Description
not-null	If the empty not-null element is present, the CMP engine will add the NOT NULL clause of the column when creating the table. By default, the JBoss CMP engine will add NOT NULL for only primary key columns and columns with SQL types mapped to Java primitive data types.
property	Used for mapping custom JavaBean such as CMP fields to multiple database columns. This is explained in detail in the next section.
auto-increment	If this element is present, the CMP engine includes the SQL fragment in the create DDL to declare the field whose value is automatically incremented.
dbindex	If this element is present, the CMP engine includes the SQL fragment in the create DDL to create an index for the field.

The following snippet shows the CMP field mapping for the LineItemEJB in the order processing application of the petstore:

```
<jbosscmp-jdbc>
   ...
   <enterprise-beans>
      ...
      <entity>
        <entity>
          <ejb-name>O_LineItemEJB</ejb-name>
          <table-name>LineItemEJBTable</table-name>

          <cmp-field>
            <field-name>id</field-name>
            <column-name>id</column-name>
          </cmp-field>

          <cmp-field>
            <field-name>categoryId</field-name>
            <column-name>categoryId</column-name>
          </cmp-field>

          <cmp-field>
            <field-name>itemId</field-name>
            <column-name>itemId</column-name>
          </cmp-field>
```

279

```
        <cmp-field>
          <field-name>lineNumber</field-name>
          <column-name>lineNumber</column-name>
        </cmp-field>

        <cmp-field>
          <field-name>productId</field-name>
          <column-name>productId</column-name>
        </cmp-field>

        <cmp-field>
          <field-name>quantity</field-name>
          <column-name>quantity</column-name>
        </cmp-field>

        <cmp-field>
          <field-name>quantityShipped</field-name>
          <column-name>quantityShipped</column-name>
        </cmp-field>

        <cmp-field>
          <field-name>unitPrice</field-name>
          <column-name>unitPrice</column-name>
        </cmp-field>

      </entity>
      ...
    <enterprise-beans>
      ...
  <jbosscmp-jdbc>
```

18.8.1 Dependent Value Classes

JBoss supports CMP fields of types other than the standard types such as primitives, strings, and date types. By default, CMP fields of types other than the standard types are serialized and stored as a blob. However, if the type conforms to the standard JavaBean naming conventions for accessors and mutators for the fields, JBoss will allow you to map the properties of the CMP field to multiple database columns. These classes should be serializable and should have public no-argument constructors.

As an example, assume that in the purchase order example, you don't want the credit card to be a separate EJB because it's entirely dependent on the purchase order. Hence, you may define a class to model the credit card:

```
package com.sun.j3ee.blueprints.purchaseorder;

public class CreditCard implements java.io.Serializable {

  public CreditCard() {}
```

```
    private String number;
    public String getNumber() { return number; }
    public String setNumber(String val) { number = val; }

    private String type;
    public String getType() { return type; }
    public String setType(String val) { type = val; }

    private String expiryDate;
    public String getExpiryDate() { return expiryDate; }
    public String setExpiryDate(String val) { expiryDate = val; }

}
```

Now you need to define the CMP field accessor and mutator in the purchase order EJB for the credit card-dependent value class:

```
public abstract CreditCard getCreditCard();
public abstract void setCreditCard(CreditCard creditCard);
```

You also need to define the credit card CMP field in the `ejb-jar.xml` file:

```
<cmp-field>CreditCard</cmp-field>
```

On the JBoss side, the first thing you need to define the schema for the **Dependent Value Class (DVC)**. You can do this either in the `jbosscmp-jdbc.xml` or `standardjbosscmp-jdbc.xml` file. I prefer to do it in the `jbosscmp-jdbc.xml` file, if only one or more of the entity beans defined in that deployment unit only uses the DVC. You do this using the `dependent-value-classes` element:

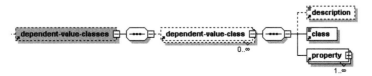

This element may contain zero or more `dependent-value-class` elements describing the schema of each DVC that's used.

The `dependent-value-class` element contains an optional `description` element, a mandatory `class` element that contains the fully qualified class name, and one or more `property` elements:

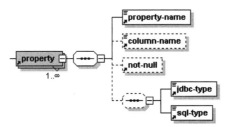

The `property` element contains a `property-name` element that contains the name of the property, an optional `column-name` element to which the `property` is mapped by default, an optional `not-null` element that has the same purpose as that in the `cmp-field` element, and an optional set of `jdbc-type` and `sql-type` elements that has the same purpose as that in the `cmp-field` element.

The type of the property can be either a simple type or a defined or undefined DVC. If it's a DVC and the column name isn't specified, JBoss will create the column name by concatenating all the nested properties. For example, if the credit card DVC has a property called `address`, whose type is another DVC, and that DVC contains a simple property called `country`, and you don't specify the column name, JBoss will assume the column name as `address_country`.

The following snippet shows the DVC declaration for the credit card:

```
<jbosscmp-jdbc>
   <dependent-value-classes>
     <dependent-value-class>
       <description>Credit card DVC</description>
       <class>com.sun.j2ee.blueprints.purchaseorder.CreditCard</class>
       <property>
          <property-name>number</property-name>
          <column-name>cc_number</column-name>
       </property>
       <property>
          <property-name>type</property-name>
          <column-name>cc_type</column-name>
       </property>
       <property>
          <property-name>expiryDate</property-name>
          <column-name>cc_expiry_date</column-name>
       </property>
     <dependent-value-class>
   </dependent-value-class>
</jbosscmp-jdbc>
```

Now you need to map this CMP field in the purchase order entity bean:

```
<jbosscmp-jdbc>
  <enterprise-beans>

    <entity>
      <ejb-name>PurchaseOrderEJB</ejb-name>
      <table-name>PurchaseOrderEJBTable</table-name>

      <cmp-field>
        <field-name>creditCard</field-name>
      </cmp-field>

    </enterprise-beans>
</jbosscmp-jdbc>
```

Now, the properties of the credit card DVC will be persisted to the cc_number, cc_type, and cc_expiry_date columns of the PurchaseOrderEJBTable. You can override the property descriptions defined in the dependent-value class element using the cmp-field element as follows:

```
<jbosscmp-jdbc>
  <enterprise-beans>

    <entity>
      <ejb-name>PurchaseOrderEJB</ejb-name>
      <table-name>PurchaseOrderEJBTable</table-name>

      <cmp-field>
        <field-name>creditCard</field-name>
        <property>
          <property-name>number</property-name>
          <column-name>cc_number</column-name>
        </property>
        <property>
          <property-name>type</property-name>
          <column-name>cc_type</column-name>
        </property>
        <property>
          <property-name>expiryDate</property-name>
          <column-name>cc_expiry_date</column-name>
        </property>
      </cmp-field>

    </enterprise-beans>
</jbosscmp-jdbc>
```

This is extremely important if you want to define small column names instead of the lengthy column names generated by the CMP engine in case of nested DVC properties. The following example shows how to define a simpler column name for a DVC containing another nested DVC property:

```
<jbosscmp-jdbc>
  <enterprise-beans>

    <entity>
      <ejb-name>PurchaseOrderEJB</ejb-name>
      <table-name>PurchaseOrderEJBTable</table-name>
      <cmp-field>
        <field-name>creditCard</field-name>
        <property>
          <property-name>address.country</property-name>
          <column-name>cc_country</column-name>
        </property>
      </cmp-field>

    </enterprise-beans>
</jbosscmp-jdbc>
```

In the previous case, the CMP engine will use the column name as `cc_country` instead of `address_country` for the country property of the credit card's `address` property.

18.9 Mapping Relationships

In these sections, you'll look at how to map the EJB relationships defined in the `ejb-jar.xml` file to a target database within JBoss. JBoss supports one-to-many and many-to-many cardinalities in both unidirectional and bidirectional navigability. JBoss supports relationship mapping based on both foreign keys as well as relationship tables. Relationship tables are similar to the association classes in the object-oriented world and are the only way to map to many-to-many relationships.

You can define your preferred relationship mapping style at a deployment unit level as follows:

```
<jbosscmp-jdbc>
  <defaults>
    . . .
    <preferred-relation-mapping>
      foreign-key
    </preferred-relation-mapping>
    <!-
    <preferred-relation-mapping>
```

```
        relation-table
    </preferred-relation-mapping>
    -->
    ...
  <defaults>
  ...
</jbosscmp-jdbc>
```

You can also specify this for individual relations. If not specified in either way, the CMP engine will use foreign key-based relations, which is the global default set in the standardjbosscmp-jdbc.xml file.

The global default is set in the same way as the deployment unit level default. The only difference is for the deployment unit level default, the preferred relationship mapping is specified in the jbosscmp-jdbc.xml file available in the \META-INF directory of the deployment unit, and for the global default, it's specified in the standardjbosscmp-jdbc.xml file available in the \conf directory of the configuration set you use. If you want, you can modify standardjbosscmp-jdbc.xml to change the global default.

The relationships specified in ejb-jar.xml files are mapped to the target database system using the relationships element in the jbosscmp-jdbc.xml file. This element may contain one or more ejb-relation elements. Each of these elements should correspond to the ejb-relation element specified in the ejb-jar.xml file. The structure of this element is as follows:

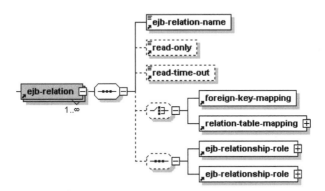

The ejb-relation-name element should map to the ejb-relation-name element in the file ejb-jar.xml. The optional read-only and read-time-out elements are used to define the relationship as read-only. This works in the same way as read-only CMP fields explained in section 18.7, "Read-Only."

If the foreign-key-mapping empty element is present, the CMP engine will use foreign keys to relate the two entities in relation. If you want to use relationship table–based mapping, you can define the details using the `relation-table-mapping` element. This is explained in detail in the next section.

The two `ejb-relationship-role` elements should correspond to the same defined in the file `ejb-jar.xml`:

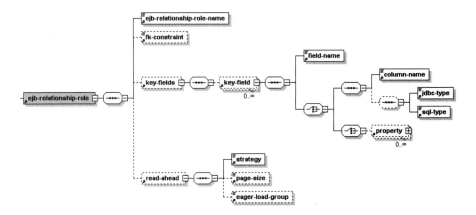

The `ejb-relationship-role-name` should to map to the same in the `ejb-jar.xml` file for that part of the relation. The `fk-constraint` element specifies whether the CMP engine should add a foreign key constraint while creating the tables. The `key-fields` element maps the primary key of the EJB that's the source of the relation to the foreign key in the table that persists the other entity in the relation.

The `read-ahead` element is used for implementing optimized reading as explained in the previous section.

The following listing shows the one-to-many unidirectional relationship between purchase order and line items in the standard `ejb-jar.xml` file:

```
<ejb-relation>
  <ejb-relation-name>PurchaseOrder-LineItem</ejb-relation-name>
  <ejb-relationship-role>
    <ejb-relationship-role-name>
      PurchaseOrderEJB
    </ejb-relationship-role-name>
    <multiplicity>One</multiplicity>
    <relationship-role-source>
      <ejb-name>PurchaseOrderEJB</ejb-name>
    </relationship-role-source>
    <cmr-field>
      <cmr-field-name>lineItems</cmr-field-name>
      <cmr-field-type>java.util.Collection</cmr-field-type>
    </cmr-field>
  </ejb-relationship-role>
```

```
    <ejb-relationship-role>
      <ejb-relationship-role-name>
        O_LineItemEJB
      </ejb-relationship-role-name>
      <multiplicity>Many</multiplicity>
      <cascade-delete />
      <relationship-role-source>
        <ejb-name>O_LineItemEJB</ejb-name>
      </relationship-role-source>
    </ejb-relationship-role>
  </ejb-relation>
```

Here, the relationship role, with line item EJB as the source, doesn't contain any Container-Managed Relationship (CMR) fields as the navigability is only from purchase order to line item. The following snippet shows how this relation is mapped to a target database in the jbosscmp-jdbc.xml file. In the generated data model, the table that persists line items will have a foreign key column that stores the primary key of the purchase order to which each line item belongs:

```
<ejb-relation>
  <ejb-relation-name>PurchaseOrder-LineItem</ejb-relation-name>
  <foreign-key-mapping/>

  <ejb-relationship-role>
    <ejb-relationship-role-name>
      PurchaseOrderEJB
    </ejb-relationship-role-name>
    <key-fields>
      <key-field>
        <field-name>poId</field-name>
        <column-name>po_id</column-name>
      </key-field>
    </key-fields>
  </ejb-relationship-role>

  <ejb-relationship-role>
    <ejb-relationship-role-name>
      O_LineItemEJB
    </ejb-relationship-role-name>
    <key-fields/>
  </ejb-relationship-role>
</ejb-relation>
```

In the previous example, the foreign key-style mapping is used and the table that persists line items will have a column called po_id to store the purchase order ID. JBoss will include this column in the DDL for the table if you've set the option to create the table on deployment to true.

Now you'll look at a bidirectional relationship.

> *None of the petstore entities involve bidirectional relationships. Hence, for the sake of the example, assume that the relationship between the purchase order and credit card is bidirectional.*

The following listing shows the one-to-one bidirectional relationship between the purchase order and credit card in the standard `ejb-jar.xml` file:

```
<ejb-relation>
  <ejb-relation-name>PurchaseOrder-CreditCard</ejb-relation-name>
  <ejb-relationship-role>
    <ejb-relationship-role-name>
      PurchaseOrderEJB
    </ejb-relationship-role-name>
    <multiplicity>One</multiplicity>
    <relationship-role-source>
      <ejb-name>PurchaseOrderEJB</ejb-name>
    </relationship-role-source>
    <cmr-field>
      <cmr-field-name>creditCard</cmr-field-name>
    </cmr-field>
  </ejb-relationship-role>
  <ejb-relationship-role>
    <ejb-relationship-role-name>
      O_CreditCardEJB
    </ejb-relationship-role-name>
    <multiplicity>One</multiplicity>
    <relationship-role-source>
    <ejb-name>O_CreditCardEJB</ejb-name>
    </relationship-role-source>
    <cmr-field>
      <cmr-field-name>purchaseOrder</cmr-field-name>
    </cmr-field>
  </ejb-relationship-role>
</ejb-relation>
```

Here, the relationship is navigable in both directions. This means a purchase order can identify its credit card, and vice versa. The following snippet shows how this relation is mapped to a target database in the `jbosscmp-jdbc.xml` file. In the generated data model, the table that persists credit card will have a foreign key column that stores the primary key of the purchase order to which the credit card belongs, and vice versa:

```
<ejb-relation>
  <ejb-relation-name>PurchaseOrder-CreditCard</ejb-relation-name>
  <foreign-key-mapping/>
```

```
    <ejb-relationship-role>
      <ejb-relationship-role-name>
        PurchaseOrderEJB
      </ejb-relationship-role-name>
      <key-fields>
        <key-field>
          <field-name>poId</field-name>
          <column-name>po_id</column-name>
        </key-field>
      </key-fields>
    </ejb-relationship-role>

    <ejb-relationship-role>
      <ejb-relationship-role-name>
        O_CreditCardEJB
      </ejb-relationship-role-name>
      <key-fields>
        <key-field>
          <field-name>id</field-name>
          <column-name>cc_id</column-name>
        </key-field>
      </key-fields>
    </ejb-relationship-role>
  </ejb-relation>
```

As you can see from the previous snippet, both sides of the relations now specify the foreign key for the table that persists the entity in the other side of the relation. The credit card table will have a column called po_id for storing the purchase order primary key, and the purchase order table will have a column called cc_id for storing the credit card primary key.

> **Please note that it isn't mandatory to define foreign keys in both the tables for bidirectional relations. Even if the foreign key is defined only for the table that persists the entity in one side of a bidirectional relation, the JBoss CMP engine will resolve the bidirectional navigability.**

18.9.1 Relationship Table Mapping

Sometimes it's difficult to map relationships in a database using foreign key mapping. A typical example is in many-to-many relations. In such cases, you can resort to using relationship tables. Relationship tables store primary keys from both tables in a relationship to implement many-to-many relations.

In JBoss, you can achieve this using `relation-table-mapping`, whose content model is as follows:

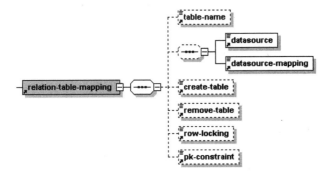

The `relation-table-mappings` element supports the following subelements:

Element Name	Description
table-name	Specifies the name of the relationship table. If not specified, JBoss will assume it's a concatenation of the two tables in relation separated by an underscore.
datasource	Identifies the datasource that'll point to the database that contains this table. If not specified, JBoss will use the default specified either deployment unit-wide or server-wide. The datasource-mapping element defines the mapping to use. If not specified, JBoss will use the default specified, either deployment unit-wide or server-wide.
create-table	See section 18.5, "Create and Remove Table."
remove-table	See section 18.5, "Create and Remove Table."
row-locking	See section 18.3.1.2, "Row Locking Template."
pk-constraint	See section 18.3.1.3, "Primary Keys."

None of the petstore entities involve many-to-many relationships. Hence, for the sake of the example, assume that the relationship between contact information and address is a many-to-many one.

The following listing shows the one-to-one bidirectional relationship between the purchase order and credit card in the standard `ejb-jar.xml` file:

```
<ejb-relation>
  <ejb-relation-name>ContactInfo-Address</ejb-relation-name>
  <ejb-relationship-role>
    <ejb-relationship-role-name>
      ContactInfoEJB
    </ejb-relationship-role-name>
    <multiplicity>many</multiplicity>
    <relationship-role-source>
      <ejb-name>ContactInfoEJB</ejb-name>
    </relationship-role-source>
    <cmr-field>
      <cmr-field-name>contactInfos</cmr-field-name>
      <cmr-field-type>java.util.Collection</cmr-field-type>
    </cmr-field>
  </ejb-relationship-role>
  <ejb-relationship-role>
    <ejb-relationship-role-name>
      AddressEJB
    </ejb-relationship-role-name>
    <multiplicity>One</multiplicity>
    <relationship-role-source>
    <ejb-name>AddressEJB</ejb-name>
    </relationship-role-source>
    <cmr-field>
      <cmr-field-name>addresses</cmr-field-name>
      <cmr-field-type>java.util.Collection</cmr-field-type>
    </cmr-field>
  </ejb-relationship-role>
</ejb-relation>
```

The following snippet shows how this relation is mapped to a target database in the `jbosscmp-jdbc.xml` file:

```
<ejb-relation>
  <ejb-relation-name>ContactInfo-Address</ejb-relation-name>
  <relation-table-mapping>
    <table-name>
      contact_info_address
    </table-name>
  <relation-table-mapping>

  <ejb-relationship-role>
    <ejb-relationship-role-name>
      ContactInfoEJB
    </ejb-relationship-role-name>
    <key-fields>
      <key-field>
```

```
            <field-name>id</field-name>
            <column-name>ci_id</column-name>
        </key-field>
        </key-fields>
    </ejb-relationship-role>

    <ejb-relationship-role>
        <ejb-relationship-role-name>
          AddressEJB
        </ejb-relationship-role-name>
        <key-fields>
          <key-field>
              <field-name>id</field-name>
              <column-name>add_id</column-name>
          </key-field>
        </key-fields>
    </ejb-relationship-role>
  </ejb-relation>
```

The data model will have a table called `contact_info_address` with a `ci_id`
column for storing the contact information primary key and an `add_id` column for
storing address primary keys. If the `create-table` option is `true`, the CMP engine
will create the necessary table and columns.

18.10 Mapping Queries

One of the major enhancements in EJB 2.0 was the introduction of EJB-QL as a means
of defining vendor-neutral queries. Even though EJB-QL is a major step forward, it's
still in its early stages and doesn't support important features such as ordering data.
Most of the container vendors have continued to offer custom query languages despite
the introduction of EJB-QL. This mainly extends EJB-QL to provide enhanced querying
functionalities. The advantage of not using anything other than EJB-QL is that your
EJBs will be portable across CMP vendors. JBoss provides the following functionalities
to extend EJB-QL:

❑ **JBossQL**
   Extends EJB-QL to provide added functionalities such as more functions,
   clauses, and keywords

❑ **DynamicQL**
   Allows you to generate JBossQL statements dynamically during runtime

❑ **DeclaredSQL**
   Allows you to compose a query statement by specifying `SELECT`, `FROM`,
   `WHERE` clauses, and so on

You can override EJB-QL for a finder or select method, using query elements nested within the relevant entity element in the jbosscmp-jdbc.xml file. When you do this, you should leave the ejb-ql element in the ejb-jar.xml file for the corresponding query as an empty element. The structure of the query element is as follows:

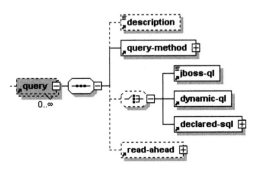

The query-method element has the same structure as the corresponding element in ejb-jar.xml file. This element is used to identify the finder or select method by specifying the method name and method parameters as follows:

```
<query-method>
  <method-name>findPOBetweenDates</method-name>
  <method-params>
    <method-param>long</method-param>
    <method-param>long</method-param>
  </method-params>
</query-method>
```

The read-ahead element is used for implementing optimized reads. This is covered in detail in section 18.11.1, "Read-Ahead Strategies."

18.10.1 JBossQL

JBossQL extends EJB-QL to support the following features:

- ❑ ORDER BY clause
- ❑ Use of parameters in IN and LIKE clauses
- ❑ UCASE and LCASE functions

The following example shows how to use JBoss-QL to return a sorted list of purchase orders from the `findPOBetweenDates` finder method by purchase order date:

```
<query>
  <query-method>
    <method-name>findPOBetweenDates</method-name>
    <method-params>
      <method-param>long</method-param>
      <method-param>long</method-param>
    </method-params>
  </query-method>
  <jboss-ql>
    <![CDATA[
      SELECT OBJECT(a)
      FROM PurchaseOrder a
      WHERE a.poDate BETWEEN ?1 AND ?2
      ORDER BY a.poDate
    ]]>
  </jboss-ql>
</query>
```

The following listing shows how to use the `like` operator to return all the contact information with family names starting with the passed string:

```
<query>
  <query-method>
    <method-name>findByFamilyName</method-name>
    <method-params>
      <method-param>java.lang.String</method-param>
    </method-params>
  </query-method>
  <jboss-ql>
    <![CDATA[
      SELECT OBJECT(a)
      FROM ContactInfo a
      WHERE a.familyName like ?1
    ]]>
  </jboss-ql>
</query>
```

Please note that when you call the finder, you should pass the wildcard search character as part of the argument as follows:

```
contactInfoHome.findByFamilyName("Ran%");
```

The following listing shows how to use the `UCASE` function to implement case-insensitive searches by family name:

```
<query>
  <query-method>
    <method-name>findByFamilyName</method-name>
    <method-params>
      <method-param>java.lang.String</method-param>
    </method-params>
  </query-method>
  <jboss-ql>
    <![CDATA[
      SELECT OBJECT(a)
      FROM ContactInfo a
      WHERE UCASE(a.familyName) = ?1
    ]]>
  </jboss-ql>
</query>
```

Please note that when you call the finder, you should convert the search string to uppercase, and JBoss will match the passed argument against the family name column values converted to uppercase:

```
contactInfoHome.findByFamilyName("Ranieri".toUpper());
```

The previous example will return all contact information records with family names set to *Ranieri*, regardless of the case.

18.10.2 DynamicQL

DynamicQL allows EJB select methods to take a dynamically compiled JBossQL statement and an array of parameters as arguments. Suppose you have an EJB home method that gives you a list of purchase order IDs falling between two dates ordered by purchase order date. You can dynamically generate the JBossQL and pass it an EJB select method to get back the required data. The only restriction is that the EJB select method should accept a string parameter representing the JBossQL that should be executed and an object array representing the parameters that should be passed to the JBossQL. The example is as follows:

```
PurchaseOrderEJB {

  //Home method
  public Collection ejbHomePOIdBetweenDates(long fromDate,
      long toDate) {

    StringBuffer sb = new StringBuffer();
    sb.append("SELECT a.poId ");
    sb.append("FROM PurchaseOrder a ");
    sb.append("WHERE a.poDate BETWEEN ?1 AND ?2 ");
    sb.append("ORDER BY a.poDate");
    return ejbSelectPOIdBetweenDates(sb.toString(),
```

```
      new Object[] {new Long(fromDate), new Long(toDate)});
}

//EJB select method
public abstract Collection ejbSelectPOIdBetweenDates(String jBossQL,
Object[] args)
throws FinderException;

...

}
```

The query description for the EJB select will look like this:

```
<query>
  <query-method>
    <method-name>ejbSelectPOIdBetweenDates</method-name>
    <method-params>
      <method-param>long</method-param>
      <method-param>long</method-param>
    </method-params>
  </query-method>
  <dynamic-ql/>
</query>
```

18.10.3 DeclaredSQL

You can use DeclaredSQL if you have a query that's impossible to be expressed using
EJB-QL or JBossQL, for example, if you want to utilize the full power of writing plain SQL.
DeclaredSQL is composed of SELECT, FROM, WHERE, and ORDER BY clauses. The structure
of the declared-sql element and its corresponding elements is as follows:

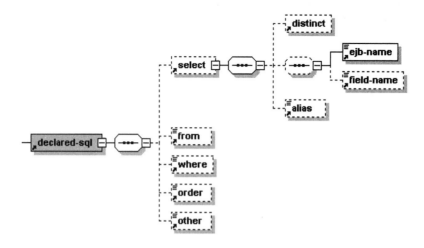

The `declared-sql` element supports the following subelements:

Element	Description
select	You can use the optional `select` element to list the columns that should be selected. By default, all columns are selected.
distinct	You can use the `distinct` empty element if you want to select distinct records. DynamicSQL for finder methods should have only the empty `distinct` element within the `select` element.
ejb-name field-name	The bean's name and the name of a container-managed persistent field, respectively.
alias	Used for defining an alias name for the entity bean table in the generated FROM clause.
from	JBoss automatically includes the entity table in the FROM clause. Any extra tables you want in the FROM clause can be defined using the `from` element. Because the CMP engine automatically includes the entity bean table in the FROM clause, the contents of the `from` element should begin with a comma.
where	Used for defining the query criteria.
order	Used for specifying sort order.
other	Used for specifying any database-specific clause that's appended to the end of the query.
alias	Used for specifying table aliases.

The following snippet shows the declared SQL to select all the line items that belongs to the purchase order with maximum value sorted by the line item ID:

```
<declared-sql>
  <select>
    <distinct/>
    <ejb-name>O_LineItemEJB</ejb-name>
    <alias>l</alias>
  </select>
  <from>
    <![CDATA[
      , purchase_order p
    ]]>
  </from>
  <where>
    <![CDATA[
      l.po_id = p.po_id
```

```
        and p.poValue = (select max(po_value) from purchase_order)
     ]]>
   </where>
   <order>l.id</order>
</declared-sql>
```

This will generate the following SQL:

```
SELECT l.*
FROM line_item l, purchase_order p
WHERE l.po_id = p.po_id
AND p.po_value = (SELECT max(p.po_value) FROM purchase_order)
ORDER by l.po_id
```

18.11 Tuning CMP Performance

One of the main complaints about EJBs (especially entity EJBs) since their inception is performance. This was mainly caused by the impedance mismatch between the object and relational technologies. However, container vendors have strived hard in the last two or three years to enhance entity bean performance. The EJB 2.0 specification aided these efforts tremendously by giving container vendors more control on how the CMP fields are persisted by abstract accessor and mutator methods. For example, because the CMP fields are mutated using abstract mutators, the containers know whether there's a field that is modified or not in a transaction. This means that the container vendors can transparently implement optimized writes depending on whether the fields are modified in a transaction.

However, EJB reads are still a problem, and container vendors provide custom solutions to implement optimized reads. JBoss provides a variety of methods to improve performance during entity EJB reads. Before looking at the JBoss features for optimized reads, you'll quickly learn about some of the performance problems associated with entity EJB reads.

One of the biggest performance bottlenecks in entity EJB reads is in reading a list of entity beans. Normally when you invoke a finder to get a list of entities, the container would issue a SQL query to get the list of primary keys matching the query criteria. After that, the first time each entity in the list is accessed in a transaction, the container issues a SQL query to get the data for that entity by specifying the primary key. This means to read 100 records, the container issues 101 queries; this is called the *n + 1 read problem* in EJBs.

Another performance issue is that when the container loads an entity at the beginning of a transaction, it loads all the fields regardless of whether they're being used within that transaction. This results in loading data that's never being used in a transaction.

JBoss solves the previous problems with the following solutions:

- ❏ Read-ahead strategies
- ❏ Load groups/optimized loads

18.11.1 Read-Ahead Strategies

JBoss provides two read-ahead strategies for loading data into entity bean instances:

- ❏ On-find
- ❏ On-load

18.11.1.1 The On-Find Strategy

In the on-find strategy, when a finder is issued, JBoss selects all the data expected for that finder from the database instead of loading just the primary keys. For example, if you issue a finder on the purchase order EJB to get all the purchase orders; so, instead of issuing this SQL:

```
SELECT poId FROM purchase_order
```

JBoss issues the following SQL:

```
SELECT poId, poDate, poStatus FROM purchase_order
```

The selected data isn't immediately associated with entity bean instances. Instead, it's kept in a cache and associated with entity bean instances, as and when the beans are accessed. For finder and select methods, the read-ahead strategy is defined in the query element for the method in jbosscmp-jdbc.xml file:

```
<query>
  <query-method>
    <method-name<findAll</method-name>
    <method-params/>
  </query-method>
  <jboss-ql>
    ...
  </jboss-ql>
  <read-ahead>
    <strategy>on-find</strategy>
    <page-size>4</page-size>
  </read-ahead>
</query>
```

299

The page-size element defines the number of records to be loaded at a time. One of the disadvantages of this approach is that the CMP engine loads all the CMP fields and foreign key fields for CMR regardless of whether they're used in the transaction. JBoss solves this problem by using named load groups. Load groups are named groups of columns that should be loaded together. Suppose you want to display all the purchase orders as a list and want to display only the ID, user ID, and date. You can define a load group for these fields and associate that to the read-ahead strategy as follows:

```
<entity>
  <ejb-name>PurchaseOrderEJB</ejb-name>
  <load-groups>
    <load-group>
      <load-group-name>list</load-group-name>
      <field-name>poId</field-name>
      <field-name>poUserId</field-name>
      <field-name>poDate</field-name>
    </load-group>
  </load-groups>
  <query>
    <query-method>
      <method-name>findAll</method-name>
      <method-params/>
    </query-method>
    <jboss-ql>
      ...
    </jboss-ql>
    <read-ahead>
      <strategy>on-find</strategy>
      <page-size>4</page-size>
      <eager-load-group>list</eager-load-group>
    </read-ahead>
  </query>
</entity>
```

In the previous example, a named load group called list, which contains purchase order ID, user ID, and date, is defined. This load group is then linked to the finder query using the eager-load-group element. This means that when this finder executes, JBoss will only select the three columns mapped to the aforementioned fields.

18.11.1.2 The On-Load Strategy

JBoss provides the alternative on-load strategy that'll load data for the next few entities that follow the current entity when the current entity is loaded (similar to a database cursor). This is under the assumption that the users access data sequentially. Again, similar to the on-find strategy, the data is kept in a cache and not immediately associated with entity bean instances. The following snippet shows how the on-load strategy can be implemented:

```
<entity>
  <ejb-name>PurchaseOrderEJB</ejb-name>
  <load-groups>
    <load-group>
      <load-group-name>list</load-group-name>
      <field-name>poId</field-name>
      <field-name>poUserId</field-name>
      <field-name>poDate</field-name>
    </load-group>
  </load-groups>
  <query>
    <query-method>
      <method-name>findAll</method-name>
      <method-params/>
    </query-method>
    <jboss-ql>
      ...
    </jboss-ql>
    <read-ahead>
      <strategy>on-load</strategy>
      <page-size>4</page-size>
      <eager-load-group>list</eager-load-group>
    </read-ahead>
  </query>
</entity>
```

If you want the CMP engine not to use any read-ahead strategy, you can specify it as follows:

```
<read-ahead>
  <strategy>none</strategy>
  ...
<read-ahead>
```

With the previous option, the CMP engine falls back to the process of lazy loading.

18.11.2 Optimized Loading

When the CMP engine loads an entity bean instance, it normally loads all the CMP fields even if all the fields aren't accessed in a transaction. JBoss allows you to specify groups of fields that should be eagerly or lazily loaded. This means the fields in the eager load group are loaded during the entity bean load, and those in the lazy load group are loaded as and when they're accessed. You can specify eager and lazy load groups at entity bean level as follows:

```
<entity>
  <ejb-name>PurchaseOrderEJB</ejb-name>
  <load-groups>
    <load-group>
      <load-group-name>eager</load-group-name>
      <field-name>poId</field-name>
      <field-name>poUserId</field-name>
      <field-name>poDate</field-name>
    </load-group>
    <load-group>
      <load-group-name>lazy</load-group-name>
      <field-name>poEmailId</field-name>
      <field-name>poLocale</field-name>
      <field-name>poValue</field-name>
    </load-group>
  </load-groups>
  <eager-load-group>eager</eager-load-group>
  <lazy-load-group>lazy</lazy-load-group>
</entity>
```

In the previous example, the purchase order ID, user ID, and date are eagerly loaded, and the e-mail ID, locale, and value are lazily loaded.

18.11.3 Read-Ahead for Relationships

As in finders and selects, you can eagerly load CMR fields when the source entity is either found or loaded. You specify the read-ahead strategy for relationships within the ejb-relationship-role element as follows:

```
<jbosscmp-jdbc>
  <enterprise-beans>
    <entity>
      <ejb-name>O_LineItemEJB</ejb-name>
      <load-groups>
        <field-name>id</field-name>
        <field-name>itemId</field-name>
        <field-name>categoryId</field-name>
      </load-groups>
      ...
    </entity>
    <entity>
      <ejb-name>PurchaseOrderEJB</ejb-name>
      ...
    </entity>
  <enterprise-beans>
```

```
    <relationships>
      <ejb-relation>
        <ejb-relation-name>PurchaseOrder-LineItem</ejb-relation-name>
        <foreign-key-mapping/>

        <ejb-relationship-role>
          <ejb-relationship-role-name>
            PurchaseOrderEJB
          </ejb-relationship-role-name>
          <key-fields>
            <key-field>
              <field-name>poId</field-name>
              <column-name>po_id</column-name>
            </key-field>
          </key-fields>
          <read-ahead>
            <strategy>on-load</strategy>
            <page-size>4</page-size>
            <eager-load-group>4</eager-load-group>
          </read-ahead>
        </ejb-relationship-role>
        <ejb-relationship-role>
          <ejb-relationship-role-name>
            O_LineItemEJB
          </ejb-relationship-role-name>
          <key-fields/>
        </ejb-relationship-role>
      </ejb-relation>

    </relationships>
</jbosscmp-jdbc>
```

This means that when the CMP engine loads a purchase order entity instance, it loads the first four line items with line item ID, item ID, and category ID.

18.12 Optimistic Locking

By default JBoss uses pessimistic locking. JBoss does this by making sure there's only one instance of an entity bean for a given database record and serializing access to the instance. This is the locking policy used by the default CMP container configuration. You can alternatively use Instance Per Transaction configuration, where each transaction will have its own instance. Even though this will tremendously improve throughput, the concurrency will be poor.

However, you can override the locking policy in the Instance Per Transaction configuration to use JDBC Optimistic Lock policy. With this configuration JBoss won't lock the instances, but it'll use the information present in the `optimistic-locking` element of the CMP descriptor to make sure the record hasn't been changed by other transactions since it was read by the current transactions. The optimistic locking policy is flexible to use any of the following for enforcing optimistic locks:

- ❏   Version number columns

- ❏   Timestamp columns

- ❏   Columns that are modified in a transaction

- ❏   Columns that are read in a transaction

- ❏   Generated ID columns

- ❏   A load group that's already defined

To use optimistic locking, you first need to define a container configuration that extends Instance Per Transaction.

```
<jboss>
  <enterprise-beans>
    ......................
    <entity>
      <ejb-name>PurchaseOrderEJB</ejb-name>
      <local-jndi-name>PurchaseOrderHome</local-jndi-name>
      <configuration-name>
        Optimistic Locking Container
      </configuration-name>
    </entity>
    ......................
  </enterprise-beans>
  <container-configurations>
    <container-configuration
      extends="Instance Per Transaction CMP EntityBean">
      <container-name>Optimistic Locking Container</container-name>
      <locking-policy>
        org.jboss.ejb.plugins.lock.JDBCOptimisticLock
      </locking-policy>
    </container-configuration>
  </container-configurations>
</jboss>
```

Now you need to specify the optimistic locking strategy to use in `jbosscmp-jdbc.xml` using the `optimistic-lockingType` element:

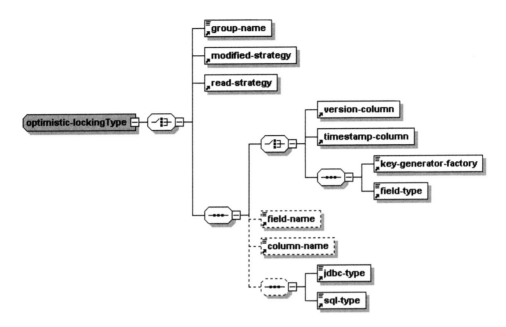

If the group-name element is present, it should point to an existing load group. JBoss will then use the fields in the load group to compare the bean state with the data in the database to find out whether the record was modified outside the transaction. If the modified-strategy element is present, JBoss will use all the columns that were modified in the current transaction. If the read-strategy element is present, JBoss will use all the columns that were read in the current transaction. If the version-column, timestamp-column, or key-generator-factory element is present, JBoss will use that to check optimistic lock violations. The following example shows how to use a version column:

```
<entity>
  <ejb-name>PurchaseOrderEJB</ejb-name>
  .....................
  <optimistic-locking>
    <version-column/>
    <column-name>version</column-name>
    <jdbc-type>LONG</jdbc-type>
    <sql-type>LONG</sql-type>
  </optimistic-locking>
</entity>
```

Here JBoss will use the value of the version column in the database to perform the optimistic lock checks.

18.13 Auditing

JBoss allows you to audit access to entity bean by allowing you to record the created user, created time, updated user, and updated time. Please note that created user and updated user will be available only when the bean is accessed within a security domain. To enable auditing, you need to use the auditType element for the entity:

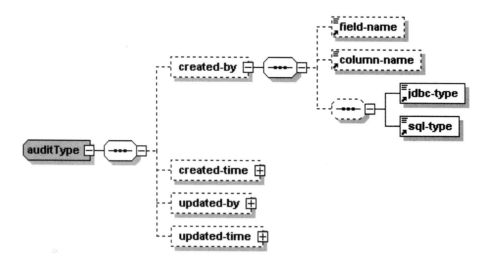

All the four child elements of the audit element have the same content structure. You can get JBoss to write directly to the database column or to the CMP field using either column-name and field-name, respectively. The jdbc-type and sql-type are relevant if you're getting JBoss to create the table during deployment. The following snippet shows how to enable auditing:

```
<entity>
  <ejb-name>PurchaseOrderEJB</ejb-name>
  ....................
  <audit>
    <created-by>
      <column-name>created_by</column-name>
      <jdbc-type>VARCHAR</jdbc-type>
      <sql-type>VARCHAR(30) BINARY</sql-type>
    </created-by>
    <created-time>
      <column-name>created_time</column-name>
      <jdbc-type>TIMESTAMP</jdbc-type>
      <sql-type>DATETIME</sql-type>
    </created-time>
    <updated-by>
      <column-name>updated_by</column-name>
```

```
        <jdbc-type>VARCHAR</jdbc-type>
        <sql-type>VARCHAR(30) BINARY</sql-type>
      </updated-by>
      <updated-time>
        <column-name>updated_time</column-name>
        <jdbc-type>TIMESTAMP</jdbc-type>
        <sql-type>DATETIME</sql-type>
      </updated-time>
    </audit>
  </entity>
```

18.14 Locking and Concurrency

Locking and concurrency are two of the critical aspects of multiuser transactional systems. Traditionally in two-tier client/server systems, locking and concurrency issues were taken care of by the underlying database system, making sure the transactions were atomic, consistent, integral, and durable. Even though the advent of middleware-based systems brought in a huge amount of benefits to enterprise applications by providing system-level services, such as data caching in the middle tier, it has also brought in an added amount of complexity in making sure that the transactions don't violate the integrity of underlying data.

18.14.1 Commit Options

Because the lifecycle of entity beans is managed between transactions and influences the concurrency options for entity beans, it's important that you have a good understanding of the commit options available for entity beans. The EJB 2.0 specification provides compliant containers the flexibility to associate the object identity of entity beans to bean instances. The specification provides the following options to the containers:

❑ Option A
The container caches entity bean instances in a ready state between transactions. The container ensures that the instance has exclusive access to the state of the entity in the persistent storage. Hence, the container doesn't need to synchronize the state of the bean at the beginning of each transaction.

❑ Option B
This is similar to Option A in the sense that the ready instances are cached between transactions. However, the container doesn't assume that the instance has exclusive access to the state in the persistent storage. This means the state of the bean is synchronized at the start of each transaction.

❏   Option C
With this option, the container doesn't cache the instance at all.
The instance is returned to the pool at the end of each transaction.

In addition to the three options listed previously, JBoss provides a fourth option:

❏   Option D
This is similar to Option A where the bean instance is cached between transactions. However, you can set a refresh rate at which the state of the bean instance is synchronized with that in the persistent store.

JBoss allows you to set the commit option you want and the refresh rate if you're using option D, using the `commit-option` and `optiond-refresh-rate` elements in the deployment descriptor. The following table shows the commit options set for the container configurations defined in `standardjboss.xml` file:

Configuration Name	Commit Option
Standard CMP 2.*x* Entity Bean	B
Instance Per Transaction CMP 2.*x* Entity Bean	B
Standard CMP Entity Bean	A
Clustered CMP 2.*x* Entity Bean	B
Clustered CMP Entity Bean	B
Standard BMP Entity Bean	A
Instance Per Transaction BMP Entity Bean	B
Clustered BMP Entity Bean	B
IIOP CMP 2.*x* Entity Bean	B
IIOP CMP Entity Bean	A
IIOP BMP Entity Bean	A

Depending on the type of the entity bean you use, JBoss will select a suitable container configuration for you. You can also extend the container configuration and override the commit option you want. If you decide to choose the commit option as D, you can optionally define the refresh rate using the `optiond-refresh-rate` element. If you don't specify it, the default value is 30 seconds.

From the previous table you can see that a standard CMP 2.0 entity bean uses the commit option B. This means if the beans are accessed within the context of a transaction (`Required`, `RequiresNew`, `Mandatory`), the bean instance is always refreshed from the database. However, if a method executes without a transaction context (`Never`, `NotSupported`) the bean state is read from the in-memory cache.

The following snippet shows how the commit option is set:

```
<container-configuration>
    <container-name>My Option-D Entity Bean</container-name>
    ...
    <commit-option>D</commit-option>
    <optiond-refresh-rate>100</optiond-refresh-rate>
    ...
</container-configuration>
```

18.14.2 Locking Policy

By default JBoss maintains only one instance of the entity bean for a given home and primary key, and it makes sure no two transactions have concurrent access to that instance in a transaction. You can set the locking policy using the `locking-policy` element. The content of this element is the fully qualified class name of the locking policy to use. The possible values for this element are as follows:

❏   `org.jboss.ejb.plugins.lock.MethodOnlyEJBLock`
This option has now been deprecated.

❏   `org.jboss.ejb.plugins.lock.QueuedPessimisticEJBLock`
This lock maintains a queue of transactions waiting for a transaction lock. When a lock is released, the threads waiting for that lock are notified.

❏   `org.jboss.ejb.plugins.lock.SimplePessimisticEJBLock`
This policy notifies all the threads blocked on transaction locks.

The default value used by the configuration sets defined in `standardjboss.xml` is `QueuedPessimisticEJBLock`.

18.14.3 Instance Per Transaction

The default commit options and locking policies supported by the standard configuration sets offer a high level of isolation with poor concurrency. For example, say transaction A acquired a lock on bean instance X and transaction B acquired a lock on bean instance Y. Now transaction A requests for a lock on bean instance Y, and transaction B requests for a lock on bean instance X. This will create an application deadlock, and one of the transactions is the victim of the deadlock and rolled back. The client can detect this by extracting the `ApplicationDeadlockException` from the `RemoteException`. With default configuration, you get a lot of application deadlocks with JBoss if your transactions aren't short-lived and access to entity beans are unordered. You can get rid of this if you decide to use the Instance Per Transaction configuration. This would mean each transaction will have its own bean instances, and you'd never get a deadlock. However, the flip side is that it's a bit risky that the bean instance in one of the transaction may have dirty data. Instance Per Transaction policy is enabled using the following container interceptors:

❑ `org.jboss.ejb.plugins.EntityMultiInstanceInterceptor`

❑ `org.jboss.ejb.plugins.EntityMultiInstanceSyncronizationInterceptor`

The `standardjboss.xml` file provides the following container configurations with Instance Per Transaction policy:

❑ Instance Per Transaction CMP 2.*x* Entity Bean

❑ Instance Per Transaction BMP Entity Bean

> The only two commit options supported with Instance Per Transaction policy is B and C.

18.15 Entity Commands

JBoss allows automatic primary key generation using entity commands. Entity commands allow you to use pluggable key generation strategies. The `entity-commands` element under the `jbosscmp-jdbc` element enumerates the entity commands that are available:

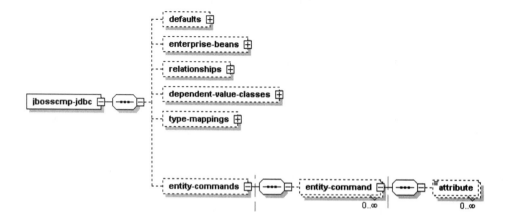

The entity-command element has the attribute's name and class. The name element defines a unique name that can be later used by individual entity beans to specify the entity command to use. The class attribute should specify the fully qualified name of the class that implements the key generation logic. These classes should implement the interface JDBCCreateEntityCommand in the package org.jboss.ejb.plugins.cmp.jdbc.

The entity-command element can have zero or more attribute elements. The attribute element has an attribute called name. The attribute elements are used to pass additional information to the entity-command object as metadata. Instead of specifying the entity-command globally, you can choose to specify it locally for the entity bean. In such scenarios you should use the class attribute of the entity-command element within the entity element to specify the fully qualifed class of the entity-create command.

Individual entity beans specify the entity-create command to use, using the entity-command element within the entity element. The name attribute of this element should specify the name of an entity command that's already defined. The following table shows some of the entity commands that are supported out of the box by JBoss:

Class	Description
org.jboss.ejb.plugins.cmp.jdbc.JDBCCreateEntityCommand	This inserts the entity with the primary key value available in the key CMP field.
org.jboss.ejb.plugins.cmp.jdbc.JDBCPkSqlCreateCommand	This command uses the SQL statement specified using the attribute named pk-sql to fetch the next primary key.
org.jboss.ejb.plugins.cmp.jdbc.sybase.JDBCSybaseCreateCommand	This command relies on Sybase identity columns to generate the primary keys.
org.jboss.ejb.plugins.cmp.jdbc.jdbc3.JDBCGetGeneratedKeysCreateCommand	This command relies on the Java Database Connectivity (JDBC) 3.0 functionality for fetching the value of autogenerated keys.

JBoss also provides a variety of other key generation commands.

311

The following snippet shows how entity commands are used:

```
<jbosscmp-jdbc>
  <entity-commands>
    <entity-command
      name="pk-sql"
      class="org.jboss.ejb.plugins.cmp.jdbc.JDBCPkSqlCreateCommand">
      <attribute name="pk-sql">
        select MY_SEQUENCE.NEXT_VAL FROM DUAL
      </attribute>
    </entity-command>
  </entity-commands>
  <enterprise-beans>
    <entity>
      <ejb-name>My Entity</ejb-name>
      .............................
      <entity-command name="pk-sql">My Entity</ entity-command>
    </entity>
  </enterprise-beans>
</jbosscmp-jdbc>
```

EAR Configuration

In this chapter, you'll look at the features available with JBoss for deploying Enterprise Archive (EAR) files. JBoss allows the deployment of standard Java 2 Enterprise Edition (J2EE) EAR files by simply copying them to the directories monitored by the deployment scanner, as discussed in section 15.3, "The Deployment Process."

19.1 The EAR Deployer

JBoss provides a deployer that's capable of deploying EAR files. This is the `org.jboss.deployment.EARDeployer` class, which implements the `org.jboss.deployment.SubDeployer` interface by extending the `org.jboss.deployment.SubDeployerSupport` class. This EAR subdeployer accepts all files and directories that end with the string `ear`. This means that the EAR deployer can deploy EAR files in both exploded and unexploded format, stored in the directories monitored by the deployment scanner.

The EAR deployer is an MBean configured in the root configuration file `jboss-service.xml` in the `\conf` directory of the configuration set you use as follows:

```
<mbean
  code="org.jboss.deployment.EARDeployer"
  name="jboss.j2ee:service=EARDeployer">
```

When this MBean starts, it registers itself with the main deployer as a subdeployer. This enables the main deployer to delegate the deployment of EAR components to the main deployer.

19.2 The JBoss EAR Deployment Descriptor

In addition to the standard EAR deployment descriptor (`application.xml`), JBoss allows a JBoss-specific deployment descriptor for EAR files. This file should be present in the `\META-INF` directory of the EAR file and should be called `jboss-app.xml`. The structure of this file is as follows:

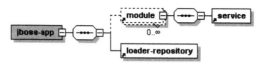

The `jboss-app.xml` file is mainly used for the following:

❑   Deploying Service Archive (SAR) components as part of the EAR

❑   Defining a named classloader repository for the EAR

19.2.1 SAR Components

In section 4.2.1.2, "JBoss SAR Components," you saw the use of SAR components for deploying MBean services within JBoss. You can deploy SAR components as part of a standard J2EE EAR application. To package a SAR component, you need to create a standard Java Archive (JAR) with the extension `sar` that contains all the MBean and supporting classes for the MBean. In the `\META-INF` directory, you need a file called `jboss-service.xml` that contains the MBean definition.

You can also deploy MBeans in exploded format. In this case, you need to make the MBean deployment descriptor visible to the SAR deployer. The easiest way to achieve this is to name the file in the format `*-service.xml` and copy it to the `\deploy` directory of the configuration set you use. In this case, you need to make sure that all the supporting classes (including the MBean class) are available to the classloader. To do this, you can create a standard JAR containing the class files and store it in the `\lib` directory of your configuration set.

For example, you can package all the datasource and Java Message Service (JMS) destination services required for the petstore application as SAR components within the petstore EAR file, instead of configuring them separately. One advantage of doing this is that you have a self-contained application without any external dependency, and it's the only deployment unit you need for deploying it on remote servers. This means you can just drop the EAR file somewhere visible to the EAR deployer, without worrying about any external configuration. This involves three main steps:

1. Package SAR files.

2. Create the JBoss EAR deployment descriptor.

3. Package the EAR.

19.2.1.1 Package SAR Files

Package the MBean services you want to deploy as a SAR file. SAR files are similar to vanilla JAR files, with the \META-INF directory containing a file called jboss-service.xml. This file should contain all the MBean definitions you require. Additionally, you can include all the dependent classes in the SAR file.

For example, if you're packaging the datasource definition for the petstore as a SAR component, you can create a jboss-service.xml file with the following contents (refer to section 8.2.1, "Configuring Datasources," for a description of this file's contents):

```xml
<?xml version="1.0" encoding="UTF-8"?>

<!-- Datasources used for Petstore -->

<server>

 <mbean
  code="org.jboss.resource.connectionmanager.LocalTxConnectionManager"
  name="jboss.jca:service=LocalTxCM,name=jdbc/petstore/PetStoreDB">

  <depends optional-attribute-name="ManagedConnectionFactoryName">

   <mbean
    code="org.jboss.resource.connectionmanager.RARDeployment"
    name="jboss.jca:service=LocalTxDS,name=jdbc/petstore/PetStoreDB">
    <attribute name="JndiName">jdbc/petstore/PetStoreDB</attribute>
    <attribute name="ManagedConnectionFactoryProperties">
     <properties>
      <config-property name="ConnectionURL" type="java.lang.String">
       jdbc:oracle:thin:@youroraclehost:1521:yoursid
      </config-property>
      <config-property name="DriverClass" type="java.lang.String">
       oracel.jdbc.driver.OracleDriver
      </config-property>
      <config-property name="UserName" type="java.lang.String">
       megadeath
      </config-property>
```

```
      <config-property name="Password" type="java.lang.String">
        euthanasia
      </config-property>
     </properties>
    </attribute>
    <depends optional-attribute-name="OldRarDeployment">
     jboss.jca:service=RARDeployment,
     name=JBoss LocalTransaction JDBC Wrapper
    </depends>
   </mbean>
  </depends>

  <depends optional-attribute-name="ManagedConnectionPool">

   <mbean
    code=
    "org.jboss.resource.connectionmanager.JBossManagedConnectionPool"
    name=

    "jboss.jca:service=LocalTxPool,name=jdbc/petstore/PetStoreDB">
    <attribute name="MinSize">1</attribute>
    <attribute name="MaxSize">50</attribute>
    <attribute name="BlockingTimeoutMillis">5000</attribute>
    <attribute name="IdleTimeoutMinutes">15</attribute>
    <attribute name="Criteria">ByContainer</attribute>
   </mbean>

  </depends>

  <depends optional-attribute-name="CachedConnectionManager">
    jboss.jca:service=CachedConnectionManager
  </depends>

  <depends optional-attribute-name="JaasSecurityManagerService">
    jboss.security:service=JaasSecurityManager
  </depends>

  <attribute name="TransactionManager">
   java:/TransactionManager
  </attribute>

  <depends>jboss.jca:service=RARDeployer</depends>

 </mbean>

</server>
```

You then need to create a standard JAR with the extension sar with the
jboss-service.xml file in the \META-INF directory. Call this file db.sar.

19.2.1.2 Create the JBoss EAR Deployment Descriptor

Now you need to create a JBoss-specific EAR deployment descriptor. This file should be called `jboss-app.xml` and should contain the following content:

```
<jboss-app>
  <module>
    <service>db.sar</service>
  </module>
</jboss-app>
```

You can have any number of `module` elements under the `jboss-app` element if you want to deploy more than one SAR component as part of the EAR.

19.2.1.3 Package the EAR

Now creating the EAR deployment descriptor you need to package the EAR file. Here, you'll need to include the `db.sar` file at the root level of the JAR and the `jboss-app.xml` file along with the standard `application.xml` in the `\META-INF` directory of the JAR file.

> *The* `application.xml` *file should include the definitions for all the standard J2EE components such as Web Archive (WAR), Resource Archive (RAR), and Enterprise JavaBean (EJB).*

The following listing shows the structure of the EAR file for the petstore application:

```
META-INF/
        application.xml
        jboss-app.xml
asyncsender-ejb.jar
...
cart-ejb.jar
...
db.sar
...
petstore.war
petstore-ejb.jar
...
xmldocuments.jar
```

19.2.2 Loader Repository

One major disadvantage of the JBoss unified classloader repository scheme is that it's impossible to have multiple versions of the same class across different EAR files because JBoss will always use the first version that's loaded. This is because the unified classloaders will use the class already present in the repository.

However, you can circumvent this problem using scoped classloading in EAR files. You achieve this by using the `loader-repository` entry in the JBoss-specific application deployment descriptor, `jboss-app.xml`:

```
<jboss-app>
  <loader-repository>
    petstore:service=LoaderRepository
  </loader-repository>
</jboss-app>
```

This EAR will use its own loader repository and will look into this repository before falling back to the default repository. The content of the `loader-repository` element should be a valid JMX object name. You can use any name for the loader repository, as long as it's a valid JMX object name.

You can also specify the class for the object that acts as the load repository using the `loader-repository-class` element. This class should implement the `org.jboss.mx.loading.LoaderRepository` interface. The default value for this class, if not specified, is `org.jboss.mx.loading.HierarchicalLoaderRepository2`.

> **In version 3.0.2 and earlier versions, because of a bug in the code, JBoss always tries to read the loader repository class from `application.xml` and not the `jboss-app.xml` file. However, in most cases, you won't need to change the default value.**

20

Additional JBoss Configuration

In this chapter you'll look at some of the custom features available with JBoss that aren't part of the standard Java 2 Enterprise Edition (J2EE) specification.

20.1 Scheduling Tasks

Many enterprise applications use some sort of scheduling to run specific tasks at regular intervals. One way of achieving this is to rely on operating system services such as cron on Unix and scheduled tasks on Windows. However, J2EE 1.3 doesn't specify any standard way of scheduling tasks as part of the specifications.

> *EJB 2.1 in J2EE 1.4 specifies a container-managed timer service that can be used for scheduling tasks.*

JBoss provides an MBean that can be used for scheduling tasks that need to be run at regular intervals. The MBean definition is as follows:

```
<mbean
    code="org.jboss.varia.scheduler.Scheduler"
    name="petstore:service=DataPopulationScheduler">
```

Obviously, you can configure the object name to something appropriate for the service you want to create.

This MBean supports the following attributes:

Attribute	Function
InitialStartDate	Specifies the instance at which the task is run for the first time. It supports the following values: ❑ NOW runs the task for the first time a second after the service starts. ❑ The number of milliseconds after January 1, 1970. ❑ A date string that can be parsed by `java.util.SimpleDateFormat`.
InitialRepetitions	Specifies the number of times the scheduled task should be repeated. If you want to repeat the task forever, you can specify the value as -1.
StartAtStartup	If set to true, the scheduler will start immediately after the MBean starts. If this is set to false, you need to explicitly invoke the MBean operation startSchedule() to start scheduling.
SchedulablePeriod	The interval in milliseconds between each call to the perform() method to run the task. This value must be bigger than 0.
SchedulableClass	This is one option for defining the task that's scheduled. In this case, you need to provide a class that implements the interface org.jboss.varia.scheduler.Schedulable. This interface defines a single method called perform() that provides two arguments specifying the time on which the scheduled task was called and the number of remaining repetitions. The scheduler will call this method at configured intervals.
SchedulableArguments	Specifies the arguments passed to the constructor of the class that implements the Schedulable interface.
SchedulableArgumentTypes	Specifies the argument types passed to the constructor of the class that implements the Schedulable interface.

Attribute	Function
SchedulableMBean	Instead of specifying a class that implements the Schedulable interface, you can specify the object name of an MBean whose method is run at regular intervals by the scheduler using this attribute.
SchedulableMBeanMethod	Specifies the MBean operation that's scheduled.

20.1.1 Scheduling Petstore Data Population

In this section, you'll write a small example to run the petstore data population at startup and then every 24 hours thereafter. To do this, you need to perform the tasks in the following sections.

20.1.1.1 Write a Schedulable Implementation

The Schedulable implementation will take the Uniform Resource Locator (URL) to the petstore's populate servlet as an argument to the constructor. Then every time the perform() method is called, it'll make a URL connection to the servlet to repopulate the petstore database:

```
package com.apress.jboss.chapter20;

import org.jboss.varia.scheduler.Schedulable;

import java.net.URL;
import java.net.URLConnection;
import java.io.IOException;
import java.io.InputStream;

public class PetstoreScheduler implements Schedulable {

  private String populateServletURL;

  public PetstoreScheduler(String arg0) {
    populateServletURL = arg0;
  }

  public void perform(java.util.Date date, long param) {

    try {
      System.out.println("Repopulating Database:" + date);
      URLConnection con =
          new URL(populateServletURL).openConnection();
      con.setDoInput(true);
      con.setDoOutput(true);
```

```
        InputStream in = con.getInputStream();
        while(in.read() != -1) {
        }
        in.close();

        System.out.println("Repopulated Database:" + date);
    } catch(IOException ex) {
        ex.printStackTrace();
    }
  }

}
```

To compile the previous class, you need to have the `scheduler-plugin.jar` file available in the `\lib` directory of the `default` configuration set in the classpath.

20.1.1.2 Write the MBean Service Descriptor

This will define the scheduler for running the task for repopulating the petstore database:

```xml
<?xml version="1.0" encoding="UTF-8"?>

<server>

  <classpath codebase="lib" archives="scheduler-plugin.jar"/>

  <mbean code="org.jboss.varia.scheduler.Scheduler"
    name="petstore:service=DataPopulationScheduler">
    <attribute name="StartAtStartup">true</attribute>
```

Next, define the name of the schedulable class:

```xml
    <attribute name="SchedulableClass">
       com.apress.jboss.chapter20.PetstoreScheduler
    </attribute>
```

Next, define the arguments and argument types:

```xml
    <attribute name="SchedulableArguments">
       http://localhost:8080/petstore/Populate
    </attribute>
    <attribute name="SchedulableArgumentTypes">
       java.lang.String
    </attribute>
```

Next, define the initial start date as NOW, the number of repetitions until server shutdown, and the repetition period as 24 hours:

```
      <attribute name="InitialStartDate">NOW</attribute>
      <attribute name="InitialRepetitions">-1</attribute>
      <attribute name="SchedulePeriod">86400000</attribute>
   </mbean>

</server>
```

The previous contents should be stored in a file called `jboss-service.xml`.

20.1.1.3 Package the SAR Component

Now you'll package the Service Archive (SAR) component. For this, create a Java Archive (JAR) file by the name `schedule.sar` with the following contents:

```
META-INF/
          jboss-service.xml
com/
    apress/
          jboss/
                chapter20/
                        PetstoreScheduler.class
```

20.1.1.4 Include the SAR in the EAR

To do this first, you need to add a `service` element in the `jboss-app.xml` file with the following contents as explained in section 19.2.1.2, "Create the JBoss EAR Deployment Descriptor":

```
<jboss-app>
   ...
   <module>
     <service>schedule.sar</service>
   </module>
</jboss-app>
```

The structure of the petstore EAR file should be as follows:

```
META-INF/
          application.xml
          jboss-app.xml
asyncsender-ejb.jar
...
cart-ejb.jar
...
petstore.war
petstore-ejb.jar
...
schedule.sar
...
xmldocuments.jar
```

Once you deploy the EAR file, you'll be able to configure the scheduler through the JMX console. You can access the MBean by clicking the JMX object link service=DataPopulationScheduler under the `petstore` domain from the JMX console home page:

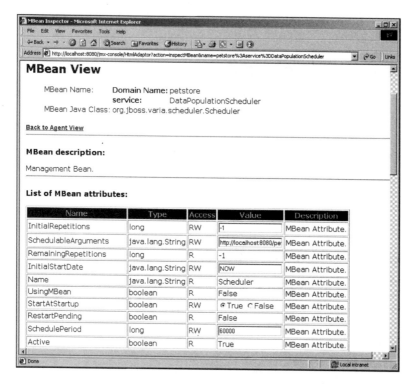

Upon first deploying the service, you might find that it doesn't work immediately. This is because you configured the scheduler to start NOW, but the SAR subdeployer runs before the `AbstractWebContainer` deployer such that the WAR hasn't been deployed yet. Thus, the URL the data scheduler needs isn't available. However, upon subsequent invocations of the scheduler, it will function fine.

20.2 System Properties

JBoss provides an MBean for populating system properties, which are useful for defining global settings. You can access system properties using the following code:

```
Object myProperty = System.getProperty("propertyName");
```

The MBean is normally defined in the file `properties-service.xml` available in the \deploy directory of the configuration set in use, and its definition is as follows:

```
<mbean
  code="org.jboss.varia.property.SystemPropertiesService"
  name="jboss.util:type=Service,name=SystemProperties"/>
```

This MBean supports the following attributes:

Attribute	Function
Properties	Specifies a set of name/value pairs of system properties. Each property should start on a new line.
URLList	Specifies a comma-separated list of URLs pointing to files in the standard Java properties file format.

The following listing shows an example of using this MBean:

```
<server>
  <mbean
    code="org.jboss.varia.property.SystemPropertiesService"
    name="jboss.util:type=Service,name=SystemProperties"/>
    <attribute name="Properties">
      myProperty=123
      yourProperty=xyz
    </attribute>
    <attribute name="URLList">
      ./conf/test.properties,http://fred.com/test.properties
    </attribute>
  </mbean>
</server>
```

The previous example sets two system properties: myProperty to 123 and yourProperty to xyz. It also reads the files test.properties stored in standard Java properties file format in the \conf directory of the configuration in use and on the URL http://fred.com/, and it sets the properties stored in those files as system properties.

Index

MethodOnlyEJBLock class,
org.jboss.ejb.plugins.lock, 309
method-permission element, 258
MinimumSize element, container-pool-conf
element, 248
minProcessors attribute, Connector element, 170
MinSize attribute, Managed Connection Pool
MBean, 103
MinThreads attribute, AJP listener, 153
MinThreads property, HTTP listener, 147
MLet service, JMX, 34
mod_jk and mod_jk2 modules, 152, 173, 175
mod_jk load balancing, 181
model MBeans, 32
modified-strategy element, optimistic-
lockingType element, 305
module-option element, login-config.xml file
monitoring services, JMX, 34
multiplicity element, ejb-relationship-role
element, 286, 288

N

name attribute
config-property element, 101
AJP listener, 153
appender element, 203
category and logger elements, 212
Engine element, 166
name element, type-mapping element, 268
name mapping, WAR deployment, 229–232
name property, javax.security.auth.login, 78, 79,
88
naming contexts and the
AbstractWebContainer class, 143
naming service. See JNDI
NamingAlias MBean and JNDI link references,
63
NamingService MBean, 57
NCSARequestLog class, org.mortbay.http, 149
NextInterceptor attribute, Security Manager, 130
not-null element, cmp-field element, 279
not-null element, property element, 282
NoTXConnectionManager class,
ConnectionManager MBean, 99
NT service, running JBoss as, 22–25
NTEventLogAppender, 209

O

ObjectName class, JMX, 33
ObjectRenderer interface, 201
OIL (Optimized Invocation Layer, JBossMQ),
115, 116–117
OILServerILService MBean, 116
one-to-many relationship mapping, 286

one-to-one bidirectional relationship mapping,
288
relationship table mapping, 291
on-find read-ahead strategies, 299
on-load read-ahead strategies, 300
OnlyOnceErrorHandler class,
org.jboss.logging.util, 203, 213
open MBeans, 32
optimistic locking, 303
optimistic-lockingType element, 304
Optimized Invocation Layer, JBossMQ, 115,
116–117
optimized loading, CMP, 301
optional-attribute-name attribute and the
depends element, 101, 103
optiond-refresh-rate element, container-
configuration element, 308
options
entity bean commit options, 307
JVM options, 55–56
startup options, 19–20
Oracle databasess, configuring a datasource,
107–110
ORDER BY clause and JBossQL, 293
order element, declared-sql element, 297
org.apache.catalina.startup package
Embedded class, 161
org.apache.commons category, 213
org.apache.jk.server package
JkCoyoteHandler class, 170
org.apache.log4j package
AsyncAppender class, 208
ConsoleAppender class, 204, 213
FileAppender class, 205, 213
Level class, 199
PatternLayout class, 201, 206, 213
org.apache.log4j.net package
JMSAppender class, 206
SMTPAppender class, 208
org.jboss package
Main class, 50
org.jboss.deployment package
Deployer interface, 218
DeploymentSorter class, 220
EARDeployer class, 313
MainDeployer class, 218
SubDeployer interface, 218, 313
SubDeployerSupport class, 218, 313
org.jboss.deployment.scanner package
PrefixDeploymentSorter class, 220
org.jboss.ejb package
InstancePool interface, 248
org.jboss.ejb.plugins package, 248, 249
interceptors, 310
JDBCCreateEntityCommand interface, 311
org.jboss.ejb.plugins.cmp.jdbc* packages, 311

forums.apress.com

FOR PROFESSIONALS BY PROFESSIONALS™

JOIN THE APRESS FORUMS AND BE PART OF OUR COMMUNITY. You'll find discussions that cover topics of interest to IT professionals, programmers, and enthusiasts just like you. If you post a query to one of our forums, you can expect that some of the best minds in the business—especially Apress authors, who all write with *The Expert's Voice*™—will chime in to help you. Why not aim to become one of our most valuable participants (MVPs) and win cool stuff? Here's a sampling of what you'll find:

DATABASES
Data drives everything.

Share information, exchange ideas, and discuss any database programming or administration issues.

INTERNET TECHNOLOGIES AND NETWORKING
Try living without plumbing (and eventually IPv6).

Talk about networking topics including protocols, design, administration, wireless, wired, storage, backup, certifications, trends, and new technologies.

JAVA
We've come a long way from the old Oak tree.

Hang out and discuss Java in whatever flavor you choose: J2SE, J2EE, J2ME, Jakarta, and so on.

MAC OS X
All about the Zen of OS X.

OS X is both the present and the future for Mac apps. Make suggestions, offer up ideas, or boast about your new hardware.

OPEN SOURCE
Source code is good; understanding (open) source is better.

Discuss open source technologies and related topics such as PHP, MySQL, Linux, Perl, Apache, Python, and more.

PROGRAMMING/BUSINESS
Unfortunately, it is.

Talk about the Apress line of books that cover software methodology, best practices, and how programmers interact with the "suits."

WEB DEVELOPMENT/DESIGN
Ugly doesn't cut it anymore, and CGI is absurd.

Help is in sight for your site. Find design solutions for your projects and get ideas for building an interactive Web site.

SECURITY
Lots of bad guys out there—the good guys need help.

Discuss computer and network security issues here. Just don't let anyone else know the answers!

TECHNOLOGY IN ACTION
Cool things. Fun things.

It's after hours. It's time to play. Whether you're into LEGO® MINDSTORMS™ or turning an old PC into a DVR, this is where technology turns into fun.

WINDOWS
No defenestration here.

Ask questions about all aspects of Windows programming, get help on Microsoft technologies covered in Apress books, or provide feedback on any Apress Windows book.

HOW TO PARTICIPATE:
Go to the Apress Forums site at **http://forums.apress.com/**.
Click the New User link.